The Western Shores of Turkey: Discovering the Aegean and Mediterranean Coasts

'…Enchanting guide…a work of genuine scholarship, lightly worn and charmingly conveyed. I fell in love with the book and stayed enamoured until the final page.' Paul Bailey, *The Sunday Times*

'…the record of a journey undertaken by a man effortlessly able to convey in depth the meaning of what he sees.' Marlena Frank, *Scotsman*, Edinburgh

Strolling Through Athens

'…John Freely's magnificent walking guide to the city.' Anthony Sattin, Book of the Week, *The Sunday Times*

Strolling Through Istanbul

'…a classic. The best travel guide to Istanbul.' *The Times*

Inside the Seraglio: Private Lives of the Sultans in Istanbul

'Freely provides a fascinating, easy-to-follow overview, beautifully researched and riveting in its detail.' Christopher Fowler, *Independent on Sunday*

'A richly coloured, highly entertaining book that I wished I'd had to hand when I strolled around the Topkapi.' Lawrence James, *The Times*

Istanbul: The Imperial City

'This is the handiest single volume to take with you as you explore this most intriguing of cities…' Robert Carver, *Scotsman*

'Freely abounds in colourful details…' Philip Mansel, *The Independent*

'This study uncovers nuggets of information while having the charm of *The Thousand and One Nights*.' Tabasim Hussain, *Literary Review*

'If you're thinking of paying Istanbul a visit, don't go without reading this book from cover to cover at least twice.' Arminta Wallace, *Irish Times*

The Lost Messiah: In Search of Sabbatei Sevi

'Everything in this book is astonishing…' *The Mail on Sunday*

'Freely reveals a superb eye for the telling detail…This is an intriguing book.' *Independent on Sunday*

'Freely's brilliantly researched tale transports the reader through a host of wonderfully arcane locations.' *The Independent*

In memory of Ralph Bates, Vasilis Mylonas,
Sotiris Peristerakis and Yorgos Spiridakis

The Cyclades

Discovering the Greek Islands of the Aegean

John Freely

I.B. TAURIS

LONDON · NEW YORK

Published in 2006 by I.B.Tauris & Co. Ltd
6 Salem Road, London W2 4BU
175 Fifth Avenue, New York NY 10010
www.ibtauris.com

In the United States and Canada distributed by Palgrave Macmillan,
a division of St. Martin's Press, 175 Fifth Avenue, New York NY 10010

ISBN 1 84511 160 5
EAN 978 1 84511 160 1

A full CIP record for this book is available from the British Library
A full CIP record for this book is available from the Library of Congress
Library of Congress catalog card: available

Typeset in Minion by Dexter Haven Associates Ltd, London
Printed and bound in Great Britain by TJ International, Padstow, Cornwall

Contents

List of Maps

Introduction

The Cyclades are the Greek islands of the central Aegean, arrayed like the stars of a spiral galaxy around their sacred centre at Delos, the mythical birthplace of Apollo. These are the quintessential Greek isles, renowned for the beauty of their seascapes, their historical monuments, and a unique way of life deeply rooted in the immemorial past of the Aegean.

I first saw the Cyclades in June of 1962, when my wife Dolores and I took our three young children to spend the summer on Naxos. We have returned to Naxos nearly every year since then, most recently in the spring of 2005, drawn back by the siren song of the Aegean isles. During those years I also explored all of the other isles of the Cyclades, travelling on inter-island ferries as well as on fishing boats and the old *caiques* that in times past were the only means of transporting people and goods around the archipelago, leading me to the rediscovery of what seemed to be a veritable lost empire of the sea.

Cycladic civilisation is as old as that of mainland Greece but with a greater continuity because of the remoteness of the islands, which as stepping stones between Europe and Asia have been involved in every act of the unending historical drama that has been played out in the Aegean since the first settlers made their homes on the islands more than eight thousand years ago. The tides of history that have washed over the Cyclades have left not only monuments but also patterns of culture that span the whole time-line of Greek civilisation, their roots extending back even into the pre-Hellenic dawn of human existence on the Aegean isles. At several periods in their history the islands have been at the centre of maritime empires whose power extended around the eastern Mediterranean, while at other times they have been remote and almost uninhabited outposts cut off from the centres of civilisation, though preserving the essentials of their Cycladic civilisation through the depth and tenacity of their cultural roots.

The Cyclades have always been a crossroads of civilisation, one maritime route bringing people back and forth between Europe and Asia Minor, another taking them between Crete and the Greek mainland, carrying with them their way of life, their gods, their ideas and their music. These maritime migrations are enshrined in the ancient myths of the Cyclades, such as the wanderings of Leto, mother of the divine twins Apollo and Artemis, described in the *Homeric Hymns*. Herodotus writes of the great population movement that brought the first Hellenes out through the islands to Asia Minor at the end of the second millennium BC, giving rise to the civilisation that produced the first philosophers of nature and the first epic and lyric poets of the Greek world. The poet Archilochus of Samos, writing perhaps a century or so after Homer, sings of unrequited love in a restless life spent at sea, as do the lyricists of today's *nisiotika tragoudia*, the 'songs of the islands', whose melodies were brought out to the Cyclades by refugees from wars in Crete and Asia Minor in the late nineteenth and early twentieth century. The modern Greek poet Odysseus Elytis writes of a moment when 'a rowing-boat went by full of suffering, laden with songs and lights that flicker like mountain-tops'. These are the song-lines of the Aegean, echoes of the past that are still heard in the Cyclades, evoking poignant memories that come from deep within the Greek soul.

My book is a guide to the historic monuments and culture of the Cyclades as well as to the way of life of the islanders, particularly their religious festivals, the *paneyeria*, which mark the passing seasons of the Cycladic year in a calendar whose cycles were established in the night of time and adapted by the successive religions that took root in the archipelago, from paganism to Christianity, celebrated in songs and dances with ancient resonances and movements.

Life in the Cyclades has changed in many ways since we first came to Naxos, particularly the development of beach resorts with their tavernas, bars and discotheques, bringing crowds of tourists to stretches of pink-white sands where once I could walk for miles without seeing anyone other than an occasional farmer on his mule. My book reflects these changes, though it leaves to other guidebooks a description of things touristic, concentrating instead on the history, monuments and culture of the Cyclades, described in the context of our own experiences with the friends we have made on Naxos and the other islands, particularly those mentioned in my dedication.

The first chapter is an introduction to the Cyclades, their people and culture, past and present. This is followed by chapters on the individual islands of the archipelago, all of which are different, one from the other, as are the various villages on each of the isles, many of them founded by refugees from either Asia Minor or Crete, others dating from prehistoric times, such is the varied character of the Cyclades. There is also an appendix with practical details that might help in exploring the islands, each of which is a world of its own, awaiting discovery.

Istanbul, 2006

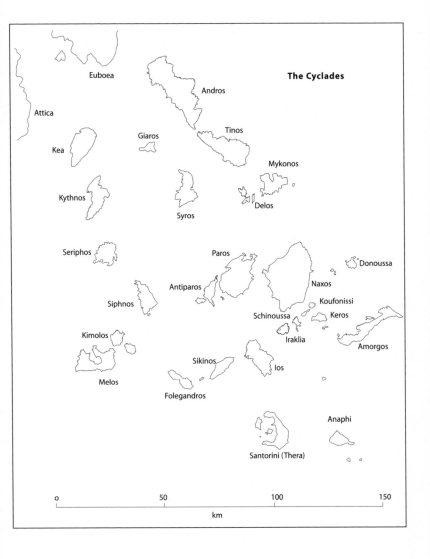

one
The Encircling Isles

The earliest reference to the islands of the central Aegean is in the Homeric Hymn to Delian Apollo, where the poet sings of the god's birth on the isle of Delos. The islands were thenceforth known as the Cyclades, or Encircling Isles, since they were set around the birthplace of the god worshipped by the first Greeks who settled in the archipelago.

When you are flying over the Aegean, as the goddess Leto did before she gave birth to Apollo on Delos, the Cyclades and the other isles around them look like the mountain-tops of a submerged Atlantis. The islands are in fact the peaks and flanks of a collapsed and engulfed plateau, now some one to two hundred metres below the surface of the Aegean.

The highest point on the Cyclades is Mount Zas on Naxos, 1,010 metres above sea level. Local legend has it that Zeus was reared in a cave on Zas after his birth on Crete, and that he was guarded there by eagles. I have seen a pair of eagles soaring over the peak of Zas, reminding me of the legend and lines from Book II of the *Odyssey*, where Telemachos sees '... a pair of eagles from a mountain crest/in gliding flight down the soft blowing wind,/wing-tip to wing-tip quivering taut'. And from the summit of Zas I have seen all of the Cyclades floating between the blues of sea and sky in what Homer, in Chapman's translation of the *Odyssey*, called the 'middle of the sable sea' between the Greek mainland, Asia Minor and Crete, whose peaks are visible to the south on the clearest of halcyon days.

A glance at the map of Greece shows that the Cyclades form the exposed heights of two ridges extending out from the Greek mainland. The south-western ridge is a prolongation of the Attic peninsula, while the north-eastern crest is an extension of the island of Euboea, the two merging at their southern end. Kea, Kythnos, Seriphos, Siphnos, Kimolos, Melos, Folegandros and Sikinos make up the south-western Cyclades; those along the north-eastern flank of the archipelago include Andros, Tinos, Mykonos, Delos, Syros, Paros, Naxos, Amorgos and Ios; while Santorini (Thera) and Anaphi represent the merging of the two ridges to the south-east.

Off to the east of the Cyclades are Ikaria and the Dodecanese, and beyond them the mountains of south-westernmost Asia Minor can sometimes be seen from Zas, particularly in the lemon light of false dawn, when the Anatolian peaks are silhouetted on the horizon and the isles look like stepping stones set between the opposing continents, which is indeed what they were when the first settlers made their way out to the islands in the night of time.

The north-eastern islands are formed of limestone, gneiss, schist and marble, the latter being used for stone vases and figurines rather than for building. Fine marble for sculptors has been quarried since antiquity on Paros and Naxos along with emery, the abrasive used in the working of stone and in tool-making. The islands along the south-western arc of the archipelago are made of volcanic rock: lava, basalt and trachyte. Melos was the main Aegean source of obsidian, the hard volcanic glass that was essential in the production of tools and weapons. Iron was produced on Seriphos, Kythnos and Andros, copper on Kythnos and possibly Seriphos, while Siphnos was renowned for its mines of gold and silver, which, according to Herodotus, made the Siphnians 'richer than any of the other island peoples'. Melos and Santorini are the remnants of craters, formed by a line of volcanic activity stretching from the Greek mainland across the Aegean to Asia Minor. The volcano on Santorini is still active, having last erupted in 1956. Its earliest known eruption, an explosion *c.* 1500 BC, may have given rise to the myth of Atlantis, the lost continent.

My first impression of the Cyclades, from the deck of a ship heading for Naxos in June 1962, was that they were as barren as the moon, without colour other than the grey-white of the rocks that penetrate through the thin earth of the terraced hillsides behind the tiered white houses of the port towns. But in hiking through the interiors of some of the islands, particularly Naxos, I came upon rich farmland, vineyards, orchards and olive groves as well as highland pastorages where herds of goats have been grazing since antiquity, as evidenced by an inscription high on Mount Zas identifying a shrine of Zeus as Protector of Flocks.

Several thousand species of flowers (*louloudia*) flourish in the Cyclades, along with flowering fruit trees, bushes, vines, herbs and weeds. Their blossoms form a floral calendar as they first appear in turn during the passing months. January brings anemones, crocuses and blossoming almond trees; February: narcissus, asphodels and Cretan irises; March: irises, white mandrake, grape hyacinth, wild garlic, wild orchid, rock rose, cyclamen, lupin, orange and lemon trees in full bloom; April: daisies, red poppies, chrysanthemums, camomile, broom and blossoming cherry trees; May: marigold, fennel, sage, oregano and flowering judas trees; June: pomegranate flowers and blossoming plum and peach trees; July: golden thistle, oleander and blossoming pear trees; August: sea daffodils and chaste-tree flowers; September: sea squill and crocus cancellatus; October: heather, sea onion, cyclamen, black mandrake and crocus cartwrightianus; November: jack-in-the-pulpit and crocus laevigatus; December: anemones, with almond trees beginning to flower at the end of the month.

Roses have been intensely cultivated in Greece since antiquity, and on the islands they bloom in olive-oil cans on the window sills and courtyard walls of houses and tavernas. And every house or taverna has a pot of basil, Greek *basiliko*, to sweeten the air with its fragrance, an aroma that can evoke memories of Greece when you are exiled in another world.

The olive has been one of the basic elements of the Greek economy since antiquity. There are olive groves on all of the islands, most notably on Naxos, where they stretch for miles across the highland plain known as the Tragaea, looking like a landlocked sea with their silver-green leaves quivering in the breeze, embowering whitewashed chapels and Venetian tower-houses, their gnarled and convoluted trunks embedded deeply in the earth, invisible hordes of cicadas chattering from their branches.

Every Cycladic village square and church courtyard is shaded by a giant *platanos*, or plane tree, some of them centuries old, as evidenced by the great girth of their bark-shedding trunks, rivalling the most venerable olive trees in their antiquity. It is a veritable Tree of Idleness, spreading its dappled shade over the village *kafenion*, where the locals take their ease after a day of working in their fields. Another distinctive element in the Cycladic landscape is the cypress, or *kiparissi*, sacred to Artemis. In the Orphic mysteries it was the symbol of resurrection, as it is still today, its spectral groves invariably shading graveyards, spectral memento mori.

Around the eighth century BC the Ionians began meeting annually at Delos, the mythical birthplace of Apollo and Artemis, the twin children of Zeus and Leto. The divine twins were the patron deities of the Ionians, and so their birthplace was chosen to be the religious and political centre of the Hellenes who settled in the islands of the central Aegean and on the western coast of Anatolia. According to the myth, Artemis was born first and assisted Leto in her delivery of Apollo, whose birthday was subsequently commemorated by an annual festival on Delos. The Homeric Hymn to Delian Apollo is both a paean to the god and a tribute to the Ionians themselves.

> Many are your temples and wooded groves ... yet in Delos do you most delight your heart; for the long-robed Ionians gather in your honour with their children and shy wives. Mindful they delight you with boxing and

dancing and song, so often as they hold their gathering. A man would say they are deathless and unageing if he should come upon the Ionians so met together. For he would see the graces of them all, and would be pleased in heart gazing at the well-girded women and the men with their swift ships and great renown.

The cult of Artemis was as strong in the Cyclades as that of Apollo. Although she was represented as a virgin huntress in classical times, Artemis is undoubtedly a fertility goddess stemming from the Great Earth Mother of Anatolia.

Another ancient myth of the Aegean is that of Theseus and his flight from Crete with Ariadne, daughter of King Minos, who led him and his men out of the Labyrinth only to be abandoned on Naxos, where Dionysos took her as his bride.

After their sacred marriage, Dionysos set Ariadne's bridal wreath among the stars, where it still sparkles as the constellation Corona Borealis. Hesiod describes their union in his *Theogony*: 'And golden-haired Dionysos took for his buxom wife brown-haired Ariadne, the daughter of Minos, and the son of Kronos [Zeus] made her deathless and ageless for him.'

The history of the Cyclades is a long and turbulent one, with periods in which the archipelago was powerful and prosperous alternating with times when it was an insignificant backwater of the Aegean.

The earliest evidence of human settlement on the Cyclades was found at Loutra on Kythnos, dating to the first half of the seventh millennium BC. The archipelago seems to have had a relatively numerous population by the third millennium BC, when more of the islands were inhabited than are today. The economy was based on agriculture and fishing along with seaborne commerce, as evidenced by archaeological finds including prehistoric carvings and paintings.

One of the first to write of this Cycladic civilisation was James Theodore Bent, who in 1885 published an article in the *Journal of Hellenic Studies* entitled 'Researches Among the Cyclades', in which he reported on the archaeological findings that led him to the discovery of 'a prehistoric empire of the sea', a civilisation that he called 'Cycladic'. Archaeologists have since unearthed numerous Cycladic sites on all of the Cyclades, including 36 on Naxos alone, most of them dating from the period 3200–1150 BC, the Bronze Age of Greece and Anatolia.

The most fascinating finds made in the Early Cycladic sites are marble statuettes placed in graves as votive offerings, most of them stylised representations of what is believed to be a fertility goddess. These are similar to figurines of the Great Earth Mother of Bronze Age Anatolia, indicating that the first settlers in the Cyclades came from Asia Minor, crossing the Aegean on the stepping stones provided by the isles, bringing their goddess with them.

Archaeological evidence indicates that *c.* 1600 BC the Cyclades came under the dominion of Minoan Crete, whose rulers had established what the Greeks later called a *thalassocracy*, or maritime empire. The principal Minoan colony in the Cyclades seems to have been on Santorini, as evidenced by the excavations at Akrotiri, with their vivid frescoes depicting life in a Bronze Age town. Akrotiri is a Cycladic Pompeii, buried in ash by a colossal volcanic explosion *c.* 1500 BC, preserving the town frozen in time until its rediscovery by the Greek archaeologist Spyridon Marinatos in the years 1967–1974.

The explosion left Santorini uninhabited for the next two centuries, and when settlers returned they and the other Cycladic islanders were under the dominion of the Mycenaean Greeks who had conquered Crete. The archipelago remained under Mycenaean rule until the mid-twelfth century BC, when a wave of invaders known as the Sea Peoples destroyed Bronze Age civilisation, beginning the Dark Ages of the ancient world.

At the end of the second millennium BC a mass migration took place, in which the Hellenes left mainland Greece and moved across the Aegean, settling in the islands and on the western coast of Anatolia, first the Aeolians, then to their south the Ionians, and finally the Dorians still farther to the south. So far as the Cyclades were concerned, the Ionians settled on all of the islands except Melos, Kimolos, Folegandros, Santorini and Anaphi, which were colonised by the Dorians, along with Crete.

Early in the archaic period (c. 750–480 BC) the Greeks began founding colonies around the Mediterranean as well as in the Black Sea and its approaches through the Hellespont, the Sea of Marmara and the Bosphorus. The Naxians joined with the Ionian city of Erythrae in Asia Minor in 734 BC to found the first Greek colony in Sicily, calling it Naxos, whose settlers went on to establish the cities of Leontini and Catana. Paros and Erythrae founded the city of Parium in the Marmara in 710 BC, and a decade or so later the Parians established a colony on Thasos.

Around 655 BC Andros established four colonies on the east coast of the Greek mainland. Then c. 630 BC Santorini founded the city of Cyrene in Libya, the first Greek colony in Africa, whose settlers went on to establish other colonies along the African coast.

The leader of the Parian colony on Thasos was Telesikles, father of the poet Archilochus, whom the ancient Greeks ranked second only to Homer. Archilochus earned his living as a mercenary soldier and died in battle on Thasos, killed by a Naxian named Corax, the Crow. One of the best of his surviving works is a three-line fragment that catches the numbing ache of unrequited passion.

> Here I lie mournful with desire,
> Feeble in bitterness of the pain gods inflicted upon me,
> Struck through the bones with love.

During the archaic period Cycladic sculptors produced the first monumental free-standing statues in the Greek world. These were larger-than-life-sized marble statues of young men (s. *kuros*, pl. *kouroi*) and young women (s. *kore*, pl. *korai*), set up in temples of Apollo and Artemis as dedicatory offerings. Three of these statues still lie in or near the ancient marble quarries on Naxos where they were carved, while others are on exhibit in museums in Athens and elsewhere in Europe. The most characteristic features of the *kouroi* are their haunting archaic smiles and the plaited hair hanging down over their shoulders, a representation of a young man idealised as Apollo. This is reminiscent of the Pythian Hymn to Apollo, written only a generation before the earliest of these statues were created: 'He is like a youth, lusty and powerful in his first bloom, his hair spread over his shoulders.'

Naxos became the strongest state in the Aegean in the mid-sixth century BC, when it came under the control of the tyrant Lygdamis, who built a formidable fleet and an army of 8,000 hoplites. After a reign of 20 years Lygdamis was deposed by aristocrats backed by Sparta. The aristocracy held power for the next quarter of a century before they were overthrown and replaced by a democratic regime. The aristocrats sailed off to the Ionian city of Miletos in Asia Minor, where they appealed to the Persian satrap Aristagoras for help in regaining power. Aristagoras referred the matter to the Persian king Darius, pointing out that a restoration of the Naxian aristocrats would be a convenient excuse for launching an invasion of Greece. Darius agreed, and in 499 BC a huge Persian fleet and army besieged Naxos for four months, after which they ran out of supplies and sailed back to Miletos.

The failure of this expedition led the Ionian cities in Asia Minor to rebel against Persian rule, but they were crushed after a five-year struggle. Darius then prepared to invade Greece, and in 492 BC his son-in-law Mardonius conquered Thrace and Macedonia. Two years later an enormous Persian fleet sacked Naxos before they were defeated by the Greeks at the Battle of Marathon.

Darius was succeeded by his son Xerxes, who in 480 BC crossed the Hellespont to begin an invasion of Greece, only to be defeated at Artemisium, Salamis and Plataea by the Greek allies, including several of the Cycladic isles. This marks the beginning of the classical period (480–336 BC), when Athens emerged as the political and cultural centre of the Greek world. Two years after their victory the Greeks founded a maritime confederacy known as the Delian League, so called because its meeting place was Delos. It soon became evident that Athens was using the League to dominate the Greek world, and so in 470 BC Naxos decided to withdraw. The

Athenians responded by attacking Naxos and demolishing its defence walls, after which they forced the Naxians to rejoin the League under far less favourable terms. This effectively broke the power of Naxos, and throughout the remainder of antiquity the island no longer played an important role in Greek history.

Thucydides considered the abortive Naxian revolt to be one of the first steps on the road that led to the Peloponnesian War, which wracked Greece in the years 431–404 BC. Most of the Cyclades sided with Athens, but Melos, because of its Dorian origins, chose to remain neutral, sending gifts to Sparta but no troops.

This led Athens to attack and conquer Melos in 415 BC, when all of the adult males on the island were put to death and the women and children sold into slavery. After Athens surrendered to Sparta in 404 BC the few surviving Melians, virtually all of them widows and children, made their way back to the island, which for the rest of antiquity was just a ghost of its former self.

The Hellenistic period began in 336 BC when Alexander the Great succeeded to the throne of Macedonia, which by then controlled all of Greece. After Alexander's death in 323 BC, the Cyclades were ruled first by the Macedonians (318–285 BC) and then by the Ptolemies of Egypt (285–241 BC), who established naval bases on several of the islands. At the beginning of the second century BC the Cyclades came under the control of Rhodes, whose domination ceased when the Romans completed their conquest of Greece in 146 BC, ending the Hellenistic era.

The most impressive monuments of the Hellenistic era on the Cyclades are the splendid watchtowers (s. *pyrgos*, pl. *pyrgoi*) one sees standing on remote hilltops. These were erected early in the Hellenistic period to watch for the approach of enemy fleets, and for two millennia afterwards they also gave shelter to the local people in case of corsair raids. They are the oldest historic landmarks on the Cyclades, erected when Alexander the Great was still in living memory.

During the early part of the Roman period (146 BC–AD 330) the Cyclades became prosperous under the mantle of the *pax*

Romana, particularly Delos, which, in addition to being a famous shrine, was an important banking centre and marketplace, particularly for the slave trade. But in the years 88–69 BC Delos was twice sacked by Mithridates VI of Pontus during his wars with Rome, disasters from which it never recovered, so that at the beginning of the Christian era it was virtually abandoned, by which time the other Aegean isles were almost deserted as well.

The centre of gravity of the Roman world shifted in AD 330, when Constantine the Great moved his capital to Byzantium on the Bosphorus, thenceforth known as Constantinople. During the Byzantine era the Cyclades were far away from the centre of power and virtually disappeared from history, left undefended against the attacks of the corsairs who ravaged the Aegean.

Christianity seems to have reached the Cyclades by the fourth century, as evidenced by the establishment of a bishopric on Santorini in 342. During the medieval era churches were built all over the Cyclades, many of them still standing, including some decorated with mosaics that represent a unique heritage of Byzantine art, created in a forgotten corner of the Greek world.

Monasteries were founded on all of the islands as well, invariably in the form of a fortified *pyrgos* patterned on the watchtowers of Hellenistic times, for the monks and nuns had to protect themselves against corsair raids. These constant raids forced the islanders to leave the coast and resettle in mountain villages invisible from the sea, facing the backs of the peripheral houses outward to create a surrounding fortification wall, with an inner citadel for a last-ditch defence.

A new era in Aegean history began in 1204, when the Latin knights of the Fourth Crusade and the Venetian fleet under Doge Enrico Dandolo sacked Constantinople. The Latins then created an empire named Romania on the wreckage of the Byzantine Empire, which they divided up among themselves, with the Cyclades falling to the lot of the Venetians.

Marco Sanudo, nephew of Doge Dandolo, recruited a force of Venetians in Constantinople and set out in a flotilla of eight ships for the Aegean in 1207, capturing Naxos after a five-week siege. Using Naxos as his base, Sanudo went on to take Paros, Antiparos, Amorgos, Ios, Sikinos, Folegandros, Melos, Siphnos, Kythnos and Syros. At the same time other Venetian adventurers occupied Kea, Seriphos, Andros, Tinos, Mykonos, Santorini and Anaphi.

By *c.* 1210 all of the Cyclades had been occupied by Venetians, and the emperor Henry of Flanders agreed to make these fiefs of Romania, the Latin empire he ruled from Constantinople, giving Marco Sanudo the title of Duke of the Archipelago. Sanudo then built a fortified castle on the acropolis of the principal town and port of Naxos, the Chora, which became the capital of the Duchy of the Archipelago. This castle, known in Greek as the Kastro, housed the duke and the other members of the new Latin aristocracy, who worshipped in a Roman Catholic cathedral that Sanudo erected within the citadel. The subject Greeks were free to worship in their Orthodox churches in the lower town and in the countryside, where they worked as serfs on the estates of their masters, a pattern repeated throughout the Cyclades. Relations between the Greeks and Latins were on the whole good and intermarriage was common, fostering a Graeco–Italian culture that still lingers on in the Cyclades, particularly in the Kastro of Naxos, where some of the former Venetian aristocracy continue to reside.

The Greeks regained control of Constantinople in 1261, though the Latins continued to hold a large part of the former Byzantine possessions, including the Cyclades. Seven years later the Byzantine admiral Licario recaptured several of the Cyclades, but all of the islands were eventually regained by the Venetians. Then in 1311 the Catalans defeated the Latin rulers of Athens, which they held until 1389, and during that period they raided Kea, Siphnos, Melos and Santorini.

A new threat appeared with the rise of the Ottoman Turks, who established their first capital in 1326 at Bursa in north-western Asia Minor. In 1344 a flotilla of Turkish corsairs sacked Naxos, slaughtering the adult males and carrying away all of the women and children to be sold as slaves. The Byzantine Empire came to an end in 1453 when the Ottoman sultan Mehmet II conquered Constantinople, which then, as Istanbul, became the capital of the Ottoman Empire.

Meanwhile the Cyclades remained under the control of the Venetians, who fought three wars with the Turks in the century following the fall of Constantinople. By then the Ottomans had reached the peak of their power under Sultan Süleyman the Magnificent (r. 1520–1566), who led his armies in a dozen victorious campaigns that expanded his empire as far as the Danube, while his fleets threatened to control the Mediterranean.

The most formidable of the Turkish admirals was a pirate from Lesbos named Hayrettin Pasha, better known to the West as Barbarossa, who in 1533 was appointed by Süleyman to command the Ottoman fleet. Four years later Barbarossa attacked the Venetian-held islands in the Adriatic and the Aegean, conquering Paros, where he killed virtually all of the men and carried the women and children off to the slave market in Istanbul. Naxos was spared the same fate when Duke Giovanni IV Crispo paid a huge sum to Barbarossa, a tribute that had to be renewed each year when the Turkish fleet reappeared in the islands.

The Latin Duchy of the Archipelago finally came to an end in 1566, by which time all of the Cyclades were under Turkish rule except for Tinos, which survived as a protectorate of Venice until 1715, when the last Venetian governor surrendered to the Ottomans.

Thus began the *Turkokrateia*, the rule of the Turks, which for most of the Cyclades lasted for more than two and a half centuries. The Cyclades on the whole fared somewhat better under Ottoman rule than did mainland Greece, for the islands were never occupied by the Turks, who merely sent a few civil servants to collect taxes and to administer the sultan's laws. The laxness of Ottoman rule was a mixed blessing, particularly as the empire declined, for the absence of the Turkish fleet left the islands defenceless against piracy once again. The bitter memories of these corsair raids are perpetuated in some of the *nisiotika tragoudia*, the 'songs of the islands', particularly the lament called *I Sklavi ton Koursaron*

(The Slaves of the Corsairs), which refers to the Barbaressi, or Barbarians.

> Sun, when you come up tomorrow
> To give light to the whole world,
> Rise for all the world,
> For all the universe.
> But in the halls of the Barbaressi,
> Sun, don't rise.
> And if you do, set quickly.
> For they have many handsome slaves
> Who suffer greatly,
> And your rays will be turned to water by their tears.

During the Russo–Turkish Wars of 1768–1774 and 1787–1792 the Greeks were led to believe that they might be liberated from Ottoman rule. A Russian fleet of some thirty warships sailed through the Cyclades in 1770, stopping off in Naxos and Paros, but four years later Russia signed a peace treaty with the Ottomans, leaving the Greeks to their fate. During the second war a Russian fleet commanded by Lambros Katsonis of Kea cleared the Turkish corsairs from the Aegean, but once again the conflict ended with Greece still under Ottoman rule.

Many from the Cyclades took part in the Greek War of Independence, which began on 25 March 1821. The *Turkokrateia* ended on the archipelago in 1832, when the modern Greek Kingdom came into being, with the Cyclades included within its boundaries, though not Crete or most of the other Aegean isles. Syros became for a time the principal port in Greece, and the other Cyclades revived as well through their renewed contacts with the Greek mainland. But otherwise there was little change in the life of the islanders, particularly in the interior mountains. This is evident from what James Theodore Bent wrote in his book *The Cyclades, or Life Among the Insular Greeks*, published in 1885, where he observes of Naxos that '… up in its lofty mountains it contains some of the most primitive inhabitants of modern Hellas, half robbers, almost heathen in their beliefs'.

The 'primitive' Naxians of whom Bent was speaking were actually Cretans, who had resettled on Naxos as well as on Melos after fleeing from Turkish oppression on Crete, where the *Turkokrateia* did not end until 1898. Another wave of refugees washed up on the Cyclades in 1922–1923, when the Greeks in Asia Minor were deported during the population exchange following the Graeco–Turkish War of 1919–1922. The refugees brought their music and poetry with them, as they had in the nineteenth century, and so even today in the mountain villages of Naxos you hear Anatolian laments and the extemporaneous Cretan rhymes known as *mantinades*, whose origins go back to Venetian times.

The Cyclades suffered under Italian and German occupation during the Second World War, when many of the islanders died of starvation. The islands recovered slowly during the two decades following the war, and then in the late 1960s many of them began attracting tourists in large numbers, accelerating their economic development, though at some cost to their traditional way of life.

Foreigners are particularly drawn to the Cyclades because of their superb beaches and the nightlife of famous islands like Mykonos, the beauty of their white cubist villages and seascapes, and their historical monuments and archaeological sites such as on Delos and Santorini. But there is another island world beyond this, and those who seek it leave behind the crowded resorts to hike out along mule tracks that wind across the thyme-scented hills, where the only sounds are the occasional tinkling of faraway goat bells and the soughing of the wind among the gnarled olive trees. The tracks lead to whitewashed roadside chapels and monasteries, Venetian tower-houses and dovecotes, Byzantine churches embowered in olive groves, a sacred well flowing from the remains of a temple of Artemis, a classical landscape in which the only reminders of the modern world are the occasional jet trails of passing airplanes.

The tracks eventually bring you to whitewashed villages perched on the tawny flanks of terraced mountains. Traces of the archaic Cycladic way of life still linger on in these mountain villages, particularly in the recurring cycle of *paneyeria*, the religious festivals whose customs, music, songs and dances preserve the oldest elements of Aegean culture.

The *paneyeria* have their roots in the pagan festivals that marked the agricultural year, part of the Bronze Age culture that extended across Europe from Greece to Ireland. The traditional Greek agricultural year recognises only two seasons, summer and winter. Summer begins with the *paneyeri* of Agios Yiorgios (St George), which in the modern calendar is celebrated on 23 April, when shepherds leave their winter folds and lead their flocks up to the mountains pastures. Winter starts on the feast day of Ayios Dimitrios, 26 October, when the flocks are driven back to their folds down in the plains. The end of winter is heralded at the beginning of March by the Procession of the Swallow, in which children proceed from house to house with a wooden effigy of a bird, singing 'A swallow came to us, she sat on a bough and sweetly sang...' I had done the same as a boy in Ireland on the feast of St Stephen, except that we carried a wren rather than a swallow, and the song we sang was 'The wren, the wren, king of all birds...'

The most popular dance at island *paneyeria* is the *syrtos*, so ancient that it appears in the *Iliad*, where Homer sings of a young woman leading a line of men through 'certain turnings and returning, imitative of the windings and twisting of the labyrinth'. Such is the continuity of culture in the Cyclades, where immemorial past and timeless present meld together in the evolutions of a village dance.

The wayfarer is always welcome at these village festivals, particularly if you come trudging up the mule track at the end of a long hike, having left the modern world to find the old Greece that some say is gone for ever. But the old Greece is still there, particularly in the Cyclades, though it reveals itself only to those who set out in search of its traces, the quest itself being part of the discovery.

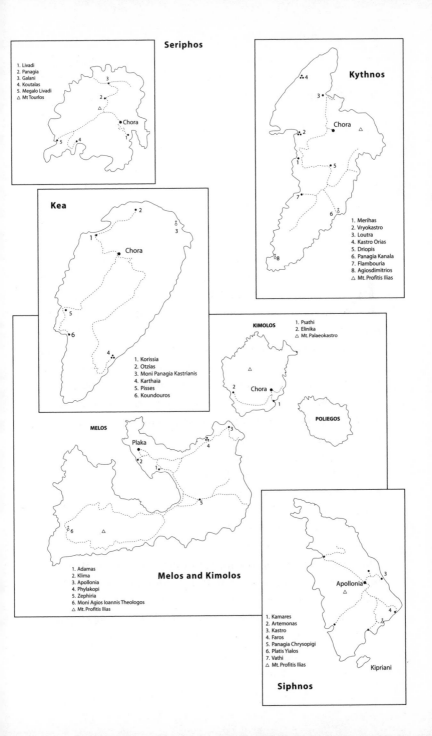

Seriphos

1. Livadi
2. Panagia
3. Galani
4. Koutalas
5. Megalo Livadi
△ Mt Tourlos

Chora

Kea

Chora

1. Korissia
2. Otzias
3. Moni Panagia Kastrianis
4. Karthaia
5. Pisses
6. Koundouros

Kythnos

Chora

1. Merihas
2. Vryokastro
3. Loutra
4. Kastro Orias
5. Driopis
6. Panagia Kanala
7. Flambouria
8. Agiosdimitrios
△ Mt. Profitis Ilias

KIMOLOS

Chora

1. Psathi
2. Elinika
△ Mt. Palaeokastro

POLIEGOS

MELOS

Plaka

1. Adamas
2. Klima
3. Apollonia
4. Phylakopi
5. Zephiria
6. Moni Agios Ioannis Theologos
△ Mt. Profitis Ilias

Melos and Kimolos

Apollonia

1. Kamares
2. Artemonas
3. Kastro
4. Faros
5. Panagia Chrysopigi
6. Platis Yialos
7. Vathi
△ Mt. Profitis Ilias

Kipriani

Siphos

two
Kea

Kea is the north-westernmost of the Cyclades and is thus the closest of the archipelago to the Greek mainland, 13 nautical miles from Cape Sounion on the Attic peninsula. I first saw Kea in June 1962 from the deck of the *Despina*, the ferry that was taking us to Naxos, steaming through the strait between Kea's southern cape and the northern promontory of Kythnos, with some of the other islands of the archipelago barely visible as sea-girt mountains in the marine mist off to the south and east. We were in the Cyclades, and I recalled the lines of Byron that had started me off on this odyssey.

> The isles of Greece, the isles of Greece!
> Where burning Sappho loved and sung,
> Where grew the arts of war and peace,
> Where Delos rose and Phoebus sprung,
> Eternal summer gilds them yet,
> Though all except their sun is set.

Kea, the ancient Keos, was known in the Venetian era as Tzia or Zea. The Irish poet Thomas Moore, Byron's friend and biographer, refers to it by the latter name in lines from his *Evenings in Greece*, where he gives a lyrical description of an island that he knew only from his reading of classical sources.

> There is a font on Zea's isle,
> Round which, in soft luxuriance smile

All the sweet flowers of every kind.
On which the sun of Greece looks down...

Kea is for the most part mountainous, with its highest peak, Mount Profitis Ilias, rising to an elevation of 570 metres above sea level. The mountain is corrugated with terraced valleys planted with vines and almond trees descending to little bays and sandy beaches. All but the northern slope of the mountain is covered with Valonia oaks, the only oak forest in the Cyclades.

The island was originally known as Hydroussa, the 'well-watered isle', so called because of its numerous springs. According to legend, its original inhabitants were nymphs who lived in these springs, but they were driven away by a huge lion, whose petrified form can still be seen on the island. One of these nymphs was Cyrene, after whom the land of Cyrenaica in Libya is named. Cyrene became the mistress of Apollo and bore him a son named Aristaeus, to whom she taught the arts of dairy farming, bee-keeping and viniculture, which he passed on to mankind. When a heatwave and drought killed all the crops on the island the Keans begged Aristaeus to help them. And so he came to Kea and built an altar on the highest peak of the island, where he offered sacrifices to Zeus. Zeus responded by sending the Etesian winds, known in Greece as the *meltemi*, the prevailing northerly breeze that cools the Cyclades even in the height of summer.

Another Kean myth tells the story of Cyparrisus, a son of Telephus, the legendary founder of Pergamum. Cyparissus, who was beloved of Apollo, spent his short life on Kea in the company of a sacred stag, whom he killed one day with his javelin. The youth was so stricken with grief that he wanted to take his own life, beseeching the gods to let him do so as he wept inconsolably. But the gods answered his request by transforming him into a cypress, the tree of sadness and resurrection, which thereafter bore his name.

Herodotus says that the Keans were Ionian colonists from Athens and that they contributed ships to the Greek fleets that won naval battles against the Persians in 480 BC at Artemisium and Salamis, sending two 50-oared galleys to the first and two triremes to the second. The Keans also fought at the battle of Plataea in 479 BC, when the Greeks won their final victory over the Persians. After Plataea, Kea was one of the 31 allies whose names were inscribed on the golden tripod dedicated by the Greeks in the sanctuary of Apollo at Delphi. The names can still be seen on the serpentine base of the column, now in the ancient Hippodrome in Istanbul, under the heading 'The following fought the war...'

During the classical era Kea had four cities: Ioulis, Korissia, Poiessa and Karthaia. These cities formed a *tetrapolis*, governed by a convention described in a lost work of Aristotle entitled *The Constitution of the Keans*. It is said that at least one of the cities, Ioulis, decreed that every person on reaching the age of 70 should commit suicide by drinking hemlock, so as to avoid being a burden to society, a harsh measure that seems to have been adopted when Kea was besieged by the Athenians in 360 BC. Plutarch, in his life of Pompey, writes of the general's astonishment at seeing a noble lady of Kea drink poison while surrounded by her family and friends, although at the age of 90 rather than 70.

The Keans were known for their modesty and sobriety, and the Roman writer Varro credits them with having introduced a greater degree of elegance in female dress. They owed their wealth primarily to trade in metals, enamels and acorns, the latter coming from the island's forest of Valonia oaks, which Bent estimated to number a million and a half trees. Kea was also noted for its wine, which the medieval Byzantine scholar Michael Psellos described as 'beneficial to the lips and mouth, sweet to the scent, and black in colour'.

Kea produced two of the great poets of ancient Greece, Simonides (*c.* 556–468 BC) and his nephew Bacchylides (*c.* 505–450 BC), both of whom were born in Ioulis.

Simonides is best known for his epigrams, particularly the one inscribed on the tomb of the Spartan heroes who died at the battle of Thermopylae in 480 BC: 'Tell them in Lacedaemon, passerby,/ That obedient to their word here we lie.'

The most beautiful of Simonides' lyric poems is perhaps 'Halcyon Days'. Here he sings of the halcyon, the mythical bird that was supposed to breed on the calm surface of the sea in mid-winter, when the gods calmed the Aegean for a fortnight, the so-called *halcyonidis meras*, which the Cyclades still enjoy in late January and early February.

> As when in the winter moon God stills
> Weather a space of fourteen days,
> And winds sleep in the season, and men have named it
> Sacred to the breeding of the bright halcyon.

Bacchylides is noted for his dithyrambs, or dramatic lyrics, the best-known of which describes the flight of Theseus from Crete, beginning with these lines:

> A dark prowed ship, carrying battle-brave
> Theseus and twice seven glorious Ionian
> young men and maidens,
> was cutting the open sea off Crete,
> for into her sails far-white-gleaming
> blew the northern winds
> by grace of renowned Athene...

According to Strabo, at the beginning of the Christian era only two of the four cities on Kea remained, the population of Korissia and Poiessa having been removed to Ioulis and Karthaia. By the thirteenth century only Ioulis survived, for Karthaia had been abandoned during the Byzantine era, when the island became a lair for the pirates who infested the Aegean.

Early in the thirteenth century Kea became the home of Michael Choniates, the former Greek Orthodox archbishop of Athens, who was exiled when the Latins took the city in 1205. A poem that Michael wrote in 1211 shows that the Latins had not yet taken Kea, but it would seem that the Venetians must have arrived soon afterwards. The island was taken by the brothers Andrea and Geremia Ghisi together with Pietro Giustiani and Domenico Michiel, each of whom ruled a fourth of their conquest. Michiel took possession of Ioulis, which he fortified with a *kastro*, one of the strongest in the Cyclades. Early in the fifteenth century Kea passed by inheritance to the Gozzadini family, who held the island until the beginning of the Ottoman era.

The *Turkokrateia* began on Kea in 1537, when Süleyman's admiral Barbarossa plundered the island, whose inhabitants either fled or were carried off into slavery. Kea remained virtually uninhabited until 1566, when a branch of the Gozzadini family on Seriphos sent a group of settlers to the island, whose population was increased later in that century by refugees from Albania.

One of the very few accounts of life on the Cyclades in Ottoman times is that of the Provençal botanist and antiquarian Joseph Pitton de Tournefort, whose *Voyage into the Levant*, translated into English by John Ozell, was published in 1718. Tournefort stayed only a day on Kea, which he refers to by a version of its Latin name.

> Being apprehensive of the inconveniences in this island, Bandetti and Famine, we tarried but 24 hours in it … The burghers of Zia generally get together when they spin their silk; they sit upon the very edge of their terrass-roofs, and let the spindle into the street, and then draw it up again in winding the thread. We found the Greek bishop in this posture; he asked us who we were, and at the same time giving us to understand that 'twas a sign we had not much to do, if we came thither only to hunt for plants and pieces of antiquity: to which we reply'd, we should be much more edified to find him reading St Chrysostom's or St Basil's sermons, than winding off bottoms of silk.

Kea revived in the late Ottoman period, when for a time its port became the principal harbour in Greece. After the establishment of the modern Greek kingdom in 1832, Syros replaced Kea as the principal port in Greece.

Today the island is known locally by its Latin name of Tzia. The principal city is still Ioulis, known today as Chora, the name generally given to the principal town of a Greek island.

Ferries land on the north-western coast at Korissia, set at the southern end of the Gulf of Agios Nikolaos, one of the finest natural harbours in the Cyclades. The harbour was a lair of pirates during the Byzantine era, and during the Russo–Turkish War of 1787–1792 it was used as a base by the Kean captain Lambros Katsonis.

The site of ancient Korissia is a short way to the west of the port, where some scattered ruins can be seen on a promontory. The Kean Kouros, now in the National Archaeological Museum in Athens, was unearthed here in 1930 by the Greek archaeologist Stavropoulos. The discovery of the *kouros* substantiated the testimony of ancient sources that at Korissia there was a temple of Apollo, for such colossal statues were dedicated in his sanctuaries. Apollo was worshipped here as Smintheus, the Mouse God – a cult first mentioned in the *Iliad*.

An inscription found on the site of the ancient city is now set into the wall of a modern house in the port at Korissia; it reads: 'I am the ancient Korissia. At some time the Romans came and conquered me. My citizens are eagerly rebuilding me. From now on I will no longer be an unimportant harbour in the Aegean.'

There are good beaches along the bay north of Korissia at Yialiskari and Voukari, a seaside village whose tavernas serve up the fish caught by the local fishermen.

Around the bay beyond Voukari there is an important archaeological site at Agia Eirene, named for a chapel on the northern horn of the gulf. Excavations by the American archaeologist J. L. Caskey beginning in 1960 unearthed a settlement that was first occupied prior to *c.* 3200 BC. During the period 1700–1500 BC a Minoan colony flourished here, a port on the trade route between Crete and the Greek mainland. The settlement continued in existence to the end of the Bronze Age, *c.* 1150 BC.

On the north coast the hamlet of Otzias has now become a popular summer resort, with a long sandy beach bordered by tamarisk trees. The village church of Agios Sozon celebrates its *paneyeri* on 7 September. Sozon was a Christian shepherd in

Lycaonia who suffered martyrdom in the reign of the emperor Maximianus, and in times past his feast day was celebrated with offerings and the sacrificing of lambs.

Bent discovered the ancient harbour works of Otzias, from where the Keans shipped a mineral called *miltos*, used to manufacture a red dye. His discovery led him to suggest that 'probably many a boat in ancient days here painted its bows and became, as Homer expresses it, "a red-cheeked ship"'.

There is another important archaeological site near Otzias on the barren headland known as Kephala, first excavated in 1898 by the Greek archaeologist Christos Tsountas and subsequently studied by Caskey. The excavations have shown that the site was first settled *c.* 3600 BC, the earliest known settlement on Kea. It was a hamlet of some fifty people, who dwelt in simple stone-built houses, cultivated crops, reared animals and collected shellfish. Their dead were buried in a nearby cemetery of cist-tombs, a pit lined with stones and covered with a large capstone.

The most important monastery on the island is beyond Otzias on the north-westernmost promontory of the island. This is Moni Panagia Kastrianis, the Monastery of Our Lady of the Castle. The monastery, founded in the early eighteenth century, houses a miraculous icon of the Virgin which is popularly believed to have protected the Keans from corsairs during the *Turkokrateia*. On 15 August all of the people of Kea make a pilgrimage here to celebrate the great *paneyeri* of the Virgin's Assumption. This is one of the most important festivals in the Greek calendar, coming at the end of a 15-day fast in honour of the Virgin. The beginning of this fast is marked by various customs, such as the cleansing of all copper cooking pots, and the offering of figs, grapes and other fruit at the church altar. This period of fasting adds to the general outburst of gaiety on the holiday itself, which is celebrated with music, song and traditional folk dancing.

The main road on the island winds up from Korissia to Chora, the capital of Kea. This was one of the first paved highways on the Cyclades, completed shortly before the Greek monarchs King Otho and Queen Amalia paid a visit to Kea in 1840. When Otto asked to see the man who built the road a peasant was brought before him, and when the king asked to see his tools the man produced a hammer, a length of string and a lead weight. Otto offered him a sum of money as a reward for his work, and he accepted only after being told that it would be an insult to turn down the royal gift.

Chora is perched on a mountainside at an altitude of 352 metres, commanding a splendid panorama of the surrounding seascape. The town is a labyrinth of winding whitewashed alleyways, some of which tunnel through the surrounding houses, dominated by the neoclassical *Demarcheion*, or Town Hall, which is surmounted by marble statues of Athena and Apollo. Bent identified the town as the site of Ioulis, capital of Kea in antiquity and again in the medieval Latin era. He found the town very odd and filthy.

> Keos is the queerest place imaginable: the flat roof of the house beneath us fitted close up to ours, and this seemed to be the universal custom, so that most of the houses are entered by the roof of the house in front. Everyone walks on the roofs as being preferable to the dark, dirty alleys, arched over for the most part, which are given up to pigs...

But I myself found Chora to be as clean and spotless as any community in the Cyclades, its pigs no longer in evidence except as pork chops served up in the local tavernas.

The town was once dominated by a Venetian fortress built soon after 1211 by Domenico Michiel, who held his fourth of the island as a sub-fief from Marco I Sanudo, Duke of Naxos. This fortress, known locally as Kastro, was for the most part destroyed in 1865. Its single arched entryway survives as the entrance to the upper town, along with part of its defence wall, the lower course of which is built from ancient marble blocks. There are also a number of ancient springs in and around the town, all of them still in use. The local archaeological museum preserves some Cycladic antiquities from the site at Agia Eirene, as well as architectural and sculptural fragments of classical Ioulis.

The patron saint of Kea is Agios Haralambos, and his *paneyeri* is celebrated on 10 February at his church in the Chora. Haralambos was renowned for his ability to protect Christians against the plague. The traditional offering made to him was an apron made of 'one-day' cloth, woven in one night by a group of women gathered together in a house, weaving to the sound of incantations that were believed to endow the fabric with magical powers so that it would be a talisman against the plague.

The Chora also has a *paneyeri* on the Feast of the Assumption on 15 August at the church of the Panagia, and those who do not make the pilgrimage to the Panagia Kastrianis celebrate the festival here.

The oldest and most fascinating antiquity on the island is about two kilometres north-east of Chora, approached by an old cobblestone road flanked by olive trees. This is the famous Leon Petrino, the archaic figure of a recumbent lion carved out of the living rock of the mountainside. This colossal sculpture, six metres long and 2.7 metres high, has been dated to the early sixth century BC. Bent thought that the lion originally may have been set at the end of a stadium, some of whose seats were visible in his time, though these have now vanished. He also suggested that this figure gave rise to the myth of the great lion who drove all the nymphs from Kea, a legend that is still part of the folklore of the island, as I learned from an old farmer whom I met when I was examining the Leon Petrino.

The monastery of Agia Anna is set high on a mountain east of Chora. The *katholikon*, or monastic church, which dates from the sixteenth century, has been completely restored in recent times. Off to the south-east there is another old monastery, of which all that survives is its small *katholikon*, dedicated to the Panagia tis Episcopi, Our Lady of the Bishop, dated by its dedicatory inscription to 1641. The name suggests that this was the seat of the Bishop of Kea, though there is no indication as to whether the church was Greek Orthodox or Roman Catholic. The centre of the island is dominated by Mount Profitis Ilias, where Aristaeus, son of Apollo and the nymph Cyrene, offered sacrifices to Zeus to end the heat and drought that afflicted the island. On the peak of the mountain there is a chapel of Agios Profitis Ilias, the Prophet Elijah, whose *paneyeri* is celebrated on 20 July. Profitis Ilias is the patron saint of rain, thunder and lightning, which suggests that he is the Christian successor of Zeus, whose attributes include Cloud-Gatherer and Sender of Lightning. Up until quite recently the Greeks customarily lit fires on mountain-tops on the feast day of Profitis Ilias, just as in antiquity they did at festivals honouring Zeus.

The villages in the centre of the island have in and around them a number of interesting churches and monasteries, some of them dating back to the Byzantine era. The hamlet of Astra, embowered by groves of oaks and almonds, has an old church of unknown date dedicated to Agios Ioannis Prodromos, St John the Forerunner, better known in the West as John the Baptist. Farther along is the monastery of Agios Pandeleimon, which dates in foundation to the Byzantine period. The hamlet of Ellinika has a church dedicated to Agios Nikolaos which has eighteenth-century wall paintings. The Byzantine church of Agioi Apostoloi in the little village of Kato Meria has wall paintings dated to the thirteenth century. Off to the west is the monastery of Agia Marina, built in the sixteenth century next to the impressive ruins of a Hellenistic *pyrgos*. The monastery celebrates the *paneyeri* of Agia Marina on 17 July, when it is the custom to cut the first clusters of grapes in the local vineyards.

The ruins of the ancient city of Karthaia lie on the south-eastern coast of the island at the Bay of Poles, flanked by two superb beaches. The site of Karthaia was first excavated in 1811–1812 by the Danish antiquarian P. O. Bronstead, in one of the earliest explorations on the Cyclades. The monuments that he excavated can still be seen, including the colossal stones of the defence walls and their gates, the cavea of the theatre, and the ruins of two temples, one of them dedicated to Apollo and the other to Artemis, the latter now marked by a little chapel dedicated to the Virgin.

The temple of Apollo was the site of an annual festival, at one of which the poet Simonides first presented his hymns (now lost) sung by a choir of maidens. A local legend is associated with one of these maidens, Ktesylla, who was so beautiful that an Athenian youth named Hermochares fell in love with her when he first saw her at the festival. They married and Ktysella accompanied Hermochares to Athens, where she died while giving birth to their first child. When the Keans learned of these they deified her as the goddess of love, worshipping her as Aphrodite Ktesylia.

There is another ancient site in the plain near the Vathypotamos River, where the ruins of a Greek theatre and a Doric temple have been identified, with fragments of other buildings scattered around the surrounding area.

The resort villages of Pisses and Koundouros are on the south-west coast. The name Pisses is a corruption of Poiessa, one of the four cities of the ancient Kean *tetrapolis*, of which little remains. Nevertheless, the drive there is worth the effort, for it passes through a beautiful rock-bound valley with fruit orchards and groves of cypresses, leading down to the best beach on the island.

The ruins of ancient Poiessa are on the summit of the sea-girt hill that forms the southern limit of the valley. The only remaining structures are a ruined temple of Apollo and a church dedicated to the Panagia Sotira, Our Lady the Saviour, which has numerous fragments of ancient marbles built into its walls. Bent concluded that Poiessa was the least of the four ancient cities of Kea, 'a place of secondary importance, a sort of fishing village – and amongst the ruins of it have been found more plummets of lines than in any of the other towns'.

During Bent's exploration of the island he picked up many gems of local folklore, including stories of the Nereids, beautiful sea-maidens who often bewitched unwary young men, particularly shepherds who spent the night under an oak tree. He writes of the wizard measures that were taken to break the Nereids' spell.

> For those who are supposed to have been struck by the Nereids when sleeping under a tree the following cure is much in vogue. A white cloth is spread on the spot, and on it is spread a plate with bread, honey and other sweets, a bottle of good wine, a knife, a fork, an empty glass, an

unburnt candle, and a censer. These things must be
brought by an old woman who utters mystic words and
then goes away, that the Nereids may eat, undisturbed,
and that in their good humour they may allow the
sufferer to regain his health.

These stories are still prevalent on Kea and the other isles of the
Cyclades, although those who have told them to me profess not to
believe in such supernatural creatures. Nevertheless, I have the
feeling that the Nereids continue to haunt their imagination, as
do other survivals of their ancient lore, for they love to talk about
such things, particularly late in the evening over a few glasses of
retsina under an ancient *platanos* tree.

Kea: population 2,415; area 132 sq km; Mt. Profitis Ilias (570 m);
ferries from Piraeus (42 mi) and Lavrion (17 mi); hotels in Chora,
Korissia and Koundouros.

three
Kythnos

K ythnos is an island steeped in ghostly legends, some of which still haunt the imagination of islanders, particularly the oldest ones, who tell tales of vampires, dragons and subterranean demons, not to mention the Nereids so popular in the folklore of all the Cyclades. These supernatural creatures are associated with some of the ancient sites on Kythnos as well as with its thermal springs, which were so popular in Roman times that the island was called Thermia, the name by which it is still known locally.

The terrain of Kythnos is rocky but relatively flat, its highest peak, Ai-Lias (a corruption of Agios Profitis Ilias), rising to only 336 metres. It is the most barren of the inhabited Cyclades, the only touches of green in its landscape stemming from a few terraced vineyards and orchards of fig trees. The Kythniotes thus have had to rely on their herds of goats, and since antiquity the island has been noted for its goat cheese, *kythneios tyros*. Bent writes that the cheese of Kythnos is 'so delicious that one does not wonder at Epicurus, who said that as often as he wished to sup most luxuriously he put Kythniote cheese on the table… Pliny tells us that it was a wild flower which grew in Kythnos which gave the delicious flavour to the cheese.'

Recent excavations at Loutra indicate a settlement dating to the first half of the seventh millennium BC, the earliest evidence of human presence in the Cyclades. Other excavations show that copper was mined on Kythnos in the Cycladic Bronze Age, and bronze tools found on the island are the earliest known in the Cyclades, dating to *c.* 2600 BC.

Kythnian tradition has it that the island was first settled by the Dryopes, a pre-Hellenic people who are said to have originated around Mount Parnassos. At the end of the second millennium BC Kythnos was resettled by the Ionians, who founded the city of Kythnos on the north-west coast of the island. The constitution of this city was praised by Aristotle in a work entitled *The State of the Kythnians*. Herodotus reports that the Kythnians supplied a trireme and a 50-oared galley to the Greek fleet at Salamis. The Kynthians also fought at Plataea, so that the name of Kythnos is among the list of cities commemorated on the Serpent Column.

During the Venetian era the island was known as Fermania, a corruption of Thermia. The island became part of the Latin Duchy of the Archipelago *c.* 1210, and in 1336 Duke Niccolo I Sanudo granted it as a sub-fief to Francesco Gozzadini of Bologna, along with other islands in the western Cyclades. When the Ottoman admiral Barbarossa attacked the archipelago in 1537 the Kythnians who were not captured and enslaved fled to other places, and for several decades thereafter the island was virtually uninhabited. The Gozzadini eventually attracted settlers to the island, which they held until 1617, paying tribute to the Turks to leave them in peace. By this time the Gozzadini had become so Hellenised that they joined the Orthodox faith, transferring the Catholic churches on the island to the native Greeks.

Kythnos was one of the first islands to join in the Greek War of Independence when it began in 1821. Two years later Kea was stricken by a plague that was still a living memory when Bent visited the island. He writes that 'there are inhabitants alive now who well remember the fearful plague which carried off seven hundred people at the time of the revolution, which, out of a population of two to three thousand, is an alarming percentage'.

Ferries land at Merihas in a deeply indented bay on the west coast of Kythnos, whereas in times past the main port was at Loutra, on the north-east shore. Messaria, the main town, is in the middle of the island between the two ports, which are connected by a paved road. Another road leads south-east from Merihas to the large village of Driopis on the spine of the island, going on from there to the shrine of Panagia Kanala on the east coast.

There is a string of excellent beaches in the two bays along the coast north of Merihas, at Episkopi and Apokrousi. The headland between these bays is known as Vryocastro, 'the Jew's Castle', which has been identified as the site of the ancient city of Kythnos. The squared stone blocks of a temple and an altar can still be seen, along with the acropolis and its Cyclopean walls, so called because in the medieval era it was thought these colossal stones could only have been put in place by giants like Cyclops or other creatures of supernatural power. Bent writes that '[t]his acropolis is built of extraordinarily large stones, and is known by the inhabitants as the Dragon's House. The superstitious always put down these Cyclopean walls to the work of dragons, who with their great strength can tear up trees and hurl great rocks, like Polyphemus of old...'

Down on a promontory opposite an islet in the bay there are the remains of the *agora*, or marketplace. There are more ruins on the islet itself, and the locals told Bent that it was the haunt of *Broukolakes*, or Vampires, a superstition that dates back to the myth of the blood-sucking evil female spirits known in ancient Greece as *lamiae*. Bent describes the exorcism that brought the remains of these 'undead' creatures out to the islet, leaving their ghosts safely isolated there, though their spirits continue to linger on in one of the legends that are perpetuated by the Kythnians.

> Hither the superstitious Kythniotes still bring the bones of those dread wandering spirits, for a Kythniote believes firmly in *Broukolakes*, dead men, who for their crimes haunt the earth and commit horrors after death. The priest opens the tomb of such a one on a Friday, being the one

day in the week in which the dead man is supposed to remain quiet in his tomb; he then puts the bones in a sack and carries them to this lonely island and turns them out of the sack. The idea is that a ghost cannot cross water.

Messaria, also known as Chora, is a typical Cycladic village, though not of great antiquity. It became the capital of the island early in the *Turkokrateia*, when the landowners were forced by corsair raids to abandon their medieval capital on the northern coast. Its oldest churches are post-Byzantine, i.e., dating to the first two centuries or so of the *Turkokrateia*, when the Byzantine style in art and architecture lingered on in the Cyclades.

Agia Triada, the Holy Trinity, is the oldest church in Chora, probably dating from the late sixteenth century. The church took on its present form, a domed single-aisle basilica, only after a series of restorations. It retains fragments of its original frescoes, as well as a number of icons by the seventeenth-century Cretan painter Antonis Skordilis. Sculptural fragments and inscriptions found in the vicinity of the church indicate that it was built on the site of an ancient temple.

The church of Agios Savvas is dated by an inscription to 1613, and bears the coat of arms of Antonio Gozzadini. Antonio and his brother Angelo, who ruled on Siphnos, were the last two barons of the Gozzadini dynasty, which came to an end when the Turks finally took their islands in 1617.

Other old churches in Chora include the Panagia Soteira (Our Lady the Saviour), adorned with a seventeenth-century *iconostasis*, or icon-screen; Agios Nikolaos, with several icons by Antonis Skordilis; and Agios Ioannis Theologos, whose miraculous icon of the Panagia Athenia is said to have floated to Kythnos after Athens was captured by the Turks.

Bent writes that when he rode south from Messaria 'we passed by the ruins of no less than four ruined monasteries, the outer walls of which were brown and crumbling, whilst inside the whitewashed church, still taken care of to a certain extent, peeps up and seems to reproach the sacrilege around it'.

The closest of these monasteries to Chora is that of the Panagia Nikous, Our Lady of Victory. All that is left of the monastery is its *katholikon*, a three-aisled basilica with two domes. During the *Turkokrateia* there was a secret monastic school in the basement of the monastery. These secret schools kept Greek culture alive during the long centuries of Ottoman occupation, when there were virtually no other institutions of learning in Greece. The church of the Panagia Nikous celebrates a *paneyeri* on the Feast of the Assumption, 15 August.

Loutra Bay on the north-east coast consists of three inlets, each with a village: Loutra, Agia Eirene, and Schinari. The village of Loutra takes its name from the thermal baths that have been in use since Roman times, one of them preserved inside the Xenia Hotel. The English traveller George Wheler, who visited Kythnos in 1675, wrote of the spa that '[i]t is much frequented by the Paralytic, Lame, and many other diseased people, being very Diaphoretic'. When Tournefort visited Loutra in 1698 he observed that 'these waters still preserve their Virtue, but have lost their Reputation, because none resort to them, but such Invalids, whom all the Mineral waters in the World will not cure'.

Queen Amalia of Greece built a modern bathing establishment at Loutra in 1856, with accommodations for over a hundred guests. Bent, in writing of this spa, observes that the Kythniotes never used the baths because of their belief that the mineral springs were haunts of the Nereids.

> But the people of the island flatly refused to use the waters; they were far too superstitious, and said that the warm springs were haunted by the Nereids, and that the devils of Hades worked below… It is certainly a dreary spot to go for a cure; not a tree near, and a hideous waste of sand, impregnated with mineral water, between the bathhouse and the sea; rheumatism for life would be preferable to a month of the burning summer spent here.

On the north-west coast there is an abandoned monastery dedicated to Agios Yiorgios (St George). The monastery is near a medieval Latin fortress known as Kastro Orias, the 'Beautiful Castle'. Bent says that in his time the locals believed the fortress to be the residence of demonic creatures, another baleful legend that still haunts the imaginative memory of Kythnians.

> They now call the spot 'the fortress of beauty,' and a more splendid situation for a fortress it is impossible to find. It crowns a rock rising 500 feet out of the sea, and is approached from the land side by only a narrow tongue of land. There is still the wall standing, which is entered by a low doorway, and inside the old churches and houses are in many cases in good preservation; but it is a desolate weird place, and full of terror to the inhabitants. Here in 1821 the people of Messaria took refuge from the Turks, in spite of the dread they have of the fearful demons (*stoichiea*) which haunt it – giants with black faces, man-eating, like the Homeric Cyclops, who guard hidden treasures of Venetian florins which have been buried in the ruins.

Kythniote tradition says that there were once a hundred churches in Kastro Orias, but of these only two have survived. The one in better repair, dedicated to Our Lady of Compassion, still retains some of its original wall paintings; the dedicatory inscription of the other bears the date 1748.

Driopis is an ancient and interesting village. It was originally known as Sillaka, and in recent times it was given its present name to commemorate the Dryopis, the non-Hellenic people who are supposed to have settled Kythnos in prehistoric times. It is a typical Cycladic village, described by Bent as being 'prettily situated on either side of a cleft watered by a brook; it is far prettier than the capital: the houses climb one above another, and there is a fair-sized hill behind it, which gives an air of importance to the place'. The oldest church in the village is Agios Minas, which has a fine seventeenth-century *iconostasis*.

Just outside the village is the famous Katafyki Cave, which extends for a distance of some 600 metres. During the *Turkokrateia* the locals took refuge in the cave whenever corsairs appeared, and in the years 1908–1914 it was successfully mined for iron. Bent was shown a great chamber in the cave where, he was told, the villagers used to dance on the Friday after Easter, though at the time of his visit it was being used as a rubbish dump. He remarks that '[t]he cave is still the object of great veneration, and only for forty days after Easter is it safe to enter it, when the Nereids' power is supposed to be dormant'.

There are several good beaches in the elongated southern half of the island, the most popular being those at Kanala on the east coast and Flambouria on the west coast, both of them extending around lune-shaped bays.

The first of these bays is named for the monastery of the Panagia Kanala, which has a miraculous icon of the Virgin that tradition says was painted from life by St Luke, though it is actually a work of Antonis Skordilis. The monastery celebrates *paneyeria* of the Virgin on 15 August and 8 September, the first celebrating her Assumption and the second her birthday. One of the old customs associated with the second of these festivals is the 'sale' of sickly children to the Virgin in the hope that they will regain their health. These children are called 'the slaves of Our Lady' and are brought back by their parents the following year, presumably healthy, as was so in the case of my old friend Dimitri Isayef, a frail child who lived out the fullness of his years after being in the Virgin's care.

The two *paneyeria* at Kanala attract people from all over the island. One song that one might hear at these festivals is *Agapi Paignidiari* (The Games that Lovers Play), an old Kythniote favourite.

> Seize this thief,
> this lazy boy.
> Let me beat his legs
> with jasmine.
> Let me beat his hands
> with basil.
> Let me beat his mouth

with a sweet kiss.
Let me bind him in chains
with my embraces.

The beach at Flambouria is named for the church of the Panagia Flambouriani. Tradition says that the Virgin once made a miraculous visit here, leaving traces of her steps all the way between the beach and the chapel. The local tourism literature says of this holy place that 'in summer lilacs in bloom in the area give off their sweet smell'.

There is still another good beach near the southern tip of the island at Agios Dimitrios. The beach is named for a seaside chapel of Saint Dimitrios whose *paneyeri* on 26 October marks the beginning of winter in the two-seasoned year of the ancient agricultural calendar. Prior to that date there is always a brief spell of fine weather known as the 'little summer of Saint Dimitrios', the Greek equivalent of 'Indian summer'.

The headland just to the south of Agios Dimitrios is known as Akri Delphines, the Cape of Dolphins, which I have passed many times in my voyages through the Cyclades, the first time when on my way from Kythnos to Seriphos. I have never seen dolphins off the cape, but I am told by my Kithynian friends that I might see them if I passed Akri Delphines in a period of calm weather, perhaps during the 'little summer of Saint Dimitrios'.

Kythnos: population 1,603; area 99 sq km; Mt. Ai-Lias (336 m); ferries from Piraeus (52 mi); hotels in Loutra.

four
Seriphos

S eriphos is associated in mythology with the hero Perseus, son of Zeus and Danae, daughter of King Acrisius of Argos. Acrisius had been told by an oracle that he would be killed by Danae's son, and so when she give birth to Perseus her father had her and the child thrown into the sea in a wooden chest, which eventually was cast up on Seriphos. There it was found by a fisherman, who reported his catch to Dictys, brother of King Polydectys. Polydectys tried to make Danae his mistress, but, aided by Dictys, she rejected him, and when Perseus came of age he protected his mother from the king's advances. Polydectys tried to get Perseus out of his way by sending him off to slay the Gorgon Medusa. Perseus succeeded in his task, and when he returned to Seriphos he turned Polydectys and his army to stone by displaying the snake-haired head of Medusa.

According to tradition, the rock formations and large stones strewn around Seriphos are the petrified forms of King Polydectys and his men, lying where they fell when they were petrified by the sight of Medusa's severed head. As Tournefort writes, referring to the ruggedness of the island, whose highest peak is Mount Tourlos: 'The mountains of Seripho are so rugged and steep, that the poets feigned that Perseus transform'd into stones the very natives of this place.'

Another curious tradition associated with Seriphos originates with Pliny, repeated by Aelian, who wrote that the frogs on the island were always silent. But Tournefort was amused to find that the frogs of Seriphos do in fact croak: 'The greatest pleasure we took on this island was to hear the Frogs croaking in the Marshes around the Port. Pliny and Elian say that they were mute in Seriphos; and recovered their voices again, if transported elsewhere; this Race of mute Frogs must needs be lost.'

Excavation reveals that Seriphos was inhabited throughout the Bronze Age, when its inhabitants supported themselves by farming, herding and fishing, as they still do today. Otherwise the principal resource of the island was its copper, which apparently was mined here as early as the third millennium BC, while iron was mined later in antiquity.

Herodotus notes that Seriphos was peopled by Ionians and contributed a 50-oared galley to the Greek fleet at Salamis. The islanders also fought at the Battle of Plataea, and the name of Seriphos is inscribed on the Serpent Column among the list of Greek allies.

Seriphos sided with King Mithradates VI of Pontus in his wars against Rome, as a result of which the Romans sacked the island in 84 BC. The subsequent history of Seriphos is that of an impoverished and defenceless pawn, subject to attacks by marauding fleets. It is mentioned as a place of banishment in Roman times, along with the islet of Giaros between Kea and Tinos, as in Juvenal's description of an exile's life in one of his satires: 'Unhappily it festers in a narrow channel of the world,/So tightly confined by the rocks of Giaros and by small Seriphos.'

During the Latin period the island was known variously as Serfento or Serfeno. Soon after 1211 it was taken by the same quartet who held Kea, namely the brothers Andreas and Geremia Ghisi together with Pietro Giustiani and Domenico Michiel. Unlike Kea, Seriphos was a desperately poor island in the Latin period and was not on the trade routes of the Venetians, its only resource being its iron mines, its sources of copper having long been exhausted.

Late in the fourteenth century a Venetian noble named Niccolo Adoldo seized control of Seriphos, killing many of the other Latin aristocrats. This led the Venetian authorities to arrest and imprison Adoldo, and in 1393 Venice took direct control of the island.

A quarter of a century later the Florentine traveller Buondelmonti found the people of Seriphos and the other isles of the Cyclades living in terror of the Turks, whose corsair fleets had become the scourge of the Aegean. He writes that he spent four years travelling through the Cyclades 'in fear and great anxiety'. At Seriphos he found 'nothing but calamity', remarking that the people lived 'like brutes' and were in constant fear that they would fall into the hands of 'the Infidels'.

Seriphos fell to Barbarossa in 1537, though apparently the Ottoman government allowed the Latins some degree of autonomy, for nearly half a century later there is a report of a fortress on the island still controlled by the Michiel family.

Ferries to Seriphos stop at Livadi, sheltered in a deeply recessed bay on the south-east coast of the island, from where a road winds up to Chora, now officially known as Seriphos.

The port at Livadi has become a popular resort, particularly because of the good beaches in its vicinity. The village celebrates two *paneyeria* each summer, the first of which takes place on 27 July at the church of Agios Pandeleimon and the second on 7 September at Agios Sozon. Pandeleimon was court physician to the emperor Galerius and suffered martyrdom in the reign of Diocletian. He is the patron saint of invalids, cripples and the blind, and is celebrated in the Greek Orthodox Church as *Iamatikos*, or the 'Healer'. An old proverb that I have heard on Seriphos says that 'All blind men and all lame men go to St Pandeleimon', and his healing powers are attested by the numerous metal ex-votos, some of them in silver, which are attached to his icon at the church dedicated to him in Livadi.

Chora is a charming Cycladic village, its whitewashed houses perched on a rocky eminence surmounted by the usual Venetian fortress, the Kastro. The gateway of what remains of the fortress bears the coat of arms of the Michiel family, with the date 1443. Fragments of the fortress are built into the walls of some of the surrounding houses. The *Demarcheion* houses a small collection of antiquities found on the island.

There are a number of post-Byzantine churches in Chora, including Agios Athanasios, Agios Eleftherios, Agios Ioannis Theologos, Agios Konstantinos, and Agios Tryphon. Tryphon is the patron saint of Seriphos and his *paneyeri* is celebrated on 1 February. He is revered as the protector of vines and fields, for he has the power to exterminate rats and caterpillars. This led Bent to suggest that Tryphon was the Christian reincarnation of Apollo Smintheus, the Mouse God, worshipped by the islanders in antiquity.

Bent remarks of Chora that '[o]f all towns in the Greek Islands, Seriphos will remain fixed in my mind as the most filthy. The main street is a sewer into which all the offal is thrown; and it is tenanted by countless pigs – for each householder has liberty to keep three.' But after complaining about this he writes of a charming street game played in the town, one that I have heard of myself in Chora, which is now spotlessly clean, its pigs here too appearing only as pork chops on taverna menus.

> In one of these narrow streets on the Tuesday after Easter the maidens of Seriphos play their favourite game of the swing (*kounia*). They hang a rope from one wall to the other, put some clothes on it, and swing, singing and swinging, one after the other. Aware of this the young men try to pass by, and are called upon for a toll of one penny each, a song, and a swing. The words they generally use are as follows: – 'The gold is swung, the silver is swung, and swung, too, is my love with the golden hair;' to which the maiden replies, 'Who is it that swings me that I may gild him with my favour, that I may work him a fez all covered with pearls?' Then, having paid his penny, he is permitted to pass, and another comes on and does likewise.

The game that Bent describes is a survival of the ancient Greek *Aiora*, or Swinging Festival, celebrated at the season when the vines were pruned. The anthropologist Martin Nilsson says that the *Aiora* is connected with the myth of Icarius, who is credited with introducing viniculture, and in his book, *Greek Folk Religion*, he has an illustration of a vase painting of the fifth century BC in which a naked youth is pushing a maiden on a swing.

The largest village in the north of the island is Panagia. This is named for the church of the Panagia, the oldest on the island, a Byzantine structure of the tenth or eleventh century, with wall paintings dated *c.* 1300. The church celebrates a three-day *paneyeri* on 14–16 August that attracts everyone on the island, and on our first visit to Seriphos we celebrated all three days with them. The dances were as lively as any I have seen on the Cyclades, and the singer, a gravelly voiced fisherman named Andoni, interspersed his lyrics with witty comments about the dancers, particularly the leading man, who would foot the bill. This reminded me of the description that Tournefort writes of this *paneyeri*, which he attended in 1700 as a guest of the Turkish governor, who held the title of *Waiwode*.

> The Waiwode of Seripho, a Turk of Negroponte...gave us a hearty Welcome, and earnestly invited us to see the Greek dance at la Madonna de la Masseria, which is the prettiest Chapel in the Island. It is certain that the Greeks here have not lost their Jocularity, nor that Genius for Satire, which shown so conspicuously in their Ancestors; they are every day making very witty Ballads; nor is there any manner of Posture they do not put themselves into, when they dance.

Seriphos is noted for its wine, and a number of its festivals, like that of St Tryphon, are associated with the various stages in viniculture. One of these is the *paneyeri* of Agios Menas on 11 November, when the wine casks are opened. When the farmers plant their vines they and their helpers pour wine on the roots, just as was done in antiquity.

West of Panagia there is a Byzantine church dedicated to Agios Stephanos, which preserves some of its original wall paintings and is well worth a visit. There are no fewer than seven saints in the

Greek Orthodox Church known as Stephanos, the one revered here being Stephen the Protomartyr, a Greek-speaking Jew who after his conversion to Christianity was stoned to death outside the walls of Jerusalem. He had been one of the first deacons appointed by the apostles to serve the needs of widows and the poor, for whom he is the patron saint. His *paneyeri* is celebrated on 26 December.

The northernmost village on the island is Galani, which Bent described as looking 'like a giant's staircase, one house above the other… [F]ew places in the world can be more out of the world than this…' On the coast west of Galini there is a sandy beach at Sikamia.

A short way to the east of Galani is Moni Taxiarchon, the Monastery of the Archangels, dedicated to Saints Michael and Gabriel. An inscription over the door of the *katholikon* bears the date 1447, six years before the fall of Constantinople. The church is adorned with beautiful frescoes which may be part of its original decoration, painted in the last twilight of Byzantium.

South-west of Chora there is a ruined Hellenistic watchtower known as Aspropyrgos, or the White Tower. The tower is the subject of a local ballad dating from the days of the *Turkokrateia* which is still sung at *paneyeria*, telling of how the Turks besieged it for 12 years before an old woman betrayed its defenders by revealing their secret source of water to the *barbaria*.

There is a secluded beach at Koutalas on the south-west coast. Koutalas was known to the Latins as Porto Catena, the Port of the Chain, for they stretched a chain across the mouth of the harbour to protect the ships inside, which were there to carry off iron ore from the mine above the bay.

Above the bay to the west there is a remarkable cavern known as the Koutala Cave, which extends for nearly 100 metres. The cave was rediscovered early in the twentieth century by Herr Gromann, who was then director of the Seriphos iron mines. The cave had been mined for its iron in antiquity, but had been blocked off by a fall of rock. Gromann found that the cave was an ancient sanctuary, as evidenced by an altar made from a stalagmite resembling a headless female figure whom he called 'the Divinity', in front of which there were the remains of burnt offerings and sacrifices. It would appear from Gromann's description that the altar, which is no longer visible, dated from the archaic period, when the iron of Seriphos was first mined.

On a hill above the bay there are the remains of a fortress called Kastro tis Grias, the Castle of the Old Woman, where there are some traces of an ancient settlement, including a few broken bits of columns and a white marble lion set as an ornament in the roof of an abandoned chapel.

On the south-west coast at Megalo Livadi there is another Hellenistic watchtower, called Psarapyrgos. The cape that forms the south-west extremity of the island beyond Megalo Livadi is known as Akri Kiklops, Cyclops Point. East of the cape, at Mesa Akrotiri, there is a marine grotto known as the Cave of Cyclops. Like a number of other places in Greece, both the cave and the cape are named for the Cyclops Polyphemos. This imaginative identification is based on the adventure that Odysseus recounts to King Alkinoos in Book IX of the *Odyssey*, where he tells of how he and his shipmates encountered the one-eyed giant in his cave when they beached their ship on an island off the land of the Cyclops.

> And in truth he was a wonder to behold, not
> Like a man, an eater of bread, but more like a wooded
> Peak of the high mountains seen standing away from the
> others.

Seriphos: population 1,399; area 73 sq km; Mt. Tourlos (486 m); ferries from Piraeus (73 mi); hotels in Chora and Livadakia.

five
Siphnos

S iphnos appears barren from the sea, but it is actually the most verdant of the western Cyclades, largely because it has a plentiful supply of water to irrigate the fields on its terraced hills and the lush olive groves in the valleys furrowing down from its mountains.

The villages of Siphnos are celebrated for their classic Cycladic architecture, their white cubist houses draped with bougainvillea and surrounded by gardens, the countryside graced by numerous monasteries, chapels, dovecotes and *pyrgoi*, of which there are more than fifty on the island.

The renowned gold mines of Siphnos were remarked upon by writers from Herodotus onwards, though they were already worked out in classical times.

The silver mines of Siphnos date back to the first half of the third millennium BC, while the mining of gold began somewhat later, and studies have shown that the Siphnians were the first to trade in these precious metals. This enriched the Siphnians, and in 526 BC they built a superb treasury at Delphi, endowing it with a tithe of their wealth to surpass the existing treasuries of all the other Greek states at Apollo's shrine. When the Siphynians sent their treasure to Dephi they asked the oracle of Pythian Apollo, the Pythia, if their prosperity would continue. She replied in her usual Delphic manner, referring to the gleaming white marble of the Siphynian *prytaneium*, or senate house:

> When the Prytanies' seat shines white in the island of Siphnos –
> White-browed all the forum – need then of a true seer's wisdom.
> Danger will come from a wooden host and a herald in scarlet.

The prophecy was fulfilled when a Samian fleet attacked the island and forced the Siphnians to pay them the enormous sum of 100 talents.

Tradition has it that the Siphnians paid their tithe to Apollo in the form of a golden egg. On one occasion the Siphnians, who were notoriously devious, attempted to hold back most of their tithe by sending to Delphi a gilded leaden egg (they also mined lead) instead of one made of solid gold, but their subterfuge was detected by the oracle, whereupon Apollo in his wrath struck the island with an earthquake and sank its mines of gold and silver into the sea.

Siphnos was still a power to be reckoned with down to the end of the archaic period, and it was one of three islands in the Cyclades that refused to give offerings of earth and water in submission to Darius, along with Seriphos and Melos. A trireme from Siphnos was part of the Greek fleet at Salamis, and the island is listed on the Serpent Column among the allies who defeated the Persians at Plataea.

At the beginning of the Latin period the island, then known as Siphanto, became part of Marco Sanudo's Duchy of the Archipelago. In 1307 Siphanto was taken by the Catalans under Januli I da Corogna, whose descendants held the island until 1456, when it passed by marriage to the Gozzadini family. The Gozzadini held power until 1617, when the island was finally taken over by the Turks.

The Latin feudal system declined under the *Turkokrateia*, and a system of local government developed on Siphnos. Despite the fact that piracy was again rife, Siphnos became one of the centres of maritime commerce in the Cyclades, with European ships stopping here to trade such things as cotton thread, textiles and straw hats in exchange for the island pottery. Local craftsmen in the 'Tsikalaria' potteries still produce the traditional earthenware for which Siphnos has long been known. Siphnos is also noted for the number of good cooks it has produced, many of whom in times past won praise as chefs in Athens and Istanbul.

George Wheler remarks that Siphnos was 'celebrated for its excellent fruits and beautiful women'. Tournefort, who visited the island in 1700, praises the island's salubrious climate and abundance, though he is critical of the morals of the ancient Siphnians.

> The isle of Siphanto is in a fine air; they especially think so who arrive there from Milo [Melos], where the sulphureous Vapours are perfectly infectious. There are men at Siphanto 120 years old: the Air, Water, Fruit, Wild-Fowl, Poultry, every thing there is excellent; their Grapes are wonderful, but the Wines not delicate, and therefore they drink those of Milo and Santorin. Their Ancestors Morals were very scandalous. When anyone was abraided of living like a Siphantine, or keeping his word like a Siphantine, it was as much as calling him a Rogue.

During Byzantine and Ottoman times the island was renowned for an institution of higher learning known variously as the School of Siphnos or the School of Agios Tafou, the Holy Tomb. According to tradition, the school had been founded during the Iconoclastic Period (729–843) by political refugees from Constantinople. It numbered among its graduates several patriarchs of Constantinople and numerous bishops, many of whom returned to spend their last days on Siphnos, enriching their old school with the knowledge they had gained in the Byzantine capital. At the outbreak of the War of Independence the school was directed by Nicholas Chrysogelos, who had initiated his students into the revolutionary movement known as Philiki Hetairia, and on 25 March 1821 he mustered those who were old enough to carry arms and sailed off with them to join the Greek forces in the Peloponnesos. During the course of the war Chrysogelos for some time served as chief aide to Capodistrias, who became President of Greece in 1827, and when he returned home after the establishment of the Greek Kingdom he was made the first *demarch* of Siphnos.

Siphnos today is far less isolated than in the past, with a daily ferry service that connects it to Athens and the other islands of the Cyclades. The ferry-landing is at Kamares, at the inner end of a bay on the north-west coast of the island. Kamares has only been in use as a port since the end of the nineteenth century, and most of the village was rebuilt in the 1950s. The oldest church in the village, dedicated to Agios Yiorgios and Agia Barbara, was built in 1785 and renovated in 1906.

The name Kamares means 'arches' or 'vaults', from the vaulted chambers cut into the cliffs around the port by miners in ancient times. Inscriptions on the walls of the chambers indicate that they were dedicated to the cult of the nymphs, who were believed to inhabit these vaults.

On the heights north-east of the port is the Monastery of Agios Simeon, which celebrates its *paneyeri* on 1 September. There are nine saints named Simeon in the Greek Orthodox Church, the one revered here being Simeon the Stylite, or Pillar-Sitter, so called because he spent the last 36 years of his life perched atop a pillar near Antioch, where he died in 459. The path to the monastery from Kamares passes the site of one of the five ancient silver mines at Vorini, east of Agios Simeon.

Excursion boats from Kamares make day trips to Heronissos, a little fishing village on the northern tip of the island, which recently has been connected to Apollonia by an asphalt road. When Bent landed here, after crossing from Seriphos in the dead of winter, he found just three houses in the village, only one of which was occupied, the one-room home and workplace of an old potter, who lived in utterly bleak and inhospitable surroundings. Bent watched the old man working at his wheel, as potters still do on Siphnos, a scene that he says 'reminded me strongly of a potter at work as represented on a certain vase in the British Museum'.

In the middle of the island there is a group of five villages that Bent describes as the 'centre of Siphniote life', the largest of them being Apollonia. Apollonia, also known locally as Stavri, has been the capital of Siphnos since 1836. The village takes its name from the fact that it was built on the site of a temple dedicated to Apollo, whose site is now occupied by the eighteenth-century church of the Panagia Ouranofotia, Our Lady of the Heavenly Light. Fragments of the temple are built into the church, which has an interesting relief of St George over its entryway. There are three other old churches in the village, those of Agios Athanasios, Agios Fanourios, and Agios Sozon, all of which are noted for their wall paintings and their finely carved wooden *iconostases*. The Museum of Popular Arts and Folklore and the house of the poet and satirist Kleanthis Triandaphillou-Rhangabi (1846–1899) are also interesting places to visit.

Less than two kilometres to the north is the large village of Artemonas, as well as its satellite villages of Ano (Upper) and Kato (Lower) Petali and Agios Loukas.

Artemonas is named for Artemis, though no remnants of her ancient temple have been found; nevertheless, the church of the Panagia Kochi is said to have been built on its site. Other notable churches in and around the village are Agios Yiorgios tou Efendi, a seventeenth-century structure with a number of fine icons of that era; the Panagia tis Ammou (Our Lady of the Sand), which has an icon with a rare depiction of the Virgin without the Christ-Child; the Panagia tou Vali, founded by a local who during the *Turkokrateia* served as the Vali, or Governor; Agios Spyridon, patron saint of Artemonas, whose *paneyeri* is celebrated on 12 December; and the Panagia tou Barou (Our Lady of the Baron), founded by one of the Latin rulers of Siphnos.

The latter church is in a quarter of Artemonas still known as Barou. Tradition has it that the Latin baron for whom it is named fell in love with a Byzantine princess who had become a nun in the nearby convent of Agios Ioannis Theologos. When the princess spurned the baron's advances his unrequited passion was released on the local women, who in time bore him so many children that the quarter of Barou was named for him, or so the story goes.

Artemonas is noted for an ancient dance performed there in the celebration on Cheese Sunday, the last day of *Apokreos*, or Carnival. (The last week of Carnival, beginning on the Monday, is called Cheese Week, for only cheese, milk and eggs can be eaten on those days, in preparation for the Lenten feast.) The festivities on the evening of Cheese Sunday in Artemonas begin with the Dance of Master North Wind, in which the village priest leads a line of dancers in the *plateia*, a survival of the ancient Greek *Boreades*, a ceremony performed to appease Boreas, the North Wind. A song that is traditionally sung at this festival is '*Tou Kyr Voria*' (Sir North Wind), beginning with these lines:

> The north wind ordered all the ships:
> 'You ships at sea, you galleys on your way,
> Get to your harbours now – I want to blow,
> Make fields and mountains white,
> Ice up the springs,
> And anything I find at sea I shall
> Hurl on to land.'

The village of Agios Loukas is named for its church of St Luke. The church of the Panagia ta Gournia (Our Lady of the Troughs) takes its name from the small stone troughs that were hollowed along the nearby stream by local women doing their laundry. The church, which has remarkable wall paintings by the Siphnian artist Agapiou, celebrates its *paneyeri* on 15 August.

The village of Kato Petali is dominated by the large church of the Panagia Zoodochos Pigi, Our Lady of the Life-Giving Spring, erected in 1894 on the site of an *agiasma*, or sacred well. On Christmas Eve the villagers traditionally give a carol concert in the church. Just outside the village to the south is the church of the Panagia Koukia, dating from 1614.

Just to the east of Kato Petali is the historic monastery of Agios Ioannis Chrysostomos, founded in 1650. The monastery was restored shortly after the establishment of the modern Greek Kingdom, and in the years 1835–1854 it housed a school for girls.

Eastward from Apollonia is Kastro, a fascinating medieval town set on the top of a sea-girt promontory high above the eastern coast. This was the capital of Siphnos both in antiquity and during the Venetian period, when the Latin rulers built the fortified upper town on the ruins atop the ancient acropolis. It was also the seat of the Orthodox Archdiocese of Siphnos from 1646 until 1848, as well as the Bishopric of Siphonomilou (Siphnos and Melos) in the years 1797–1852.

Archaeological excavations have shown that the site was settled as early as the first half of the third millennium BC, and that it was continually inhabited throughout antiquity. Remnants of the ancient acropolis walls have been found on the north-west slope of the hill, along with house foundations dating from the eighth and seventh centuries BC. Foundations of an archaic temple of the seventh century BC have been found beneath the foundations of the Venetian fortress, which itself dates from the early fourteenth century.

Kastro is a good example of the fortified medieval towns that can still be seen on the Cyclades. Its outer houses are joined to one another so as to form a continuous defence-wall, with another circuit of houses within encircling a citadel, whose arched entryway is still in use. The outer houses are dwellings of two or three storeys where the Greek commoners lived, while the inner and higher buildings were the homes of the Latin aristocracy. A number of old houses in Kastro still bear Latin coats of arms, including one of the da Corogna family dated 1365.

There are a number of post-Byzantine churches in Kastro, the oldest of which are Agios Ioannis Theologos, founded in 1566; Koimisis tis Panagia (the Dormition of the Virgin), dating from 1593, with an ancient altar and pavement in a local style of popular art; Eftamartyrios (The Seven Martyrs); Agios Stephanou; and next to the latter beside the entryway to the citadel is Agios Ioannis Theologos, dated 1617, which from 1687 to 1835 was the site of the famous School of the Holy Tomb. The old Roman Catholic cathedral of St Anthony of Padua up until recently served as the local archaeological museum, but that is now housed elsewhere in Kastro. Near St Anthony there is a marble stele with an inscription bearing the name of Baron Januli II da Corogna, with the date 1374.

The harbour installations of the medieval town can be seen to the south-east of Kastro at Seralia. Seralia is a corruption of the Italian Seraglio, the name by which the castle of the Latin barons in Kastro was known in former times. The last Latin baron to rule in Kastro was Angelo Gozzadini, who fled to Rome after the island was taken by the Turks in 1617. Two other interesting villages south of Apollonia are Exambela and Katavati.

The name Exambela is a corruption of the Turkish *Aksham Bela*, meaning 'Trouble in the Evening', because of the turbulent nature of the village during the *Turkokrateia*, when it was a lively intellectual centre, as it continues to be up to the present time. Just outside the village, on the road to Faros, is the monastery of the Panagia Vrisianis (Our Lady of the Fountain), dating from 1642.

The *plateia*, or village square, in Katavati has a bust of Apostolos Makraki (1830–1905), the philosopher and theologian, who is buried in the family church of the Panayia Evangelistrias. Other churches in the village are Agios Yiorgios and the Panagia Angelokistis, whose last name implies that it was built by the angels.

South of Katavati is the chapel of Agios Andreas, founded in 1701. Excavations made near the chapel in 1899 by Christos Tsountas unearthed evidence of a settlement dating back to the third millennium BC, which apparently continued in existence through the Mycenaean age to the Hellenistic period. The excavations were renewed in 1970–1980 by Barbara Philippaki, who uncovered a large section of the Mycenaean wall which surrounded the acropolis in the twelfth century BC. She also unearthed an outer circuit wall with a defence-tower and two gateways, as well as the ruins of at least five buildings, probably houses, all of which date to the eighth century BC.

The southernmost villages on the island are Faros, Platis Yialos and Vathi, the first two of which are on the south-east coast and the third on the south-west shore. All three villages are accessible by road, but it is more rewarding to hike to them along the old *monopati*, or mule paths, which have been in use since antiquity, where every now and then a farmer mounted on his mule will bid you good day as he passes – an indication that you are back in the old Greece that has otherwise disappeared under the onslaught of tourism.

The *monopati* that leads from Apollonia to Faros passes two ruined Hellenistic towers south of Exambela, the second of them near the abandoned monastery of Moni Vrises.

Faros is a fishing village at the north-east bend of a large bay on which there are several sandy beaches. Faros means 'Lighthouse', taking its name from a beacon on the eastern promontory of the bay, standing next to the Monastery of Stavros (the Cross). Bent was of the opinion that Faros rested on the site of the ancient city of Minoa mentioned by the chronicler Stephanos of Byzantium.

On the western promontory of the bay is the Monastery of the Panagia Chrysopigi, Our Lady of the Golden Spring. The monastery stands on a rocky islet that has split off from the rest of the promontory, to which it is connected by a bridge. Chrysopigi was founded in 1650 after a miraculous icon of the Virgin was discovered on the islet by two fishermen. According to tradition, the islet was originally connected to the rest of the promontory, but the Virgin broke it off when two women fled to her church to escape pirates who were pursuing them. The Panagia Chrysopigi is revered as the Protectress of Siphnos, having saved the islanders from a plague in 1676 and from a swarm of locusts in 1928. Local fishermen and mariners bring their sons here for baptism, which is performed in the open above the sea, in the belief that this will give them the strength they need for a seafaring life. The Virgin's *paneyeri* is celebrated here on 15 August.

Platis Yialos is on the coast south of Faros. The village has long been a centre for the island's 'Tsikalaria' pottery, and in recent years it has also become a popular summer resort, since it has the best beach on Siphnos.

Excursion boats from Platis Yialos make daily trips south to the uninhabited islet of Kipriani, which lies off the southern tip of Siphnos. At the northern end of the islet there is a chapel dedicated to the Panagia Kipriani, built in 1742. According to tradition, the chapel was built by a pious Siphniote lady called Kypria in memory of her son, who had drowned at sea; and in honour of her own name she caused the clay of the brick intended for the building of the church to be mixed with Cypriot wine instead of water.

There is another monastery of the Virgin on a hillside north of Platis Yialos. This is dedicated to the Panagia Vouno, Our Lady of the Mountain, founded in 1813, whose *paneyeri* is celebrated on 15 August. The *katholikon* of the monastery would seem to have been built on the site of an ancient Doric temple, as evidenced by the column drums that form part of its structure.

On the peninsula that forms the eastern side of the bay at Platis Yialos are the remains of Aspro Pyrgos, the White Tower, the best-known of the ancient watchtowers on the island. The Greek archaeologist Christos Tsountas excavated a site on this peninsula in 1899, discovering an Early Cycladic settlement and cemetery.

The *monopati* that leads from Apollonia to Vathi passes along the eastern flank of Mount Profitis Ilias, the highest peak on Siphnos, rising to a height of 678 metres. High on the mountain there is an abandoned monastery dedicated to Agios Profitis Ilias o Psilos, 'The Tall One', which celebrates its *paneyeri* on 20 July. This is the oldest and most important monastery on the island, probably dating from the tenth century, and in times past the people of Siphnos gathered here to pray for rain in times of drought. The view from the monastery is superb, encompassing all of Siphnos and its surrounding isles, with Seriphos to the north and to the south Melos and Kimolos.

Farther along the *monopati* to Vathi passes the church of the Taxiarchis, which retains fragments of its beautiful wall paintings. After traversing two saddles the path comes to the Monastery of Agios Nikolaos Tiaerina, which has a tap with running water in its courtyard, a good place to rest before starting down the last stretch of the path to Vathi.

Vathi is an old settlement of potters on an almost landlocked bay with a long sandy beach. There is an excellent taverna on the beach near the seaside Monastery of the Taxiarchis Evangelistrias (the Archangel of the Annunciation). The *katholikon* of the monastery appears to date from the late Byzantine period, with a bell-tower added in later times. The church is very picturesque, with its whitewashed dome and walls reflected in the turquoise shallows along the golden strand. The feast day of the Annunciation is celebrated here with a *paneyeri* on 25 March, which is also a national holiday, since it marks the beginning of the Greek War of Independence in 1821. When Bent stopped here he found the monastery inhabited by an aged monk who seemed to subsist entirely on food left over from these *paneyeria*.

> On the day of the festival of the archangel quantities of sailor pilgrims come to visit the spot, and the old monk collects in a basket the remnants of the loaves that they leave behind them; and when we saw him all the food he had to subsist upon were these hard crusts, which he moistens with water, olives, and a few herbs. He sleeps on a bed of leaves, and if not a hermit in name he is so in deed.

The monastery is now uninhabited, but the *katholikon* is well maintained and is open for the *paneyeri* of the Annunciation, with dancing at the taverna after the celebration of the liturgy in the church. This is the survival of an ancient festival celebrating the beginning of spring, when the swallows return from the south. The swallow-songs that were sung by Greek children, and perhaps still are today, are remarkably similar to one recorded in the mid-first century AD by Athenaeus, which for me evokes the arrival of spring in islands like Siphnos, catching the season's spirit on the wing.

> See! See! The swallow is here!
> She brings a good season, she brings a good year;
> White is her breast and black is her crest;
> See, the swallow is here.
>
> If you give us but a little, then God send you more;
> The swallow is here! Come, open the door;
> No greybeards you'll see, but children are we;
> O we pray you to give us good cheer.

Siphnos: population 2,414; area 77 sq km; Mt. Profitis Ilias (678 m); ferries from Piraeus (76 mi); hotels in Artemonas, Kamares, Faros, Vathi and Platis Yialos.

six

Melos and Kimolos

Melos is always romantically associated with the famous statue of the armless Venus de Milo in the Louvre. Her many devoted admirers included the German poet Heinrich Heine, who rose from his 'mattress grave' and went to the Louvre to see his beloved goddess for the last time.

> With great difficulty I dragged myself to the Louvre, and I almost collapsed when I entered the great hall where the blessed Goddess of Beauty, our beloved Lady of Milo, stands on her pedestal. I lay a long time at her feet, and wept so profusely, that even a stone must have pitied me. The goddess did indeed cast me a sympathetic glance, but one so comfortless that she seemed to be saying 'Don't you see, I have no arms and therefore I cannot help you.'

Melos and Kimolos, together with the uninhabited isles of Antimelos and Poliegos, form the southernmost end of the western Cyclades, which since antiquity have been stepping stones between the Greek mainland and Crete. This chain of islands from Kea to Melos formed the maritime boundary between the Aegean and the *Myrtoon Pelagos*, the sea between the Cyclades and the Peloponnesos. Melos, the largest and most populous of the chain, is also washed by the *Kritikos Pelagos*, the sea between Crete and the Cyclades, so that it has always been a hub of the eastern Mediterranean.

Ferries land at Adamas, commonly known as Adamata. The port is on the north-eastern side of the Gulf of Melos, one of the largest natural harbours in the Mediterranean, measuring some four miles across from east to west, penetrating so deep into the waist of Melos that it almost cuts the island in half. It is believed that this enormous bight was originally the caldera of a volcano, which in the Pliocene era, some five million years ago, erupted explosively and let the sea pour in through its shattered north-west side, forming the present gulf. This would seem to account not only for the almost bifurcated shape of Melos but also for its hot springs and caves and fantastic rock formations, with their multitudinous eroded shapes and variegated colours, as well as the island's abundance of minerals. Melos was famous for its obsidian, the hard black volcanic glass used for the making of tools and metals, which was the island's main export in the Early Bronze Age, the earliest marine commerce in the Aegean.

Excavations at Phylakopi, on the north-east coast, show that Melos has been inhabited since the mid-third millennium BC. During the years 1800–1450 BC the island was strongly influenced by Minoan civilisation on Crete, whereas in the later part of the Bronze Age the Mycenaeans were dominant, for by then they controlled Crete. Thus the tides of history flowed back and forth between Crete and the Peloponnesos through the western Cyclades, as they still do today.

Around 1100 BC Melos was colonised by Dorians from Lacedaemon in the Peloponnesos, and throughout the rest of antiquity the island remained Dorian in its culture. According to Herodotus, the people of Melos, together with those of Seriphos and Siphnos, were the only ones in the archipelago who refused to make token offerings of earth and water to the heralds of Darius. Thucydides writes that at the outbreak of the Peloponnesian War in 431 BC Melos and Thera were the only Aegean islands that refused to join the Athenian alliance, undoubtedly because they both had been colonies founded by Dorians from Lacedaemon. In 426 BC the Athenians sent a force of 2,000 hoplites to subdue the people of Melos, but to no avail. The following year the Athenians attacked again and apparently were victorious, for an inscription discovered on the Acropolis in Athens records that in 425 BC the Melians paid a tribute of 15 talents, as much as Naxos and Andros, the richest of the Cyclades. However, the Melians continued to be rebellious, and in 416 BC the Athenians put them down savagely, slaying all the adult males and selling the women and children into slavery, after which the island was occupied by 500 Athenian *clerurchs*, or colonists.

The surviving Melian exiles were brought back to their island by the Spartans after the final defeat of Athens in 404 BC, which ended the Peloponnesian War. The island seems to have revived in late antiquity and the early Byzantine era, as evidenced by the extensive remains found at Klima, site of the ancient capital of Melos. Any revival was short-lived, however, as the city of Melos seems to have been utterly destroyed in a series of severe earthquakes that shook the island from the sixth century through the eighth, so that it disappeared until unearthed by archaeologists more than a thousand years later.

Melos was one of the islands conquered by Marco Sanudo in 1207, becoming part of the Latin Duchy of the Archipelago. Sanudo governed Melos and Naxos directly while sending governors to the other islands. He and his successors often made Melos their home, travelling back and forth to their capital at Naxos. Whenever the Duke of Naxos was not present on Melos, one of his sons was often residing there as governor.

After the reconquest of Constantinople by the Byzantines in 1261, the native Greeks of Melos and other islands in the archipelago revolted against Latin rule under the leadership of a monk, whose name is not mentioned in the sources. The duchy was at the time ruled by Marco II Sanudo, grandson of Marco I, who assembled a fleet of 16 galleys and quickly put down the rebellion. The duke pardoned all of the rebels except the monk, who was bound hand and foot and thrown from a cliff into the sea.

In 1304 a Catalan fleet attacked the Cyclades, ravaging Melos as well as Kea, Siphnos and Santorini. Seven years later the Catalans captured Athens, which they ruled until 1388. Meanwhile they attacked Melos again in 1329, carrying away some 700 captives to be sold as slaves.

During the *Turkokrateia* Melos prospered more than most of the other Cyclades, since it was the home of many of the mariners employed by the corsairs, most of them French, who at that time were the scourge of the Aegean. One of these corsairs, a Greek named Captain Ioannis Kapsis, made himself master of Melos in 1677, but three years later he was captured by the Turks and executed in Istanbul. Turkish retribution then made life intolerable for the Melians, causing a large number of them, together with refugees from Samos, to sail off to England under the leadership of the Archbishop of Melos, Georgirenes. When the islanders arrived in London they were welcomed by the Duke of York, the future King James II, who allowed them to buy homes in what is now Soho's Greek Street, which takes its name from them. Soon afterwards they bought a plot on Hog Lane, afterwards to be called Crown Street, where they built the first Greek Orthodox church in England.

The English traveller Bernard Randolph gives an interesting description of the island, particularly its vulcanism, in his *Present State of the Islands in the Archipelago*, published in London in 1687.

> It has a very faire harbour, large and secure against all winds. Here privateers do usually come to make up their fleets, at their first coming into the Archipelago… Here are several hot places for men to sweat, at the side of the hills, which in some places are so hot as to rost an egg, if put between the hollow of some stones. All the whole island is esteemed to have fire under it, which is thought to consume the stones, which are very like to honeycombs, being all hollow.

When Tournefort stopped here in 1700 he found that the Meliotes were still serving as pilots for ships sailing through the archipelago, though they regretted the loss of the profitable piracy mart that

had ceased only two decades before with the downfall of Captain
Ioannis Kapsis.

> The Meliotes are good sailors, being much used to the
> Archipelago, they serve as Pilots to most ships trading
> thither from abroad. When the French corsairs were Masters
> of the Sea in the Levant, this island abounded with all
> manners of accommodation... Merchandise used to sell
> cheap, the Burgher retailed them again with good Advantage,
> and the Ships Crews made Consumption of the Products
> of the Country. The Ladies likewise made no ill hand of it;
> they are as arrant Coquettes as at Argentiere [Kimolos]:
> they all make use of the Powder of a seaplant to beautify
> themselves; it gives a ruddiness to their cheeks, but it soon
> goes off, and spoils the complexion... Tho the air of
> Melos is very unwholesome, and the Inhabitants subject
> to dangerous Distempers, yet they lead a merry Life.

The present port town of Adamas was a mere hamlet at
the beginning of the Latin period, but by the last quarter of the
seventeenth century it had became a prosperous town, its
development based principally on its corsair market. The town
went into decline after the French pirates were put down; then
revived as a port in the early nineteenth century, only to fade into
obscurity again when Syros supplanted Melos as the maritime
centre of the archipelago.

A revolt against Ottoman rule broke out in 1770 among the
mountaineers of Sfakia in south-western Crete, and in its aftermath
thousands of Cretan refugees fled to the Cyclades, many of them
taking refuge in the town of Zephiria in Melos. When Zephiria
was stricken by a plague in 1835 they moved to Adamas, where
their descendants remain today, as evidenced by the Cretan names
(which usually end in '*akis*') on shop signs.

Adamas is now a prosperous little port screened by tamarisk
trees, its renewed life stemming both from tourism and the revival
of its maritime trade. The church of Agia Triada has some
outstanding icons by Cretan painters, and Agios Haralambos has

a beautiful carved wooden *iconostasis* dating from the fourteenth century. Both of these churches were founded by the Cretan refugees who had abandoned Zephiria, and their icons and *iconostases* originally adorned the churches they left behind in Sfakia after their abortive revolution against the Turks. The most prominent church in Adamas is that of Christ and the Virgin, distinguished by its clock-tower at the highest point in the town. Another place of interest in the vicinity is the Mining Museum of Melos, less than a kilometre south of the port, with exhibits and memorabilia exhibiting the extraction of the minerals for which Melos has always been noted.

There is a small sand beach a short way west of Adamas at Langada. There are many other good beaches all around the island, some of which are accessible by boat from Adamas. Those on the north coast there are Firopotamos, Mandrakia, Sarakiniko, Agios Konstantinos and Apollonia; on the gulf Platina, Chivadolimni and Emporeios; and on the south Paliochori, Agia Kiriaki, Tzigrado, Firiplaka, Provatas and Gerontas, the latter being a small cove with black sand backed by grottos and natural rock arches.

The capital of the island is Plaka, officially known as Melos, some 3.5 kilometres north-west of Adamas. Plaka is one of five communities that cluster together on the heights of the peninsula that forms the eastern arm of the great gulf, the others being Plakes, Tripiti, Triovasalos and Pera Triovasalos.

Plaka is an attractive Cycladic town that developed on the site of the ancient city of Melos. Cyclopean stones of the city's east gate can still be seen, along with the baptismal font of an early Christian basilica. The town is surmounted by the usual Venetian fortress, the Kastro, which has been destroyed except for some walls and a few churches. The surviving churches include the Panagia Skiniotissa, which was probably the Latin cathedral; the Madonna di Rosario, a Catholic chapel; the Panagia Elousa (Our Lady of Compassion); and the Panagia Thalassitras (Our Lady of the Sea). The latter dates from the thirteenth century; over its side door are the arms of Giovanni IV Crispo (r. 1517–1564), the last

Duke of Naxos to rule over the Cyclades before they fell to the Turks.

Other notable churches in Plaka are the Panagia Korfiotissa and the Mesa Panagia. These and the other churches of the Panagia celebrate their *paneyeri* on 15 August.

Plaka also has two museums of some interest, one devoted to archaeology and the other to history and folklore. The entrance hall of the Archaeological Museum has a plaster copy of the famous Venus de Milo, found on Melos in the nineteenth century and now in the Louvre in Paris. The museum collection includes objects from the Neolithic era, particularly samples of the obsidian that was widely exported by Melos, terracotta animal figurines of the Early Cycladic period, and Mycenaean pottery. The Historical and Folklore Museum, housed in a nineteenth-century neoclassical mansion, has a collection of historical documents, memorabilia, local handicrafts and folk costumes, which the local women were still wearing at the time of Bent's visit.

> For the headdress they have a padded foundation, edged with gold lace, over which they twist the muslin hand-kerchief; their jacket is of purple silk edged with fur, and their skirt is of satin spangled with white flowers; a stomacher of silvered brocade, and a silk gauze apron edged with old Greek lace, and dainty little shoes complete the costume.

The acropolis of the ancient city of Melos was on the ridge between Tripiti and Plaka. The rest of the city was laid out on the slope leading down to the present seaside hamlet of Klima, which is on the site of the ancient harbour. Excavations have revealed pottery sherds of the Middle Cycladic and Mycenaean periods, tombs of the Geometric period, and other remains indicating that the city was occupied continuously from antiquity through the medieval Byzantine period. The findings indicate that the acropolis of the ancient city was the hill of Profitis Ilias, a conical eminence to the north-west. The hill is named for its crowning chapel of Agios Profitis Ilias, built in 1810 by the Sfakians who abandoned

Zephiria. Below the Kastro, in the area that Bent called the 'vale of Klima', there are the well-preserved remains of the Roman theatre, as well as the ruins of a temple known to the locals as 'the palace of the king of Melos'.

The necropolis lay on the hillside outside the city walls to the north-east. The tombs include the vast galleries of Early Christian catacombs cut into the tufa rock, which, the locals assured Bent, were inhabited by Nymphs and Nereids. Excavations have revealed that the catacombs comprise a system of underground passages some 180 metres long with several corridors and three large funerary chambers, where some two thousand burials are estimated to have been made in the third and fourth centuries AD. Within the catacombs archaeologists discovered a small mortuary chapel, which is probably the earliest Christian sanctuary on the Cyclades. Other evidence of this Early Christian community on Melos has been found near the stadium of the ancient city, where the remains of a three-aisled basilica and a baptistery have been unearthed.

Locals point out the place where in 1820 a peasant named Yiorgios Kentrotas unearthed the armless marble figure of Aphrodite that came to be known as the Venus de Milo, the most famous and enigmatic statue that has survived from the ancient Greek world. Louis Brest, the French consul in Smyrna, immediately tried to buy the statue, but Kentrotas asked for more than he was willing to pay. Brest thereupon sent word to the French ambassador in Istanbul, who sent a young nobleman named Count de Marcellus with instructions to buy the statue and bring it back to the Ottoman capital. Meanwhile Kentrotas sold the statue to an Armenian priest, who hoped to present it to a high official in the Ottoman government. When Marcellus arrived on the French warship *Estafette* he found that the statue was about to be loaded on a merchantman for shipment to Istanbul by the Armenian priest. A pitched battle ensued on the beach before Marcellus finally took possession of the statue, which was bought as a gift for Louis XVIII and eventually made its way to the Louvre.

The picturesque fishing village of Mandrakia is on the north coast of the island north-east of Plaka. The coast east of Mandrakia is called Sarakinikio, famous for its white pumice landscape of eroded cones, its variegated seaside rocks of sandstone and limestone worn into sensuous contours by the wind and waves.

Apollonia is a seaside village on the north-easternmost peninsula of Melos opposite Kimolos. The village has recently developed as a summer resort, for it has a sand beach fringed by tamarisk trees, and it is also a convenient base for visiting the archaeological site at Phylakopi and the Papafranga Caves.

Phylakopi was first excavated by the British School of Athens in 1896–1899, and again in 1974–1977 by the British archaeologist Colin Renfrew. These excavations revealed three separate levels of human occupation, dating respectively to the Early, Middle and Late Cycladic periods, spanning the epoch from the early third millennium BC to the end of the second millennium BC. Both Minoan and Mycenaean pottery were found in the third stratum, indicating that a changeover of cultures took place during that period, perhaps occasioned by the volcanic explosion on Santorini *c.* 1500 BC. The most important monuments from the latter period are a shrine and a palatial structure known as a *megaron*, both of them Mycenaean. The shrine contained a large terracotta figurine apparently representing a fertility goddess, whom the archaeologists christened Our Lady of Phylakopi, now in the archaeological museum in Plaka.

The Papafranga Caves, to the south-west of Phylakopi, comprise three sea caverns yawning side by side in the tufa cliffs, their entrances spanned by natural rock bridges. The caverns are named for a priest who is supposed to have hidden his ships there for safety from the pirates who raided the Aegean during the *Turkokrateia*. Those exploring the caves by boat can go out to Glaronissia, 'Gull Isles', a group of three tiny islets made up of hexagonal spires of basalt, some of them rising as high as 20 metres above the sea.

The half-abandoned village of Zephiria dates back to the eighth century BC, still bearing the name by which the island was known before it was called Melos. The village is also known as Palaeochora, or sometimes as Chora, since for a thousand years it was the capital of Melos, from the medieval Byzantine era until 1835, when its population began to abandon it because of the plague. It was never a healthy place, as is evident from Tournefort's description of the town.

> The town contains near 5,000 souls, and is prettily built, but abominably nasty; for when they make an Erection of a House, they begin with the Hogsty, beneath an Arch even with the Ground, or a little lower, and always fronting the Street: in a word, it is the Jakes of the whole House. The Ordure that gathers there, joined to the salt marshes on the sea-side, the mineral Exhalations of the Island, the Scarcity of good Water, to infect the Air, that it breeds very dangerous Distemper.

Zephiria has since been repopulated to some extent, but it still has the haunting air of a ghost town, with many abandoned old houses and churches. A number of the churches were built or taken over by the Sfakiote refugees from Crete, and when the plague forced them to abandon Zephiria they carried their icons with them and built new churches with the same name where they resettled, such as that of Agios Haralambos in Adamas.

On the narrow waist of the island between the gulf and Provata Bay there is a thermal establishment known as Loutra Provata, which is still much frequented by rheumatics. The heart of the spa is an underground chamber within what Bent believed to be a volcanic crater, where the temperature is still as steaming hot as it was in his time, 'hotter than the hottest room in any Turkish bath I ever knew'.

The hamlets of Panagia and Kipos on the west side of Provata Bay are both named for old roadside chapels of the Virgin. The one at Kipos is the Panagia tou Kipou, Our Lady of the Garden, which local tradition dates to the fifth century.

The western half of the island is sparsely settled, since a large part of it is taken up by the ramparts of Mount Profitis Ilias, the highest peak on Milos at 748 metres above sea level.

The monastery of Agia Marina lies under the north-east flank of Mount Profitis Ilias. When Bent and his party passed this way they found the monastery abandoned and in ruins, but the local peasants who had squatted there gave them food and shelter, perpetuating the medieval tradition of monastic hospitality that still lingers on in the Cyclades even today. 'Here we were told that we should get our breakfast,' he writes, 'but it consisted only of rye bread, with black mastic berries in it, coffee, and a pull at a public raki bottle.'

The monastery of Agios Ioannis Theologos, St John the Theologian, is in the remote south-western corner of the island. The Theologian is venerated here as Sideroyianni, or Iron St John, a strange attribute that may stem from the mineral deposits that since antiquity have been mined here on the slopes of Mount Profitis Ilias. Bent's account of his ride out to the monastery of Iron St John is a classic, evoking the sense of what travelling in the interior of the Cyclades was like in times past, and what it still can be today when venturing off the beaten path.

> For a second time on Melos we had a female muleteer, an intelligent girl of about ten, who busied herself for us in gathering the red arbutus berries (still called *koumari*), which are just now ripe, and the gorges were lovely with them. We passed by cleft after cleft of oleander, and locust trees, wild olives, cedars and wild mastic, the black berries of which our damsel made us taste: they are simply horrid, and the taste of varnish, but the peasants here are very fond of them, and put them instead of anise seed into their bread… And through the bright green carob trees the views of the red mountain and blue sea were exquisite.

Remote as it is, the monastery of Iron St John is the goal of two annual pilgrimages that the Meliotes still make on the *paneyeria* of the Theologian, 8 May and 25 September. Local tradition holds that in one of these *paneyeria* during the *Turkokrateia* pirates were seen to be approaching and the pilgrims took refuge in the monastery, whose gates were closed and barred with iron through the intercession of St John. One pirate climbed up on the dome of the church and tried to fire down upon the crowd in the courtyard, but his hand was paralysed and he dropped the pistol, which is still preserved in the treasury of the monastery, or so I was told.

There are two famous marine caves on Akri Psalidi, the south-westernmost peninsula of the island, one on either side of the promontory. The western cave is Sykia, known in English as the Emerald Cave; the eastern is Klephtiko, Thieve's Cave, whose spectacular spires of offshore rocks have earned it the name of the 'Marine Meteora'.

After Bent's visit to Iron St John's he and his wife made their way to Adamas, where they waited for a boat to take them to the next island on their itinerary. While they waited Bent spent his time listening to the songs and stories of the Meliotes, here again catching the spirit of the Cyclades on the wind, preserving the memory of a time that would now otherwise be lost.

> And all this time we were lodged in a most humble house, in a very quiverful of children, but the people were kindly disposed, and did everything they could to amuse us in the evenings; they sang for us, they played the lyre for us; and very pretty were the words of some of their songs, though the music was to us monotonous, drawled out for us by that hideous music of the Eastern Church, so distasteful to a Western ear; but the beautiful idea is present in every song.

One of the songs they would have heard that evening, and which is still sung today at *paneyeria* on Melos, is an old Meliote favourite, *O Apohairetismos Pros Ton Naftin* (Farewell to the Sailor).

> The Stone on which you trod
> to get into your boat –
> Let me go and find it,
> cover it with tears.
> And in that place you're going to,
> My darling, where you'll drop anchor,

Lots of girls will see you
and you'll forget me.
And if you forget me, oh my love,
And find yourself another mate,
May they sell you as a slave,
And take you to the coast of Barbary,
put you in irons, a chain around your neck,
And may you sigh and say you're wearing them for me.

***

Kimolos lies just off the north-westernmost cape of Melos, from which it is separated by a strait barely a kilometre wide, the Diavolos Polloni. It is the smallest of the permanently inhabited islands of the western Cyclades, with a population of just 799. Virtually all of the inhabitants live in Chora, on the ridge above the port at Psathi, about a kilometre by road. The island is generally barren and lacking in water, except in the Dekas Valley in the south-west, where there are vineyards and orchards of olive and fig trees, for which Kimolos was noted in antiquity.

Kimolos was also renowned in antiquity for its *terra Kimolia*, a chalk-like material used to make fuller's earth, which the ancients used for washing clothes and for medicinal baths. According to Tournefort, 'The Terra Cimolia, so highly esteemed by the Ancients, is a white chalk, very heavy, without any taste, abounding in a small grit that sets one's teeth on edge.' This *terra Kimolia* can still be seen today forming the silver-white cliffs that fringe part of the island's coastline. The colour of these cliffs led medieval Latin mariners to call the island Argentiere, 'the Silver One'.

Kimolos was one of the islands taken in 1207 by Marco I Sanudo, becoming part of the Duchy of the Archipelago, ruled by his descendants and the succeeding dynasty of the Crispi. Giovanni II Crispo ruled over Melos and Kimolos before succeeding as Duke of Naxos in 1418. During the early years of the *Turkokrateia* Kimolos was one of the Cyclades retained by the Gozzadini family on payment of an annual tribute to the

Ottomans, but then in 1617 the island finally came under direct Turkish rule.

Tournefort writes that Argentiere, as he calls it, became prosperous in the late seventeenth century as a notorious lair of French corsairs, who cohabited with the local women and gave the island a very unsavoury reputation, until finally they and the other pirates in the Aegean were put down by the King of France.

> In fine, this island is becoming wretchedly poor ever since the King put down the French corsairs in the Levant. Argentiere used to be a place of their Rendezvous, where they spent in terrible Debaucheries the booty they took from the Turks; to the great advantage of the Ladies, who are none of the coyest or ugliest: this is the most dangerous rock to split upon in all the Archipelago; but he must be a real Ignoramus that can't avoid it. The whole trade of the Island consists of this sort of rough Gallantry, suitable enough to Sailors who have none of the nicest Stomachs: the Women have no other Employment than making Love and Cotton Stockings.

The Chora, also known as Kimolos, is a walled Cycladic town of medieval aspect, very much like Kastro of Siphnos, with an outer ring of houses forming the external defence wall and an inner ring surrounding a citadel. The outer part of the village, known as Exo Kastro (Outside the Kastro) or Neo Chorio (New Village), was built from the late sixteenth century onwards, while the inner part, called Meso Kastro (Inside the Kastro) or Palio Chorio (Old Village), dates back to the thirteenth and fourteenth centuries. There were originally towers at each of the corners, of which only one has survived. The citadel, or Kastro proper, has outer gateways in the middle of its south side and in its north-east corner, with an inner gate in the south-west corner leading to a small *plateia* centred on the Roman Catholic cathedral. Kastro, which is now virtually abandoned, was the capital of Kimolos during the Latin period, which ended here in 1617 when the reign of the Gozzadini gave way to the *Turkokrateia*.

There are a number of post-Byzantine churches in the Chora, most notably the cathedral, dedicated to the Panagia Evangelistria, dating from 1614, which celebrates its *paneyeri* on 15 August. Other are Christos (1592), the Taxiarchis (1670), Agios Ioannis Chrysostomos (1680), and the ruined Catholic church of the Madonna di Rosario. The impressive church of the Panagia Hodegitria (Our Lady who Points the Way) was dedicated in 1873.

There is a small archaeological museum in the Chora, with objects from excavations on the island. The exhibits include a remarkable collection of ceramics dating from the Geometric, Hellenistic and Roman periods. The Afentakeion Foundation also has a collection of antiquities, mostly pottery and sherds.

The beaches closest to Chora are on the south-east coast at Psathi, Goupa and Klima; others are at Aliki (south), Kambana (south-west), and Prasso (north-east). At Ormos Vroma, a large bay on the north-east coast of the island near Prasso, there are several caves that the surging sea has carved out of the rocks. The largest of these is the Vromolimni Cave, within which there is a smaller cavern that has not yet been explored.

Palaeokastro, the highest peak on Kimolos, rises to a height of 364 metres north of the island's centre. The peak takes its name from Palaeokastro, the capital of Kimolos from antiquity down through the medieval Byzantine period, whose ruins are on the summit of the mountain. One can still see the ancient Cyclopean walls of the acropolis and the ruins of the medieval fortress, brooding a thousand feet above the sea.

There is an important archaeological site on the south-western coast at Elinika. Excavations here and at the offshore islet of Agios Andreas have unearthed a settlement and cemetery dating back to the Mycenaean period, the latter half of the second millennium BC. It has been suggested that this was a colony of refugees from the Greek mainland, who brought their personal wealth and skills with them and engaged in wide-ranging maritime commerce. The settlement apparently continued in existence well into the Christian era, perhaps even into the Middle Ages. Finds in the cemetery indicate that during the Geometric period, the ninth and eighth centuries BC, local potters produced fine ceramics. A grave stele in tufa from the seventh century BC found at Elinika has a relief depicting the upper half of a female figure, believed to be the oldest representation of a human being in stone from the archaic era in Greece. Votive objects buried with the dead indicate that trade took place between Kimolos and Corinth in the Archaic period; later the islanders also traded with Athens, until well into the Hellenistic period. An inscription records a judgement by Argos settling a dispute between Kimolos and Melos concerning the ownership of Poliegos.

The people of Kimolos in times not long past lived in fear of vampires, the dread *Broukolakes*. They believed that anyone on the point of death who cursed himself or was cursed by an enemy became a vampire, so that his body would not decay in the earth, allowing him to wander about at night attacking man and beast to suck their blood. There is no peace for the vampire in Hades, they believe, nor peace for his relatives on earth, for he returns to his home and 'feeds on his own', bringing with him plague and death, so that the grass dies and flowers wither around his grave and the herds who graze there die and dogs howl ominously in the night.

The locals used to rid themselves of this menace through a rite of exorcism carried out by a priest who accompanied the family of the supposed vampire to his unquiet grave. There they prayed to God to have mercy on the accursed creature, after which the priest poured boiling water mixed with vinegar on the grave. This seemed to do the trick, as Bent noted, for '[a]fter this ceremony it is observed that the ghost stops his wanderings; many affirm that whilst the service is going on they hear the rattle of bones as they settle in the grave'.

A more cheerful tradition that is still remembered, if not actually practised, is one associated with Agia Ekaterini, St Catherine of Alexandria, whose *paneyeri* is celebrated on 25 November. On the eve of the *paneyeri*, young girls gathered to bake Saint Catherine's cakes, which were made from three handfuls of flour and three of salt mixed by an old widow. The girls ate the salty cakes, each of them hoping that she would dream of being offered a glass of water by a handsome young man who was destined to become her husband, through the intercession of Saint Catherine. Bent, after describing this practice, remarks: 'I do not doubt that sooner or later they will find helpmates, for they were pretty girls, with an Ionian type of countenance, round faces, and those curious almond-shaped eyes.'

Such are the legends and traditions of Kimolos, where you still see girls with round Ionian faces and almond-shaped eyes.

Melos: population 4,714; area 158 sq km; Mt. Profitis Ilias (748 m); ferries from Piraeus (86 mi); airport; hotels in Adamas, Paliochori, Provatas and Sarakiniko.

Kimolos: population 799; area 36 sq km; Mt. Palaeokastro (364 m); ferries from Piraeus (88 mi); rooms in Chora and Psathi.

Andros

● Chora

1. Gavrion
2. Fellos
3. Makrotandalo
4. Kalivari
5. Varidi
6. Amolochos
7. Vitali
8. Agios Petros
9. Moni Zoodochos Pigi
10. Batsi
11. Katakilos
12. Arnas
13. Ateni
14. Palaeopolis
15. Zagora
16. Melida
17. Menites
18. Messaria
19. Apikia
20. Stenies
21. Moni Panachrantou
22. Korthi
23. Agia Moni
△ Mt Petalon

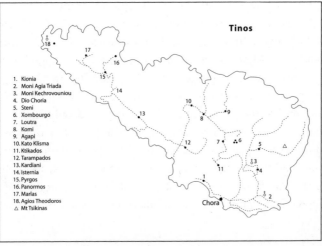

Tinos

1. Kionia
2. Moni Agia Triada
3. Moni Kechrovouniou
4. Dio Choria
5. Steni
6. Xombourgo
7. Loutra
8. Komi
9. Agapi
10. Kato Klisma
11. Ktikados
12. Tarampados
13. Kardiani
14. Isternia
15. Pyrgos
16. Panormos
17. Marlas
18. Agios Theodoros
△ Mt Tsikinas

Chora

seven
Andros

Andros is the northernmost of the Cyclades, separated from the southern end of Euboea by a strait less than three nautical miles wide, the infamous Kafireos, where I have encountered the roughest seas that have ever tossed me about the Aegean. When we crossed this strait to approach the rock-bound coast of Andros for the first time I was reminded of T. S. Eliot's lines:

> Paint me a cavernous waste shore
> Cast in the unstilled Cyclades,
> Paint me the bold anfractuous rocks
> Faced by the snarled and yelping seas.

At its south-eastern end Andros is separated from the opposing tip of Tinos by an even narrower strait, the two islands forming the first links in the short chain of the north-eastern Cyclades, which extends on to Mykonos and its companion isles of Delos and Rhenea.

Andros is the second largest of the Cyclades after Naxos, which it compares with in ruggedness, its highest peak – Mount Petalon – rising to 994 metres above sea level, surpassed only slightly by Mount Zas and another Naxian peak. The range of steep mountains is unbroken by plains, the rugged heights separated only by small ravines and three green and well-watered valleys. Unlike most other Aegean islands, the mountain streams of Andros do not dry up in summer. This continuous and copious supply of water is responsible for the great fertility of the island, which brings forth a cornucopia of oranges, lemons, figs, mulberries, grapes and olives, the latter two used to produce an abundance of wine and olive oil.

The northern and western parts of Andros are populated principally by ethnic Albanians, descendants of Christian Epirotes who began migrating to Greece in the fourteenth century when the Turks first invaded their homeland. In Bent's time the Albanians on Andros still spoke *Alvanetika* and dressed in their distinctive Epirote costumes, the men kilted and wearing Phrygian caps. But today they have been more or less assimilated, with all except a few of the older people now fluent in Greek, although in their homes they still speak Albanian.

The landscape of Andros takes on aspects of a Japanese silk-screen painting because of the terracing of its tiered hillsides, where the Andriotes have laid out their elongated strips of little farms, orchards and vineyards at great expenditure of labour over many generations. The soil is retained on the steep slopes by dry stone walls (*xerolithos*) set closely together with horizontal and vertical slabs of schist, with the distinctive orthostats known as *stimata* marking property boundaries. There are marvellously constructed stone huts called *kellia*, or sometimes *barbakedes*, and also enclosed threshing floors with curving windowed walls known in Greek as *skepos* and in Albanian as *gardi*, as well as dovecotes with elaborate facings in slabs of schist instead of the brickwork used elsewhere.

There are also numerous *pyrgoi* of a type distinctive to Andros, the oldest going back to the third century BC, most of the others dating from the Latin period.

Those areas of Andros that are not used for farms, orchards, vineyards and pasturelands are for the most part covered with aromatic pine forests, vast woods of mulberry trees, dreaming groves of cypresses, and vast silver-green inland seas of gnarled olive trees, making this the greenest and most heavily wooded of the Cyclades.

Andros first appears in history during the Lelantine War, which began *c.* 700 BC as a dispute between the two cities of Chalcis and

Eretria. At the beginning of the war Andros, Tinos and Kea were controlled by Chalcis. But by the time the war ended both Chalcis and Eretria had lost considerable power, while Andros became independent. Then *c.* 655 BC Andros founded four colonies on the peninsula of Chalcidice, one of which was Acanthus, later to be called Stagira, the birthplace of Aristotle.

When Darius invaded Greece in 490 BC his forces seized Andros and Euboea before landing on the mainland, and after their defeat at Marathon the Persians retained both islands as naval bases. The Persians apparently still controlled Andros at the time of Xerxes' invasion of Greece in 480 BC, for the Andrians played no part in the Battle of Salamis. Themistocles, who commanded the Greek fleet at Salamis, demanded an indemnity from Andros and other islands for having aided Xerxes, and when the Andrians refused he sent a fleet to besiege them, an incident described by Herodotus in Book VIII of his *Histories*.

Themistocles eventually lifted his siege of Andros, and in the flush of victory after the Battle of Plataea the following year the collaboration of the Andrians with Darius apparently was forgotten. Andros joined the Delian League in 477 BC and soon, along with the rest of the Cyclades, lost its independence and became part of the Athenian maritime empire. The island at that time must have been at the peak of its prosperity, for the levy imposed upon Andros by Athens was the same as those of Naxos and Melos, the wealthiest isles in the Cyclades. In 448 BC Athens established a *clerurchy* on Andros, confiscating the best land and distributing it to 250 Athenian settlers. This tyranny aroused great bitterness, and in later conflicts, particularly during the Peloponnesian War, Andros sided with the enemies of Athens whenever possible. Today, ironically, Andros is a favourite holiday destination for Athenians.

During the Byzantine period the Andriotes became very prosperous from the silk that they produced from their groves of mulberry trees and shipped off to western Europe. This prosperity was the main reason why culture on Andros remained on a high level throughout the medieval Byzantine era, as evidenced by a renowned school that flourished there for more than four centuries after Justinian closed the Platonic Academy at Athens in AD 529. Michael Psellos (1018–1079), one of the most brilliant scholars in the history of Byzantium, taught at the Andrian Academy early in his career, after which he went on to become professor of philosophy at the newly founded imperial university at Constantinople and then prime minister under the emperor Michael VII (r. 1071–1078). One of his students at the Andrian Academy was Leo the Mathematician, who followed him to Constantinople, where he wrote a commentary on Archimedes and other mathematical works that are landmarks in the history of medieval science.

Andros was one of the islands taken in 1207 by Marco Sanudo, who assigned it as a sub-fief to his cousin Marino Sanudo, another nephew of Doge Enrico Dandolo. After Marino's death the island reverted to the then Duke of Naxos, Marco II Sanudo, grandson of Marco I. From then, until the end of their dynasty in the second half of the fourteenth century, the Sanudi dukes styled themselves 'Lords of the Duchy of Naxos and Andros', regularly spending time in what is now the Chora of Andros.

After Francesco Crispo began a new dynasty in Naxos in 1383, he married off one of his daughters to Pietro Zeno, son of the Venetian governor of Negroponte (Euboea), whom he made lord of Andros *c*. 1402. When Zeno died in 1427 he was succeeded by his son Andreas, who ruled until his death in 1437, after which Venice took control of Andros to prevent a war of succession between several petty Latin warlords. Three years later the Venetian Senate assigned the island to Crusino I Sommaripa, lord of Paros, whose descendants ruled Andros until Barbarossa's terrible raid of 1537.

The Turks did not formally annex Andros until 1566, when the admiral Piyale Pasha took possession of the island, leaving the Andriotes unharmed after they agreed to submit to the sultan's rule and pay an annual capitation tax. Thereafter Andros was scarcely troubled by the Turks during the two and a half centuries in which they ruled the Cyclades.

After the Greek War of Independence Andros prospered through maritime commerce, its ships making their way as far as Russian ports on the Black Sea. This prosperity is still evident in the handsome mansions of wealthy merchants and captains in the village of Stenies.

One remarkable Andriote of this period was Theophilos Kaires, who was born in Chora in 1784, and then after attending primary and secondary school in Istanbul went off to university, first at Pisa and later at Paris. He returned to Greece at the outbreak of the War of Independence, representing Andros in the first national assemblies. Kaires was a philosopher and a scholar of encyclopedic knowledge, but above all he was an idealistic social reformer, and his mission in life was to establish an orphanage on Andros where poor, homeless children could find shelter and obtain a good education. After the conclusion of the War of Independence, Kaires toured Europe to raise funds for his orphanage, which he and his sister founded on Andros in 1835. At the outset the orphanage housed some thirty children, but within five years the enrolment rose to 600, as the fame of the institution spread throughout Greece.

Kaires had very unorthodox religious beliefs, embodying what he called 'theosophia', which he expressed simply as 'Fear of God and Love of Man'. This soon brought down upon him the wrath of the Greek Orthodox Church, and in 1839 he was tried by the Holy Synod and convicted as a heretic. Kaires was first imprisoned in a monastery on Skiathos and then in another on Santorini, after which he was banished from Greece. He found refuge in London, where he stayed for two years, returning to Andros soon after the Greek Kingdom adopted its first constitution in 1844. Kaires resumed work in his orphanage, which had declined greatly in his absence, but in 1852 he was once again tried by the Holy Synod and convicted of heresy, dying in Syros prison on 28 December of that year. His orphanage is no longer in existence, but its school is still functioning in the Chora, where a statue has been erected to honour his memory. Long before the statue was erected Bent wrote this tribute: 'The love of Theophilos Kaires is not yet dead on Andros; he is undoubtedly the greatest light that has ever shone amongst them.'

Today the main port of Andros is on the north-west coast at Gavrion, which has a decent beach and numerous tavernas where Athenians whoop it up on their summer holidays. The town is of little interest itself, but it is a good base to explore the northern end of the island, particularly the villages of Kato and Ano Fellos, Makrotandalo, Hartes, Kalivari, Varidi, Amolochos and Vitali, which are populated almost entirely by ethnic Albanians.

Near Ano Fellos there is an ancient quarry said to be the source of the marble used to build the Temple of Poseidon at Cape Sounion. The Fellos villages, Lower and Upper, share two old churches, one dedicated to Agios Haralambos and the other to the Metamorphosis, or the Transfiguration of Christ. Bent took the two villages to be one, which he described as 'a clean and hospitably inclined place, very picturesque, and with houses for the most part decorated with old china plates built into the walls... They have glorious views from here over the snow-capped peaks of Euboea...' The two villages celebrate the *paneyeri* of the Transfiguration on 6 August, when it is the custom to bring the first baskets of grapes to the church to be blessed and then distributed among the congregation.

At Makrotandalo there is a ruined Venetian *pyrgos*. On a hill above Kalivari and Varidi there are the remains of a medieval fortress called Vryocastro. At the beautiful village of Amolochos there is a ruined Venetian mansion known as the Pyrgos of Mastro-Yannoulis. South of Vitali there is another ruined Venetian *pyrgos* called Kastellaki, the Little Castle. The road to Vitali goes on to the bay of the same name on the north-east coast, where there is a sandy beach.

At Agios Petros, three kilometres north-east of Gavrion, there is an exceptionally well-preserved *pyrgos*. This is one of the two finest and best-preserved structures of its type in the Cyclades, the other being the Pyrgos Chimarou on Naxos, both of them watchtowers and signal beacons of the Hellenistic era, probably dating from the third century BC. The *pyrgos* at Agios Petros is cylindrical in form,

21 metres in circumference and 20 metres high, built of colossal stone blocks. The tower appears to have had five or six storeys, but the upper floors and the inner spiral staircase have disappeared.

About two kilometres south-east of Agios Petros is the monastery of the Panagia Zoodochos Pigi, Our Lady of the Life-Giving Spring. This is one of the oldest of the 13 extant monasteries on Andros; its deed of foundation is dated 1535, though much of its structure appears to date from more recent times. The monastery, which once housed a thousand monks, was abandoned in the late Ottoman period and reopened in 1928 as a convent. There is a splendid *iconostasis* in the *katholikon*, and the library contains some very old and valuable books and manuscripts.

Like other places dedicated to Our Lady of the Life-Giving Spring, the monastery is built around an *agiasma*, a holy well or spring. Bent had reason to believe that the *agiasma* here was the one referred to by Pliny, who writes that on Andros there was a festival called the Dionysia, where the god turned the water of a spring into wine when he visited the island. Today the festival is celebrated on the Friday after Easter, the *paneyeri* of the Panagia Zoodochos Pigi, who is thanked for her gift of life-giving water.

The next village south of Gavrion along the coast road is Batsi, the largest town on the western side of the island. Batsi is now the main destination of the tourists who come to Andros, drawn there by its long sand beach shaded by tamarisk trees around a scimitar-shaped bay.

At Batsi a road leads inland to the mountain villages of Katakilos, Remnata and Arnas, the latter surrounded by woodlands high on the northern slope of Mount Petalon. Katakilos is renowned for its island music and dances. Farther to the north is Ateni, a hamlet at the head of a verdant valley that comes down to the sea in a pair of beautiful sand beaches.

The site of the ancient capital of Andros is on the coast eight kilometres south of Batsi at Palaeopolis, abandoned early in the Byzantine era because of pirate raids. A farmer digging in his field here in 1832 discovered two larger-than-life marble statues, one a representation of Hermes Psychopompos, the Conductor of Souls, and the other a feminine deity known as the Matron of Herculaneum. This discovery caused such a sensation that the young King Otho of Greece came out to Andros with his father, King Ludwig I of Bavaria, and when they saw the statues they bought them for the new Archaeological Museum that was founded in Athens by royal decree the following year.

The site of the ancient city is approached by a stairway that leads down from the road to the sea. Amid the greenery there are the remains of the city walls, a gate, and the ruins of a round tower, as well as scattered architectural fragments and pottery sherds. Excavations in 1956 uncovered the site of the *agora*, or marketplace, where there are the remains of a portico and commemorative statue bases.

There is another archaeological site on the coast six kilometres to the south, near the crossroads at Stavropeda. About half a kilometre beyond the crossroads there is an unmarked pathway by the chapel of Agia Triada leading to the archaeological site at Zagora, which is on a prominent headland. Excavations that began here in 1960 have unearthed a settlement dating from the Geometric period, the most important structure being a small temple that may have been dedicated to Athena. It is believed that this settlement was founded by Ionians from Attica *c.* 900 BC, but for some unknown reason it was abandoned about two centuries later and never reoccupied. It is possible that Zagora was abandoned to found a new settlement at Palaeopolis, since the latter site has a far more abundant supply of water. This has always been the determining factor in life on the Greek islands, which is why the patron saint of Andros is Our Lady of the Life-Giving Spring.

The present capital of Andros is at Chora on the east coast, approached from the crossroads at Stavropeda by a road that cuts across the waist of the island. The road passes the prettiest and most interesting villages on the island, most notably Melida, Aladino, Menites, Messaria, Mesathouri, Ipsila and Apikia. As Tournefort writes of his journey through this valley, which Bent called the Vale of Andros: 'Going out of this Burgh [Chora], you enter one of the finest Champagnes in the world: on the left is the Plain of Livadi, i.e., agreeable spot: it is planted with Orange, Lemon, Mulberry, Jujeb, Pomegranate, and Fig Trees; nothing is to be seen but Gardens and Rivulets.'

There are a number of interesting old churches in the Vale of Andros. One of these is in Melida, the first of the villages one passes on the road from Stavropeda to Chora. The village church in Melida is dedicated to the Taxiarchis Michaelis, and dates from the eleventh century.

Near Aladino, at the place known locally as Lasthinou, there is a cave known as Chaos, where there are several chambers with remarkable stalactites.

The village church in Menites is dedicated to the Panagia Koumoulos, the Virgin of the Plentiful. On the façade of the church there is a fountain framed by a beautiful relief dating from the eighteenth century; below there is a large public water tank whose seven interconnected spouts are in the form of lion heads, a work of the Venetian era. The church is renowned for the supposedly miraculous stream of water that flows through it and emerges in this fountain.

The locals claim that this stream is the one mentioned by Pliny in his description of the Dionysia that was celebrated on Andros, but Bent disagreed, for he felt that the *agiasma* at Zoodochos Pigi was the true site, although he was very favourably impressed by Menites. As he writes: 'No, we must look elsewhere for our temple of Dionysos. Every house at Menites was gay with flowers – for without they are sweet-smelling or useful for something a Greek despises flowers. Inside, too, the houses were clean, and for the most part stocked with boxes for the lemon trade.'

Messaria is a charming old village now largely abandoned. This seems to have been the second capital of Andros in the eighteenth and early nineteenth century, after the ancient city at Palaeopolis had been abandoned and before Chora became the capital. One of the old mansions in Messaria has above its door an escutcheon with a relief of the double-headed eagle of Byzantium, while others have the winged lion of St Mark, symbol of the Serene

Republic of Venice. The oldest church in the village is dedicated to the Taxiarchis Michaelis, and was perhaps the cathedral of Andros while Messaria was the capital. An inscription in the church records that it was built in 1157, during the reign of the emperor Manuel I Comnenos. Another interesting old church in Messaria is dedicated to Agios Nikolaos and is dated 1732, though it has been completely rebuilt in recent years.

The Byzantine church of the Koimisis tis Theotokou at Mesathouri is dated to the twelfth century. At Ipsila there is another Byzantine church dedicated to the Taxiarchis Michaelis, dated to the eleventh or twelfth century.

Apikia is renowned for its spring of mineral water, believed to be a cure for rheumatism and arthritis; this is bottled under the name of Sariza and sold all over Greece. North of Apikia there is an old monastery dedicated to Agios Nikolaos; founded in the eighteenth century, it is noted for its carved wooden *iconostasis* and its treasury of sacred vessels, liturgical vestments and embroideries.

Chora, the capital of Andros, has an unusual and dramatic setting, its houses built on a tongue of rock that projects out into the bay, with the promontory ending in a craggy islet connected to the mainland by a stone bridge. The battered ruins of a medieval tower surmount the islet, known as Mesa Kastro, the bastion of the fortifications built by Marino Sanudo when he established his capital here soon after 1207. Only some fragments remain of the fortifications that he built around the periphery of the peninsular town, known as Kato Kastro, whose steep rocky sides separated the two anchorages of Paraporti and Emborios, which now serves as the town beach.

The main street of Chora, which is paved in marble and closed off to traffic, is lined with handsome stone houses of the early nineteenth century, the grandest being the neoclassical mansion of the Stylianidis family, with its arcaded balcony. The attractive *plateia* is named for Theophilos Kaires, whose commemorative statue stands there, along with a beautiful baroque street fountain bearing the date 1818.

Just off the square is the Archaeological Museum, whose most famous exhibit is the Hermes of Andros, returned from the National Archaeological Museum in Athens along with the Matron of Herculaneum, the two most important finds from the site at Palaeopolis. The town also has an interesting Maritime Museum as well as a Museum of Contemporary Art. In the square at the far end of the peninsula there is a bronze statue of 'The Sailor', by the sculptor Michaelis Tombros, some of whose other works are exhibited in the Museum of Contemporary Art.

The cathedral of Andros, dedicated to Agios Yiorgios, is built on the foundations of an older church believed to date from the sixteenth century. Near the *plateia* there is an old chapel dedicated to the Panagia Zoodochos Pigi, with a sacred spring in its crypt and an *iconostasis* bearing the date 1717. Close by there is a Roman Catholic church dedicated to Agios Andreas, with an inscription recording that it was reconstructed in 1749. Among the other old churches in the town are two dedicated to the Virgin, the Panagia Palatiani (Our Lady of the Castle) and the Panagia Hodegitria (Our Lady the Guide).

Another old chapel dedicated to the Virgin is the Panagia Theokepasti (Our Lady of the Roof of God), dating from 1555, which takes its curious name from the legend of its foundation. It seems that when the construction materials arrived in a ship the priest had money enough to pay for everything except the wood for the roof, for which the captain demanded an exorbitant price. When the priest said that he could not pay for the roof the irate captain sailed away, but his ship soon encountered a violent storm. The sailors prayed to the Virgin, promising her that if she spared their lives they would force the captain to sail back to Andros, where they would donate the wood to the priest as an offering to her. Having survived, they did so, after which the priest completed the church and dedicated it to Our Lady of the Roof of God.

Around the bay north of Chora, at Gialia, there is a sandy beach shaded by eucalyptus trees. On the hills above is Stenies, a large village of tiled single- and two-storey houses facing east towards the sea through a bower of trees. The finest houses in the village were built by ship captains and maritime merchants, whose gateways are often decorated with carvings of early nineteenth-century sailing ships. Stenies is dominated by a Venetian *pyrgos* that originally belonged to the Venetian aristocrat Bistis and is now owned by the Mouvelas family.

Moni Panachrantou, the grandest of all the monasteries on Andros, is set at an elevation of 230 metres in the mountains south-west of Chora. Tradition has it that the monastery was founded by the emperor Nicephoros II Phocas (r. 963–969) but there is no documentary proof of this, and the earliest record in its archives is a note stating that Moni Panachrantou was repaired in 1608. At one time the monastery housed some 400 monks, but today there are only five in residence. The monastery is under the jurisdiction of the Ecumenical Patriarch of Constantinople, hence it is called *stavropigiou*, a privileged status for which it pays annually to the patriarch an *oka* (about 2.75 pounds) of beeswax. The most important relic in the treasury is the head of Agios Pandeleimon, which is exhibited to those who come to celebrate the saint's *paneyeri* on 27 July.

Ormos Korthiou is a huge bay that cuts deeply into the south-eastern end of the island, fringed with sand beaches. On the northern horn of the bay there are the ruins of a Venetian fortress known as Apano Kastro. There is an abandoned Byzantine church near the village of Palaeokastro, whose name comes from the exiguous ruins of an ancient fortress.

The southernmost villages on the island are in the region inland from the bay, which Bent called the Vale of Korthi. In the countryside around Episkopia and Kapparia deserted Venetian dovecotes stand amidst the olive groves, and in the vicinity of Korthi and Aidonia there are a number of Venetian *pyrgoi*, some of them still occupied by descendants of the original owners.

Mount Profitis Ilias, the second highest peak on Andros, rises to an elevation of 682 metres near the southern tip of the island. On the southern slope of the mountain there is a deserted monastery known as Agia Moni. Bent was told this was once the site of the most popular *paneyeri* in the Cyclades, but the pilgrims had long since abandoned Agia Moni in favour of the famous shrine of the Virgin on Tinos. 'Everywhere the same complaint is made, "Before the world went to Tenos they came here...;" nearly every island complains of the disrepute into which its miracle-working shrine has fallen within late years.'

The Virgin is honoured in churches of the Panagia throughout the island on her feast days, the most spirited festival being on 15 August at Korthi, which has replaced the one at Agia Moni as the most popular *paneyeri* on Andros. The setting could not be more beautiful, the village square embowered within an olive grove in the Vale of Korthia, the sounds of the lute, the *bouzoukia* and the violin echoing under the stars as dancers circle the floor while the vocalist sings *nisiotika tragoudia*, 'songs of the islands', perhaps the old favourite called *I Tragoudistra* (The Songstress).

> From a window, a beautiful girl was singing,
> The breeze took her song, carried it down to the sea
> And all the ships that heard it cast anchor and tied up.
> And a Frankish ship, a frigate of love,
> Didn't take in its sails, nor move on,
> And back from the stern the captain shouted:
> 'Sailors, strike sail, leap to the rigging,
> Let's listen to the girl who sings so sweetly
> And hear the tune of her beautiful song.'
> The sweetness of the tune and her sweet singing
> Made the helmsman turn and make for the land,
> And the sailors hung aloft on the masts.

Such are the siren songs of the Cyclades.

Andros: population 10,112; area 383 sq km; Mt. Petalon (994 m); ferries from Piraeus (89 mi) and Rafina (36 mi); hotels in Batsi, Gavrio, Chora, Korthi and Agios Petros.

eight
Tinos

Tinos is famous throughout the Greek world for its miracle-working shrine of the Panagia Evangelistria, Our Lady of the Annunciation, which dominates Chora, the port and capital of Tinos, at the south-eastern end of the island. Multitudes of pilgrims flock to the Chora on the two principal feast days of the Virgin, 25 March and 15 August, the first celebrating her Annunciation and the second her Assumption, better known to the Greeks as the *Koimisis tis Theotokou*. Both days are national holidays, 25 March also commemorating the beginning of the Greek War of Independence in 1821, leaving all of Greece free to journey to Tinos for the Virgin's *paneyeria*, which are three-day celebrations. These two *paneyeria* are undoubtedly the survival of ancient pagan festivals, the first of them marking the spring equinox and the second mid-summer.

The first reference to Tinos is found in Book VIII of Herodotus' *Histories*, where he describes the prelude to the Battle of Salamis. Tinos had been one of the islands that had submitted to Xerxes, its citizens manning a warship in his fleet, but when the Greek allies gathered at Salamis the Tinians deserted from the Persian fleet and joined their compatriots, bringing them news that the enemy was about to attack them there. As Herodotus writes in conclusion, 'For this service the name of the Tinians was afterwards inscribed on the tripod at Delphi amongst those states who helped repel the invader.'

Strabo notes that Tinos was famous for its temple of Poseidon, whose festival, the Poseideia, attracted celebrants from all of the surrounding islands. 'Tinos has no large city,' he writes, 'but it has the temple of Poseidon, a great temple in a sacred precinct outside the city, a spectacle worth seeing. In it they have built great banquet halls – an indication of the multitude of neighbours who congregate there and take part with the inhabitants of Tinos in celebrating the Posidonian festival.'

The Poseideia was celebrated from the fourth century BC until late antiquity, outlasting the much more ancient festival of Apollo on Delos. A fragmentary verse, written during the reign of Augustus (r. 27 BC–AD 14), wonders '…who would have thought to see Delos abandoned and Tinos continuing to thrive'.

After Marco Sanudo conquered the Cyclades in 1207 he gave Tinos as a sub-fief to the Ghisi family, along with Mykonos. This dynasty ruled Tinos and Mykonos until 1390, when Giorgio III Ghisi died without heirs, having bequeathed the two islands to Venice. In 1407 the Venetian Senate gave Tinos and Mykonos to Giovanni Quirini, lord of the isle of Astypalaia, known to the Latins as Stampalia. Tinos and Mykonos reverted to Venice in 1430, and thenceforth they were under the control of a Venetian governor, the Provveditore Generale, who had his headquarters at Tinos in the mountain fortress of Sant Helena, known to the Greeks as Xombourgo. The Turks made numerous assaults on Tinos during the seven wars between Venice and the Ottoman Empire, but in all except the last of these conflicts the fortress of Sant Helena held out, even when the rest of the island was overrun.

During one of the Turkish raids on Tinos, probably in the late 1580s, they captured a young girl named Anastasia, the daughter of a Greek priest. Such was her beauty that Anastasia was brought to the imperial harem of Topkapi Saray, the great palace of the Ottoman sultans in Istanbul, where she was given the Turkish name of Kösem. Around 1604 Kösem became the favourite concubine of the young sultan Ahmet I (r. 1603–1617) and bore him seven children, including the future sultans Murat IV (r. 1623–1640) and Ibrahim (r. 1640–1648). Kösem was the power behind the throne during the reigns of her two sons and on into the early years of the reign of her grandson Mehmet IV (r. 1648–1687). In 1651 she was killed in the harem by Mehmet's mother.

By the beginning of eighteenth century the Venetians had all but given up in the Aegean, as is evidenced by Tournefort's description of the fortress of Sant Helena: 'Fourteen badly dressed soldiers formed the garrison, seven of whom were French deserters. The Provveditore's post did not bring in two thousand crowns.'

The fortress of Sant Helena was finally surrendered to the Turks in 1715 by the last Venetian governor of Tinos, the Provveditore Balbi, who then fled to Venice and was sentenced to life imprisonment for his cowardice. The last Venetian fortresses on Crete surrendered to the Turks that same year, ending the Latin period in the history of the Aegean. But the Venetian presence still lingers on in many ways, one being the relatively large number of Roman Catholics among the population, more than in any of the Cyclades other than Syros.

The young Irish traveller James Caulfeild, Viscount Charlemont, visited Tinos in 1749 and found that the island was faring well under the rule of the Ottomans, to whom they paid a yearly tribute through an agent on the island, the only Turk resident there.

> The island of Tino ... possesses also the privilege of being free from the visits of the Captain Pasha ... This freedom from oppression is easily to be observed in the state of the country, which is beautiful and well cultivated, and in the appearance of the inhabitants, who are industrious, well clothed, happy, and lively ... The dress and manners of the inhabitants bespeak their affluence, and content is visible in every countenance, but that which most strikes the traveller's eye, is the wonderful beauty of the women, to which their dress not a little contributes, which, far different from the other islands, is to the last degree elegant and graceful ... They are sprightly and affable, and peculiarly remarkable for their skill and agility in dancing, a talent which we put to the test in a ball which

was given by our Consul, at which all the belles of the island
were assembled, and jollily danced with us till midnight,
not only Greek dances, but minuets also, the knowledge
of which they have probably retained from the instruction
of their old masters, the Venetians...

During the first year of the Greek War of Independence a Tinian
nun named Pelagia had a dream in which the Virgin revealed to her
the location of a miraculous icon. The next morning Pelagia told the
prioress of the convent about her dream, and soon afterwards the
locals unearthed the icon at the spot where the Virgin had indicated
that it was buried, on a farm just above the port town of Agios
Nikolaos, the present Chora. The discovery of the icon caused great
excitement among the Tiniotes, particularly after several miraculous
cures were attributed to it. An extensive church complex was then
erected on the site to house the icon of the Evangelistria, known
as Panagia Megalochari, the Virgin of Great Joy, and pilgrims from
all over the Greek world began congregating there on the Virgin's
two annual feast days. This tremendous influx of pilgrims brought
about a financial boom on Tinos, particularly in Agios Nikolaos,
where hotels, restaurants, cafés and shops were built to accom-
modate visitors and sell them souvenirs and religious trinkets,
transforming the sleepy little fishing village into a thriving town.

On the occasion of the last festival before Greece entered the
Second World War, 15 August 1940, the Greek cruiser *Elle* was
torpedoed in Tinos harbour by an Italian submarine. This atrocity,
in which nine Greek sailors lost their lives, was the prelude to the
Italian invasion of Greece through Albania, which began on 28
October of that same year. The two annual feast days of the Virgin
continued to be observed during the war years, but there were
virtually no visitors, since Tinos and the other Cyclades were
occupied in turn by the Italians and Germans, many of the
islanders dying of starvation. Pilgrims began returning to Tinos
again at the end of hostilities, though not in large numbers until
Greece recovered from the effects of the Second World War and
the civil war that followed. Now the festivals of the Virgin are more

popular than ever, particularly the *paneyeri* in mid-August, when all of the ferries in the Aegean disrupt their schedules for three days to carry pilgrims to and from Tinos. For three days the island captures the attention of the entire Greek world just as Delos did at the dawn of history.

When Bent visited Tinos for the first time, on the eve of the festival on 25 March 1844, he was told by a local church official that 'no less than 45,000 strangers from all parts of Hellas – Egyptian, Cypriote, Cretan Greeks, Greeks who had travelled days and weeks from the innermost recesses of Asia Minor – all were assembled here to worship'.

> The narrow pier, the harbour, the windows, the balconies, the roofs of the houses encircling the harbour, were darkened by an endless crowd. We could not turn when drawn once into the crush; scarcely could I move my hand as we were borne involuntarily through the little agora toward the broad street which led directly to the temple. The whole street before us was like a dazzling dream – costumes, nationalities without end … This long street is a perfect medley of chaplets, knives, games, crosses, sweets, fresh fruits, linen, holy pictures, ornaments, cooking utensils – everything, in fact, to supply the appetites, religious and carnal, of the pilgrims, many of whom bivouac on the hillside to avoid the extortion of the town.

The market street that Bent describes has now been replaced by a broad avenue that leads up from the port to the shrine of the Panagia Evangelistria, a gleaming edifice in white marble, completed in 1831. The approach is through a vast marble-paved courtyard around which there are arranged 120 cells in a double arcade. Among other functions, particularly in sheltering pilgrims during the festivals, these cells and other structures in the complex house seven collections associated with the shrine and its history, many of the objects having been donated by grateful pilgrims who believed that they were cured here by the Virgin. The Byzantine Museum has an exhibition of post-Byzantine icons, of which there are more in the sacristy, along with liturgical vestments, sacred vessels and religious woodcarvings. The Museum of the Panagia contains representations of the Virgin from all over the world. The Museum of Tinian Artists exhibits modern works of local painters, while the Sochos Museum is devoted to paintings by the Tinian artist Andoni Sochos. The Sculpture Museum exhibits statues by local sculptors, and the Papadopoulos Museum houses works by modern Greek artists outside Tinos.

Ornate stairways on either side of the baroque façade lead to the upper church, the cathedral of Tinos. The interior of the cathedral is an astonishing sight, its walls and *iconostasis* festooned with shining tin (and a few silver) ex-voto plaques, glowing with hundreds of offertory candles, and crowded with long lines of pilgrims waiting expectantly to kiss the sacred icon of the Virgin, whose features are so obscured by layers of gold and silver plaques that they are visible only through peepholes. Bent writes, 'The silversmiths were here driving a rattling trade, selling silver legs, arms, eyes, hearts, steamers, cows, as tributes of thankfulness to be hung in the church by some pilgrim whose safety from disaster came under any of these heads.'

Below is the crypt-like church of the Evresios, or Discovery, which was built over the spot where the miraculous icon of the Virgin was originally discovered through the dream of Sister Pelagia, who is now venerated as a saint in the Greek Orthodox Church. This is the most sacred part of the shrine, for it is from there that the healing powers of the Virgin are believed to emanate on the days of her festival.

There are two churches in Chora dedicated to St Nicholas, one of them Greek Orthodox and the other Roman Catholic, both of them standing down by the port, the site of the old village of Agios Nikolaos. The original village seems to have been built on the ruins of the ancient city of Tinos in the medieval Byzantine period, and during the Venetian era it served as the port of Xombourgo. After the Venetians abandoned Tinos in 1715 the inhabitants of Xombourgo moved down to the port, along with many other Tiniotes, and thenceforth Agios Nikolaos became the capital of the island under the new name of Chora, its development accelerating rapidly after the founding of the Evangelistria shrine. The remains of the ancient town wall can be seen to the north-west of the church precincts, where a complex of Late Roman buildings was unearthed in 1973.

Some architectural fragments of the ancient city of Tinos are preserved in the Archaeological Museum, housed in a building erected in 1969 in the style of a typical Tenian *peristerione*, or dovecote. There are also exhibits here from several other archaeological sites on Tinos, including Xombourgo, Vryokastro and Kionia.

Kionia is north-west of Chora along the shore, beyond the beach at Stavros. Archaeologists of the French School first excavated the site in 1901–1903, identifying it as a sanctuary of the sea god Poseidon and his wife Amphitrite. According to Pliny, the islanders revered Poseidon as a healing deity, and also because he drove away the vipers that infested the island in remote antiquity, when it was known as Ophioussa, the Isle of Snakes. Excavations were resumed for two campaigns in 1973–1974 by the French School, exposing the foundations of an enormous sanctuary some 170 metres in length. This shrine was founded in the fourth century BC and centred on a temple of Poseidon, which in the following century was also dedicated to 'sea-moaning Amphitrite', as she is referred to in one of the *Homeric Hymns*.

The monastery of Agia Triada, the Holy Trinity, is east of town, approached via the road going to the beaches at Agios Sostis, Agia Kyriaki and Agios Ioannis sto Porto, the medieval Venetian port on the south-eastern coast of the island. The *katholikon* of the monastery, which was founded *c.* 1610, has a beautiful *iconostasis* of carved wood, dated 1764. The monastery also has an interesting museum, its exhibits including local arts and handicrafts, weapons used in the Greek War of Independence, books from the monastic library, and also rooms of the 'secret school' that operated in Agia

Triada during the *Turkokrateia*. The most interesting artworks are the marble slabs called *pheggites*, which decorated the lintels of doors or windows, carved in the form of sun disks, stars, cypresses, ships, crosses and miniature arcades. These *pheggites* are seen everywhere on the island, on houses, chapels, dovecotes and gateways, the work of anonymous stonecutters, the oldest known example bearing the date 1778.

Along the coast south of the monastery there is a headland known as Akroterion Ourion, the Heavenly Cape. Excavations on the promontory, at a site known as Vryocastro, have unearthed a settlement dating back to the third millennium BC, which appears to have remained in existence until the eighth century BC.

The most densely settled part of Tinos is the region north of the Chora, where a score of pretty villages cluster in the foothills above the coastal plain, which terminates in a chain of mountains that extends all the way to the north-western end of the island. En route to these villages one is struck by the number and variety of the old dovecotes on all sides, far more than on Andros, many of them with little family chapels attached. Most of these are relics of the Venetian period, when the Latin aristocracy were the only ones allowed to keep doves and raise them for food. (An old document refers to the '*droit du colombier*' held by the Latin aristocrats on Tinos.)

The villages of Triantaros, Dio Choria, Bermnados and Arnados were originally fortified medieval settlements on the south slope of Kechrovouni, the mountain that rises to the north-east of the Chora. Above them looms the fortress-like Moni Kechrovouniou, a convent dedicated to the Dormition of the Virgin. This is one of the largest and most renowned convents in Greece, its fame stemming from the fact that Sister Pelagia was living here when the Virgin appeared to her in a dream and revealed where the miraculous icon was to be found. According to tradition, the first religious community was established here in 842, although there is no record of the convent before the twelfth century. The archives of Kechrovouniou record that in 1749 the convent was placed under the jurisdiction of the Patriarch of Constantinople, as is still the case today. The *katholikon* has an exceptionally beautiful *iconostasis* of carved wood covered with gold, which tradition holds was made in Constantinople just before the Byzantine capital fell to the Turks in 1453. The most precious icon in the church is an ancient painting of the Panagia tis Kolonas, Our Lady of the Column. Beside the church there is a little chapel dedicated to the Panagia Zoodochos Pigi, which encloses a sacred well. The convent also has a museum exhibiting its collection of post-Byzantine icons. Also of interest is the chapel where Sister Pelagia had her vision of the Virgin, and near it is the chapel of Agia Pelagia, who was beatified in 1971.

The villages of Kechrovouni are unusually picturesque, particularly Dio Choria, which owes its name to the fact that it is a constellation of two settlements. The village is a labyrinth of clustering Cycladic cubes, its only street actually tunnelling through the lower storey of the houses that it passes, with little flights of steps allowing the villagers to make their way up and down from one roof to another. Bent and his party stopped here on what the Greeks called *Kathara Deftera*, or Clean Monday, the last day of Carnival and the first day of Lent, which the villagers of Dio Choria were celebrating on the roofs on their houses; eating, drinking, and dancing to the music of primitive bagpipes.

> Close to Arnades are two villages called Dio Choria...and here we came in for some of the gaiety incident on the first day of Lent; the sound of music and revelry filled the valley, and from afar we descried the cause. All the villagers had turned out on the roofs, and on this flat surface were dancing away vigorously. As no other flat surface occurs in or near the village they were driven to make a ballroom out of their roof.

North of Kechrovouni there is another galaxy of villages, including Potamia, Kechros, Tzados, Mesi, Falatados and Steni. Near Steni is the Roman Catholic monastery of St Francis, which dates from 1680 and has a remarkable seventeenth-century *iconostasis* in its *katholikon*. Close by the monastery stands one of the most beautiful dovecotes on the island.

Steni is on the west slope of Mount Tsiknias, the highest peak on Tinos, rising to a height of 729 metres. According to mythology, Tsiknias was the abode of Boreas, god of the north wind. Boreas had two sons named Zetes and Kalais, who accompanied Jason on his epic voyage on the ship *Argo* in his quest for the Golden Fleece, along with Hercules and other heroes. On their return voyage the brothers quarrelled with Hercules, who killed both of them and buried their bodies on Mount Tsiknias. Hercules then placed two pillars on the summit of Tsiknias to mark their grave, and thereafter these stones trembled whenever the north wind blew over the mountain. The north wind blowing over Tsiknias was dreaded by seafarers in antiquity, and pilgrims on their way to the festival of Apollo on Delos always poured a libation to Boreas when their ship passed this way.

North-west of Kechrovouni is Xombourgo, the rocky mountain on which the Latin dukes built the fortress of Sant Helena, the last Venetian stronghold on the Cyclades. The best approach to the summit, which has an altitude of 564 metres, is from Xinara, the seat of the Roman Catholic Archbishop of Tinos, a heritage of Venetian days.

Archaeological excavations have revealed that there was a settlement on Mount Xombourgo from the eighth to the fifth century BC. Among the structures unearthed there were the remains of a temple, defence-walls, and tombs, all dating from the Archaic period. It has been suggested that this was the capital of Tinos during the Archaic period, after which the site was abandoned. At the beginning of the Latin period the Ghisi dynasty built the fortress of Sant Helena on the peak of the mountain, and this was strengthened by the Venetians when they took control of the island.

The Venetians enclosed the highest part of the mountain with two concentric defence walls, each with a single gate. The inner defence circuit, the Kastro, enclosed the governor's palace, army barracks, several churches and cisterns, while the outer wall surrounded the Bourgo, or town, which comprised the mansions of the Venetian aristocracy, churches, cisterns, storage places for food, and subterranean hiding places for the people of the surrounding villages in the event of corsair raids. The largest of the churches was the Roman Catholic cathedral of Santa Maria Maggiore, known to the Greeks as Agia Maria tis Meizonos.

A second unfortified settlement developed outside the Bourgo, inhabited by the peasants from the surrounding countryside. This settlement was known as Xombourgo, 'Outside the Town', and in time the entire mountain came to be called by this name. When the Venetian governor surrendered to the Ottomans in 1715, the Turks destroyed the fortress of Sant Helena and the surrounding town, so all that survives of Kastro, the Bourgo and Xombourgo are a few fragments of the walls and piles of stones from the other buildings. Thus Xombourgo is a ghost town, still appearing much as Bent describes it:

> ... covered with ruins around the rock which is bright with an orange-coloured lichen; and two ruined churches with curious towers, half Oriental, half Italian, recall memories of the Queen of the Adriatic. Everything is now delivered up to the jackals and the ravens; not a house has a roof on, the cellars full of water and lovely maidenhair; but the streets can still be traced ...

There are a number of characteristic Tinian villages clustered around Mount Xombourgo, most notably Tripotamos, Xinara, Koumaros, Loutra and Krokos, all of them showing the architectural influence of Venetian rule, which was focused on this region.

The most interesting of these villages is perhaps Loutra, named for its mineral baths, no longer in use. Loutra is noted for its Ursiline school, founded in 1862 by an Englishwoman named Miss Leeves. There is also a Jesuit monastery, which has a remarkable library of some five thousand volumes, including works published in Venice as early as 1480. The local Roman Catholic church of St

Ignatius was built before 1658, the date of an inscription recording a restoration. Many of the older houses have very attractive marble fanlights over their doors, while others have Venetian coats of arms.

North-west of Xombourgo is the crossroads village of Komi, where there are some fine old houses of the late Ottoman period. East of that is Agapi (Love), a medieval settlement built on the slope of a hill astride a stream that flows through the village, where it once turned four watermills. North of Agapi is the church of Panagia Vourniotissa, Our Lady of the Mountain. The Virgin's title refers to the mountain known as Kleftovouni, the Mountain of Thieves, from the tradition that it was once a lair of bandits. On the western side of the mountain a fertile valley leads down to the coastal hamlet of Loutra on Kolympidra Bay, where there are a pair of sandy beaches, one of them with a taverna and rooms to rent.

North-west of Komi there is a group of four villages – Kato Klisma, Karkados, Kalloni and Aetofolia – which are considered to be the prettiest on Tinos. Kato Klisma is particularly picturesque, for many of its houses are built in the style of the numerous dovecotes seen in the surrounding fields. The village church in Kalloni, dedicated to Agios Zacharias, is considered to be the finest on Tinos and is well worth a visit. The church of Agia Triada in Aetofolia is dated 1747.

North-west of Chora there are two pairs of villages, divided by the Rachi ridge, with Ktikados and Chatzirados to the south and to the north Tarampados and Kampos. Ktikados, which has access to the sea via a secondary road to Kionia, served as a naval supply base during the Venetian era. The large and handsome village church, dedicated to the Panagia Ipapanti, dates from the Latin period. Another church in the village, dedicated to Agios Stavros (the Holy Cross), has a bell-tower dated by an inscription to 1121. Chatzirados is distinguished by the line of old windmills that still stand on the hills behind the village. Outside Tarampados there is a particularly striking group of Venetian dovecotes on the terraced hillside. The village of Kampos has the only working windmill on the island.

Midway along the sparsely settled western coast is the attractive village of Kardiane, whose church was built before 1664. The Arcadian setting of the village is much the same as that which Bent describes.

> ... mid-day found us at Kardiane, a pretty place climbing up the mountain side, and overhanging the sea, like a Riviera village, with a tall white church tower and pretty balconies to each house. We lunched in one of these festooned with vines, and having large amphorae picturesquely stuck about at haphazard; also lovely gourds which were drying a rich orange colour, plants of geranium in full bloom; and through olive trees we peeped down on the sea beneath us as we consumed our meal.

Beyond Kardiane is Isternia, a picturesque village with arcaded streets that has now become one of the artist colonies on Tinos. The village houses have over their doors and windows the same kind of fanlights as in Loutra. North-west of the village is the church of Agios Athanasios, dated 1453, the year that Constantinople fell to the Turks. The church of Agia Triada is the scene of a *paneyeri* celebrated on 15 June. On the coast below Isternia is the seaside hamlet of Agios Nikitas, where there is an isolated sandy beach.

The largest village at the northern end of the island is Pyrgos, renowned for its quarries of white, black and green marble, as well for its gifted sculptors and artisans. The works of the local sculptor Yannoulis Chalepas are exhibited in his family home, which has been converted into a museum, and other artists and artisans exhibit in their ateliers. The village grammar school, founded by Capodistrias in 1830, also houses a School of Fine Arts.

The houses in Pyrgos are among the most interesting in Tinos, many of the entryways and windows surmounted by the distinctive fanlights seen in Loutra and Isternia. The two oldest churches in the village both date to the Venetian period; one is dedicated to the Presentation of the Virgin and the other to the Panagia Eloussa, Our Lady of Pity.

The *plateia* in Pyrgos centres on a seven-spouted spring within a Venetian fountain-house in marble, dated 1784, which Bent mentions in his description of the village.

> It is a very flourishing place, and the centre of the marble district, from whence come all those marble window tops we had admired elsewhere, and in the centre of the village they have erected an elaborate marble well, and a marble cage in which the washerwomen work, in the middle of the agora… Pyrgos is one of the prettiest villages of the islands, being quite Alpine in character, as it is, in a hollow surrounded by mountains. A river leaping from rock to rock runs down the central street and is spanned by a pretty wooden bridge. From the demarch's house, which is higher than its neighbour, we had a lovely view over almond trees, now in blossom, cypresses, mingled with the yellow and white houses, with the rugged peaks of Mount Profitis Ilias of Tenos as a background…

South-west of Pyrgos is the monastery of the Panagia Katapoliani, founded in 1786. Another site of interest in the vicinity is Agia Thekla, where archaeologists have discovered a tomb of ashlar masonry similar to the famous *tholos* tombs at Mycenae. This is the only *tholos* tomb known in the Cyclades, and it has been dated to the fourteenth or thirteenth century BC, when the archipelago was under Mycenaean influence.

Much of the marble on Tinos is shipped from Panormos, a little port in a deeply indented bay on the north-east coast. The marble comes from the quarries of Kokkinokremna on the north coast and is worked by men from the village of Marlas, north of Pyrgos. The village is also noted for its thermal springs, whose sources are believed to be under Mount Profitis Ilias, the northern-most peak of Tinos, looming over the hydra-headed peninsula that faces across the narrow strait towards the southern end of Andros.

South of Marlas the road passes through the mountain villages of Marmados and Ismail on its way to the seaside hamlet of Agios Theodoros on the north-westernmost cape of the island. There are 22 saints in the Greek Orthodox Church named Theodore, and I have never learned which of them is venerated in the chapel here. Like many of the tiny churches on the Greek islands, this is undoubtedly a family chapel, where a liturgy is celebrated once a year on the feast day of the saint. But throughout the rest of the year most of the chapels are open, and whenever I visit them, as here, I always find them clean and well cared for, with the remains of guttered candles below the icon of the saint and a pot of basil in a window incensing the air, a sacred refuge for the wayfarer. Whenever I rub my hands on the basil on my balcony time stops, and I am transported back to the little church of Agios Theodoros on Tinos.

Tinos: population 8,614; area 84 sq km; Mt. Tsiknias (729 m); ferries from Piraeus (86 mi) and Rafina (62 mi); hotels in Chora, Agios Sostis and Agios Ioannis.

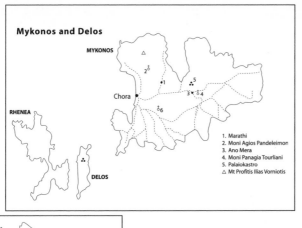

Mykonos and Delos

MYKONOS

Chora

RHENEA

DELOS

1. Marathi
2. Moni Agios Pandeleimon
3. Ano Mera
4. Moni Panagia Tourliani
5. Palaiokastro
△ Mt Profitis Ilias Vorniotis

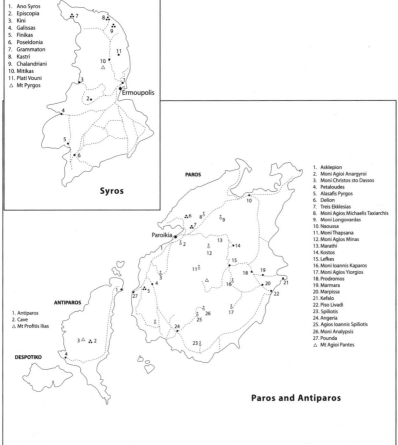

1. Ano Syros
2. Episcopia
3. Kini
4. Galissas
5. Finikas
6. Poseidonia
7. Grammaton
8. Kastri
9. Chalandriani
10. Mitikas
11. Plati Vouni
△ Mt Pyrgos

Ermoupolis

Syros

PAROS

Paroikia

ANTIPAROS

1. Antiparos
2. Cave
△ Mt Profitis Ilias

DESPOTIKO

1. Asklepion
2. Moni Agioi Anargyroi
3. Moni Christos sto Dassos
4. Petaloudes
5. Alasafis Pyrgos
6. Delion
7. Treis Ekklesias
8. Moni Agios Michaelis Taxiarchis
9. Moni Longovardas
10. Naoussa
11. Moni Thapsana
12. Moni Agios Minas
13. Marathi
14. Kostos
15. Lefkes
16. Moni Ioannis Kaparos
17. Moni Agios Yiorgios
18. Prodromos
19. Marmara
20. Marpissa
21. Kefalo
22. Piso Livadi
23. Spiliotis
24. Angeria
25. Agios Ioannis Spiliotis
26. Moni Analypsis
27. Pounda
△ Mt Agioi Pantes

Paros and Antiparos

Delos archaeological site

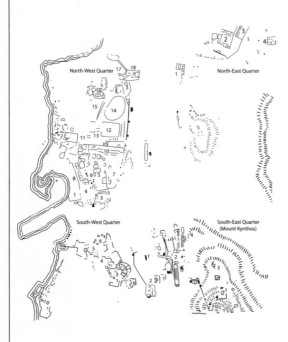

North-West Quarter
1. Agora of the Compitaliasti
2. Sacred Way
3. Agora of the Delians
4. Stoa of King Philip
5. Sanctuary of Apollo
6. House of the Naxians
7. Sanctuary of the Bulls
8. Stoa of the Naxians
9. Temple of Artemis
10. Stoa of Antigonus
11. Sanctuary of the Twelve Gods
12. Agora of the Italians
13. Shrine of Leto
14. Sacred Lake
15. Terrace of the Lions
16. Headquarters of Poseidoniasts
    of Berytos
17. House on the Lake
18. Granite Palaestra

North-East Quarter
1. Sanctuary of the Archigetis
   (Archigesion)
2. Gymnasium
3. Stadium
4. Synagogue
5. Archaeological Museum

South-West Quarter
1. House of the Dolphins
2. House of the Masques
3. Theatre
4. House of the Trident
5. House of Cleopatra
6. House of Dionysos

South-East Quarter (Mount Kynthos)
1. House of the Herms
2. Sarapieions
3. Sanctuary of the Syrian Gods
4. Summit of Mount Kynthos

nine
Mykonos and Delos

Mykonos in antiquity was one of the least important of the Cyclades, while today it is more widely known than any other island in the archipelago. This great change was brought about by tourism, which began here when travellers used Mykonos as a base for visiting the archaeological site on its companion isle of Delos. Then, in the mid-1950s, Mykonos was 'discovered' and soon became an internationally famous summer resort. This tourism boom has totally transformed life on Mykonos, a transition that the islanders have adjusted to with surprising resilience and grace.

Legend has it that the island was named for the hero Mykonos, son of Anios, who himself was the son of Apollo by the nymph Rio. Local myth also holds that the many huge boulders on the island are the petrified remains of the giants slain by Hercules. The English traveller George Wheler writes of another legend concerning the association of Hercules with Mykonos in *Journey to Greece* (1682): 'The poets fancy this to be the burial-place of the Centaurs, unconquered by Hercule.'

According to ancient tradition, the first colonists on Mykonos and its satellite isles of Delos and Rhenea were Ionians led by Hippocles, son of Neleus and grandson of Kodros, known in mythology as the last King of Athens. Throughout antiquity the people of Mykonos considered themselves to be Ionians, looking upon Athens as their mother city, though the arrogance of the Athenians eventually strained the loyalty of the islanders.

Mykonos is mentioned by the geographer Scylax of Caryanda, who, *c.* 500 BC, compiled an atlas for the Persian king Darius. Scylax describes Mykonos as a *dipolis*, or 'two-citied' island, while other ancient sources differ in saying that it had either one or three cities.

At the beginning of the invasion of Greece by Darius in 490 BC, the Persian fleet anchored off Rhenea, whereupon the people of Mykonos fled to Tinos. After the Greek victory at Marathon the Persian fleet anchored off Mykonos, and only after it departed did the Mykoniotes return to their island.

Around 1207 Mykonos became part of the Latin Duchy of the Archipelago under Marco I Sanudo. His son and successor Angelo Sanudo granted Mykonos as a sub-fief to the brothers Andrea and Geremia Ghisi in 1261, along with Tinos. When the Ghisi dynasty came to an end in 1390 the two islands came under the direct rule of Venice.

Mykonos fell to Barbarossa in 1537, and the only islanders who escaped death or enslavement were those who fled to Tinos. This left Mykonos virtually deserted, but after the departure of the Ottoman fleet many of the refugees returned from Tinos. It appears that the Venetians briefly retook Mykonos in 1545, and again during the fifth (1645–1669) and sixth (1684–1699) wars between Venice and the Ottoman Empire. But by 1715, when the last Venetian fortresses on Tinos and Crete surrendered to the Turks, Mykonos had already been formally annexed by the Ottoman Empire.

Ottoman rule on Mykonos was as remote as it was elsewhere in the Cyclades, with the Captain Pasha arriving annually to receive the capitation tax, which was collected by a local *Voivode*, or governor. Then in 1616 the people of Mykonos reached an agreement with the Sublime Porte, or Ottoman government, giving them virtual autonomy in the conduct of their affairs. This agreement, signed by representatives of the people and clergy on 8 October of that year in the church of Profitis Ilias in the Chora, created the Community of Mykonos, which governed the internal affairs of the island for the remainder of the *Turkokrateia*.

During the *Turkokrateia* many Mykoniote sailors resorted to piracy in order to make their fortunes, joining forces with the French corsairs who preyed on ships in the Aegean. The harbour at Mykonos became a lair of pirates and the Chora prospered as a market for their loot. Since the men were usually off at sea, the town was at most times inhabited principally by women and children, as George Wheler remarked when writing of his visit to Mykonos in 1675.

> The greatest part of the Inhabitants are Pyrats, and this place is a great Staple for their prey: Here they keep their Wives, Children, and Mistresses, the greatest part of the Town seems to consist of Women; who deservedly have a greater reputation for Beauty than Chastity; the Men being most of them abroad, seeking their Fortune. Our Captain had here a Seraglio of them, when he was a Corsair in these seas... But these being now antedated, he wanted new game of his coming thither; and therefore found a pretty Virgin for his Mistress, which he bought of her Brutal Father, as Provision for his Voyage to Constantinople.

Mykoniote sailors, hoping to throw off the yoke of the *Turkokrateia*, served in the Russian fleet during the Russo–Turkish war of 1768–1774, and some of them took part in the destruction of the Ottoman fleet at Cheshme on 26 June 1770. During the years 1770–1774, when the Russians controlled the Cyclades, the Mykoniote captain Andonis Psaros played an important part in the administration of the archipelago.

By the end of the *Turkokrateia* Mykonos had one of the largest fleets in the Aegean, rivalling the islands of Hydra, Spetses, Chios and Psara in its maritime trade. At the beginning of the War of Independence the Mykoniotes placed their entire fleet of 24 armed vessels at the disposal of the Greek government, complete with their captains and crews. The Mykoniote contingent of 22 vessels joined the fleet of Admiral Jakomaki Tombazes of Hydra, and they participated in the first Greek naval victory of the war, when a fireship from Psara sank a Turkish man-of-war off the coast of Chios. The following year the Ottoman Captain Pasha landed a force on Mykonos, where the islanders, despite the absence of their mariners, fought back under the leadership of the heroine Mando Mavroyennis and forced the Turks to flee. Mando was raised to the rank of general for her victory over the Turks, and she is now honoured by a commemorative bust in the *plateia* that bears her name in Chora.

The new Greek government took measures to eliminate piracy as early as 1826, when Constantine Metaxas, the *Eparch* of the Cyclades, mounted a successful campaign against them and captured 59 pirates, 'destroying their ships by fire opposite the town of Syros', as he notes in his memoirs. Among those he captured was the Mykoniote corsair whom he calls 'the terrible Mermelachas', who retired to his home in Mykonos after he was released from prison. Mermelachas lived on until 1854, and his tombstone can still be seen in the graveyard of the church of Agia Sotira tou Kastro in the Chora. During his latter years the bearded old pirate was revered as a folk hero, a Robin Hood who robbed the rich to help the poor, his fame perpetuated by a jingle that was recited in Mykonos for long afterwards: 'Have a care for me, have a care for me,/Mermelachas with the beard.'

After the War of Independence, when Syros was the main port in Greece, many Mykoniote mariners and merchants went there to make their fortunes, returning to Mykonos when they retired to build fine houses in the Chora, which developed into what is generally agreed to be the prettiest port in the Cyclades.

There are two churches of Agios Nikolaos along the Yialos, the sand-fringed inner end of the harbour. One of these is the larger red-domed church at the centre of the waterfront; the other is the smaller blue-domed chapel at the west side of the port by the little mole known locally as Molonaki ('Little Mole'). The larger one is dedicated to St Nicholas of Myra, known in the West as Father Christmas or Santa Claus, while the smaller one is named for St

Nicholas of Kadena, known locally as Agios Nikolaos tou Yialou. Both churches date from the Venetian period, although they have been reconstructed in more recent times.

The large arcaded building behind St Nicholas of Kadena on the *paralia*, or waterfront promenade, is the Demarcheion. This was erected in 1772 by Count John Voinovich, who at the time was the Russian consul on Mykonos.

The oldest church in the Chora is the very beautiful Panagia Paraportiani, which stands on the promontory that forms the western arm of the port, the medieval Kastro. The church is the most frequently photographed attraction on Mykonos, an iconic emblem of all the Cyclades. Paraportiani, which means 'Beyond the Postern Gate', actually consists of four interconnected chapels on ground level and one above. The lower chapels are dedicated, respectively, to Agios Eustathius, Agioi Cosmas and Damian, Agia Anastasia and Agios Sozon; the one above, reached by an outer staircase on the east side of the complex, is dedicated to the Panagia. The two oldest churches are those of the Panagia and Agioi Cosmas and Damian, both of which are believed to date from before 1425, while the two other chapels are thought to have been added in stages during the sixteenth and seventeenth centuries.

On the promontory beside the Paraportiani is the Mykonos Folklore Museum, housed in a restored nineteenth-century mansion that originally belonged to the Mykoniote sea captain Nikolaos Malouchas. The museum was founded in 1962 by Professor Vasileios Kyriazopoulos, whose intent it was to preserve examples of local folk art and other objects illustrating Mykoniote life of times past, and since then the collection has been augmented by similar ethnographical material from other parts of Greece. It includes a wonderful assortment of old Mykoniote musical instruments, including types that are still played at island *paneyeria*. One of the songs that are heard at these *paneyeria* is an old Mykoniote favourite that may have originated in Crete, its refrain praising the grace of the leading dancer.

> How fair is he who leads the dance,
> How beautifully he foots it.
> Angelically he treads the ground
> And hearts are rent asunder

The Mykonos Folklore Association has also opened to the public a typical Mykoniote dwelling known as Lena's House, which is in the quarter of the Chora known as Tria Pigadia, the Three Wells. The house was donated to the Municipality by Yiorgios Drakopoulos, who is also the founder of the adjacent Aegean Maritime Museum.

Lena's House is a very attractive example of a prosperous Mykoniote home of the nineteenth century, with fine period furniture and décor of the type that a local sea captain would have acquired on his voyages around the Mediterranean and the Black Sea.

The Aegean Maritime Museum is housed in a mansion that originally belonged to the Mykoniote sea captain Nikolaos Z. Sourmelis. The exhibits in the museum illustrate the history of seafaring in the Aegean from antiquity up to the beginning of the modern era, with the emphasis on Mykonos. One of the exhibits is a portrait of Mando Mavroyennis (1796–1848), the Mykoniote heroine of the Greek War of Independence.

The Municipal Library is in a mansion built in 1735 by Mando's grandfather, Nikolaos Mavroyennis, *Voivode* of Mykonos. The library has a large collection of rare works on history and sociology bequeathed to it by the Mykoniote historian Ioannis Meletopoulos. Some of these books are on display in the library, along with an exhibition of ancient Cycladic coins and seals, most of which were collected by the Mykoniote numismatist Ioannis Svoronos.

The Archaeological Museum is housed in a neoclassical structure dating from the early twentieth century. Most of the objects here were found on the islet of Rhenea, which served as the necropolis of Mykonos from the mid-fifth century BC till the end of antiquity.

Two other Mykoniote cultural institutions are its Municipal Art Gallery and the School of Fine Arts. The gallery and the school, a branch of the School of Fine Arts at the University of Athens, are open to both foreign and Greek artists, and have played an important role in establishing Mykonos as an international art centre.

It has been said that Mykonos has at least one church for each day of the year, but even this may be a modest estimate, for one authority has counted more than five hundred on the island, most of them tiny family chapels. At least thirty of them are named for St Nicholas, for he is the patron saint of mariners, and probably an even greater number are dedicated to the Virgin. The churches of the Virgin include both the Roman Catholic and Greek Orthodox cathedrals, which stand almost side by side in the northern part of Chora.

The Roman Catholic cathedral is dedicated to Our Lady of the Rosary. This is the only Catholic church on Mykonos, dating from the Venetian period; an inscription records that in 1668 it became the property of Don Leonardo Xanthakis, who restored it nine years later.

The Greek Orthodox cathedral is dedicated to the Panagia Pigadiotissa, Our Lady of the Holy Well. This has been the Orthodox cathedral only since its dedication in 1878. Before that the church of Agia Eleni in the Kastro was the cathedral, and though replaced as the seat of the bishop it retains pride of place as the starting point of the great Epiphany procession, which wends its way from there to Tria Pigadia, led by a sailor carrying an ancient cross. It is here that the Great Blessing is performed, while white doves are released as a symbol of the epiphany. The procession then proceeds along the main street to the harbour at Molonaki, where the presiding priest throws the cross into the sea, after which young men dive in to retrieve it. When one of them comes up with the cross the crowd cheers and all of the boats in the harbour sound their horns and all the churches peal their bells, while everyone exchanges the greetings of the day. Ancient *kalanda* are still sung by children at this time, as on Christmas Eve and New Year's Day, celebrating the baptism of Christ: 'Epiphany has come/illumination of the world/and great rejoicing in the Lord/By Jordan river/stands our good Mary/and thus she begs St John/it is in your power/to baptise the child of God.'

Two other old churches in the Kastro are Agia Moni and Agios Dimitrios, the latter distinguished by the ancient marbles built into its structure. Aside from the two seaside chapels of St Nicholas, other old churches in the Chora are 'Panachra'; Agia Kyriaki; Panagia tis Gati (Our Lady of the Cats); and a group of four chapels in the Limni quarter. The four chapels are dedicated, respectively, to Our Lady of Limni, Agios Vassilios, Agios Dimitrios, and Agios Ioannis Chrysostomos; together they are known as Koutsombolis, or the Gossipers, because they huddle side by side and seem to be whispering to one another.

The *meltemi*-swept cove on the northern side of the Chora is called Alefkandra. The name comes from the Greek verb *lefkaino*, 'to whiten', because in times past the women of the Chora came here to do their laundry in the surf, 'whitening' their clothes on the strand. The eastern side of Alefkandra is known as Venetia, Little Venice, because of the way its picturesque old houses project out over the sea on stilts or corbels, like *palazzi* on the Grand Canal.

The promontory that forms the western arm of Alefkandra Bay is known as Kato Myli, the 'Low Mills', taking its name from the line of windmills along the ridge, one of the iconic picture-postcard views of Mykonos. (Ano Myli, the 'High Mills', refers to the windmills on the Chora's southern heights.) The Mykonos Folklore Society has restored one of these, the Bonis Windmill, which is now operating just as it did in times past, used as a source of power to grind grain for the farmers of the island. There are no houses on Kato Myli, for ancient legislation forbids the erection of any building on such heights, so as to leave the *meltemi* free to fill the sails of the windmills and keep them grinding grain, which the Mykoniote historian Nikolaos Angelstrakis so poetically calls 'the slavery of the winds'.

Many of the beautiful old houses of the Chora have now been converted into hotels, restaurants, cafés, bars, discotheques, boutiques and art galleries, particularly along the *paralia*. Contrasting with this, many of the island men retain their traditional livelihoods, beaching their fishing boats and *caiques* along the shore beside the chapel of Agios Nikolaos tou Yialou, selling their catch on the *paralia*. There they are often joined by Petros the pelican, the mascot of Mykonos, successor to the original pelican who landed here as an orphan of the storm in 1954.

The new commercial port and yacht marina is beyond the Chora to the north on Tourlos Bay, ending at the beach resort of Agios Stephanos. A secondary road continues on to Fanari, the lighthouse at Akri Armenistris, the north-westernmost cape of Mykonos, dominated by Mount Profitis Ilias Vorniotis, the island's highest peak (372 m).

South of the Chora is the Megali Ammos beach, and beyond that is the Diakofti Peninsula, an 'almost island' that is joined to the mainland by a narrow isthmus. There are beaches on both sides of the isthmus, at Ornos on the south and Korfos on the north, and there is another beach on the west side of the peninsula at Agios Ioannis. Archaeologists have unearthed two Mycenaean chamber tombs on the isthmus, which has led to the suggestion that one of the ancient cities of Mykonos was located here. Another and even more ancient site has been discovered on the northern tip of the peninsula at Anavulousa, where pottery sherds and fragments of obsidian indicate a settlement of the Late Neolithic era or Early Bronze Age.

The most popular beaches are on the southern coast, beginning with Psarou, Platys Yialos and Paraga, followed by Paradise and Super Paradise, whose names indicate the degree to which tourism has transformed Mykonos. Super Paradise is a nudist beach, as is the next beach to the east at Elia. There are more beaches farther to the east at Kalo Livadi, Agia Anna, Dimasto and Kalafatis, as well as two on the north at Ftelia, popular with windsurfers, and Panormos, considered to be the best beach on Mykonos, the latter pair situated on the huge gulf that cuts nearly halfway across the island on that side.

About a third of the way between Chora and Ano Mera, the only large village in the interior of Mykonos, a dusty track leads to Panormos Bay on the north coast via the hamlet of Marathi. Some two kilometres north-west of Marathi is the monastery of Agios Pandeleimon. The monastery, founded in 1665, has post-Byzantine icons and an important collection of old manuscripts.

The name Ano Mera, 'the Upper Place', is also applied to the fertile countryside around the village, the most beautiful region in Mykonos. The landscape is dotted with the little farmsteads known as *choria*, which usually consist of a farmhouse with two or three rooms in a row, along with a courtyard, barn, hayloft, dovecote, storehouse and stable, all in dazzling whitewashed stone.

A short way to the east of Ano Mera is Moni Panagia Tourliani. The monastery was founded in the mid-sixteenth century, although in its present form it dates from a reconstruction in 1767, with the impressive marble belfry added in 1806. There is an interesting museum in a hall of the monastery, in which are exhibited old embroideries, liturgical vessels, ecclesiastical vestments, wood-carvings and post-Byzantine icons, including some outstanding works of the Cretan school dating from the latter part of the sixteenth century, as well as a splendid Florentine *reredos* dating from the late sixteenth century. There is also a fountain, dated 1806, in which the water spout is in the form of a woman wearing a crown, a figure known locally as 'the Queen'. The most prized treasure of the monastery is a miraculous icon of the Virgin, who is revered as the protectress of Mykonos, honoured by a *paneyeri* celebrated here on 15 August. Each year on the first Sunday in Lent the icon is carried in procession to the church of Agia Kyriaki in Chora, where it remains until the Saturday before Palm Sunday, when it is conducted back to Tourliani.

The hill just to the north of Ano Mera is crowned by the ruined fortress known as Palaiokastro. The fortress probably dates from the reign of the Ghisi dynasty, when it may have been built on the ruins of a Byzantine fortress. Excavations have revealed evidence of a Middle Cycladic settlement on the south slope of the hill, and on the summit there are traces of occupation dating from the Archaic and Classical periods. These finds have led some authorities to identify Palaiokastro as one of the two cities referred to by Scylax, the Kastro in Chora undoubtedly being the other one.

On the slope of the Palaiokastro hill there is a convent dedicated to the Panagia Palaiokastriani, Our Lady of the Old Castle. The convent is supposed to have been founded in the eleventh century, though an inscription over the door of the *katholikon* bears the date 1771. The church has three ancient icons, one depicting the Virgin, the second St Mark, and the third Agia Filareti, the latter being the only depiction of this little-known saint I have ever seen.

About a kilometre to the south-east of Ano Mera is the monastery of Agios Yiorgios Ambelokipon. The monastery was founded at the end of the sixteenth century, but from its appearance it seems to have been rebuilt within the last century.

Mykonos has long been famous for its *moerologia*, or funerary laments, some of which Bent heard at the funeral of a young man named Parados, who left a young wife and several small children. The laments were sung by a woman named Zachara at the house of the deceased.

> The *moerologista* Zachara came in shortly after we arrived; the kinswomen were all seated around the corpse; the afflicted widow and her children were groaning audibly on the divan, and had their hair down ready for the customary tearing and shaking. The entrance of Zachara was the commencement of that demonstrative grief in which the Greeks love to indulge: they all set to work to sing in mournful cadence about the merits of the deceased, keeping in time with their feet and beating their knees with their hands; then suddenly with a fearful shriek, the widow went off into an ecstasy of grief. She tore her hair, she lacerated her cheek, she beat her breast, she scratched her bare arms, until at length two or three women rushed forward to restrain her in her extravagant grief; her poor

little children lay crouching in a corner, terrified beyond measure at what was going on and screaming with all their might.

At that point Zachara 'rushed forward, fell on the corpse, kissed it, and rose to commence her dirge in that harsh and grating voice that the Greeks love, but which is so distasteful to Western ears'.

I yearn to mourn for the dead one
Whose name I dare not say,
For as soon as I hear of the lost one
My heart and my voice gave way...

That was Zachara's prologue, Bent writes, and after that the grief and lamentations were renewed with fresh vigour. Zachara then sang of the loneliness of the living and the horrors of death, and in that strange language of hyperbole she wondered how the sun could venture to shine on so lamentable a scene as the present. While she sang, the other mourners were wild with grief, until sheer exhaustion demanded a pause, during which the company refreshed themselves with raki, biscuits, figs, and other small refections which had been laid out on a table in the corner of the room. Then the tide of grief flowed on again, and presently another well-known *moerologista* dropped in, ... a relative of the deceased.

She and Zachara then sang verses alternately, and together they reminded one forcibly of the Carian women of antiquity who were hired for the same purpose, and one's mind wandered back to a Greek chorus – that of Aeschylus especially – where the virgins at the gate of Agamemnon indulge in all of the most poignant manifestations of grief, beating their breasts, lacerating their cheeks, and rending their garments... This prolonged agony of mourning continued for two long hours; occasionally to relieve the paid lamenters, some of the kinswomen would take up their parable and sing a verse or two, sending messages of love and remembrance to friends who had gone before to the shades of Hades; and great was my relief when the priests arrived with their acolytes bearing the cross and lanterns to convey the corpse to the grave.

So far as I know *moerologia* are still sung at wakes on Mykonos, though I have never heard one myself on the island. But an old woman on Naxos once sang for us part of a threnody that she had heard years ago on Mykonos, and one couplet from the lament still lingers in my memory: 'For you spring weeps and summer weeps for you,/The nightingales in their nest weep for you and the birds in the trees.'

***

Delos is an isle of ghosts, uninhabited since antiquity, when even the remains of those buried there were removed to its companion isle of Rhenea. James Stuart and Nicholas Revett describe the desolation of Delos in their *Antiquities of Athens*, the first volume of which was published in 1762.

This island, once so celebrated, the seat of religion, religious ceremonies and pompous processions, is now an uninhabited desert, everywhere strewn with ruins, so various and well wrought, as to evince its once populous and flourishing condition. The only animals we saw here, besides rabbits and snakes, were a few sheep brought occasionally from Myconos, a neighboring island, to crop the scanty herbiage which the ruins will permit to grow...

Boats leave the port of Mykonos every morning for Delos, a voyage of about 25 minutes, returning late in the afternoon the same day. The boats dock on the western side of the island, which has an area of only 3.43 square kilometres, with its highest hill, Mount Kythnos, rising to a height of just 112 metres. Despite its tiny size Delos was once the hub of the Cycladic world, where the Ionian Greeks came to worship and celebrate at the place where Leto gave birth to at least one of her divine twins, as the poet sings in the Homeric Hymn to Delian Apollo.

> Rejoice, blessed Leto, for you bare glorious children, the
> lord Apollo and divine Artemis who delights in arrows;
> her in Ortygia, and him in rocky Delos, as you rested
> against the Kynthian hill hard by a palm-tree by the stream
> of Inopus.

The name Ortygia, or Quail Island, has caused considerable confusion in classical topography, because there were half a dozen different places in the ancient Greek world with that name, which was also applied to Delos itself, as well as to Rhenea, which was so identified by Strabo. In any event, mythology agrees that Artemis was born first and was able to assist Leto when she gave birth to Apollo. Leto's labour in giving birth to Apollo lasted nine days, her agony ending only with the arrival of the goddess Eilithyia, protector of women in childbirth, who served as midwife.

The hymn to Delian Apollo was sung at the beginning of each celebration of the Delia, the great festival at which the Ionian Greeks honoured Apollo along with his sister Artemis and their mother Leto. This and other songs were sung by choirs of maidens, who are themselves praised in the penultimate section of the hymn.

> And there is this great wonder besides – and its renown
> shall never perish – the girls of Delos, hand-maidens of
> the Far-shooter; for when they have praised Apollo first
> and also Artemis who delights in arrows, they sing a
> strain telling of men and women of past days, and charm
> the tribes of men. Also they imitate the tongues of all men
> and their clattering speech: each would say that he himself
> were singing, so close to truth is their sweet song.

During the Archaic period Delos became the religious centre and symbolic capital of an Ionian *thalassocracy* called the Delian Amphictyony. From the seventh century BC until *c.* 550 BC this league was dominated by the Naxians, who erected a colossal marble statue of Apollo next to a treasury they built to house their dedicatory offerings to his shrine.

The mid-sixth century BC saw the rise of several powerful tyrants in the Greek world, three of whom in turn took control of the Delian Amphictyony, namely Lygdamis of Naxos, Polycrates of Samos, and Peisistratus of Athens. When Peisistratus took control of Delos, *c.* 540 BC, he ordered that the island be 'cleansed', a curious purification described by Herodotus: 'The object of this was to obey the injunction of an oracle, and the method he adopted was to dig up all the dead bodies which were buried within sight of the temple and re-inter them in another part of the island.'

Within two years of the end of the Persian Wars in 489 BC Delos had become the symbolic capital of the Delian League. By 454 BC the domination of Athens over the League was so complete that the Athenian leaders transferred the funds of the alliance from Delos to the Parthenon, Athena's temple on the Acropolis, adding to their already enormous resources and increasing the antagonism that eventually led to the Peloponnesian War.

The Athenians under Nicias purified Delos once again in 426 BC, apparently on the advice of an oracle, according to Thucydides. A few years after they purified the island the Athenians initiated the Delian Games, a quinquennial çelebration that Thucydides traced back to ancient times, probably part of the ancient Ionian feast of the Delia.

The reorganised festival appears to have been far more sumptuous than in earlier times, as evidenced by Plutarch's description of the *theoria*, or pilgrimage, that Nicias led *c.* 418 BC, when he built a bridge between Rhenea and Delos 'beautifully gilded with ... dyes and crowns and hangings'. The Athenian *theoria* included several contingents, including priests and priestesses, singers for the two choirs, musicians, actors, dramatists, poets and athletes for the various competitions, as well as horses for the equestrian events and oxen to be slaughtered at the *hecatomb*, or sacrifice, and then eaten at the farewell banquet. The dignitaries in charge of the pilgrimage were ambassadors bearing precious offerings to the shrine, always including a golden crown for Apollo.

The final defeat of Athens in 404 BC, at the end of the Peloponnesian War, brought about the dissolution of the Delian League. At that time Delos was liberated from Athens, and the

Delians themselves took over the administration of Apollo's sanctuary for a time, though the Athenians seem to have re-established their control of the shrine by 392 BC. The rapid recovery of Athens in the quarter-century following the end of the Peloponnesian War allowed her to reconstitute the Delian League in 377 BC, with Delos once again serving as its religious centre. But then in 338 BC, after the Greek allies were defeated by Philip II of Macedon at Chaeronea, Athens was forced to dissolve the Delian League. Nevertheless, Philip allowed the Athenians to retain control of Delos itself as long as they remained his faithful allies.

During the Hellenistic and Roman eras Delos emerged as an important emporium and financial centre. This was because the Delian festival attracted multitudes of pilgrims, providing a ready market for all kinds of goods, and the sanctity of the island seemed to guarantee security for the funds deposited in the sanctuary of Apollo. In 167 BC Rome declared Delos to be 'free of taxes' and gave it over to the Athenians, who established a *clerurchy* there. Thereafter magistrates from Athens administered the affairs of Delos and its sanctuaries, while the Athenian *clerurchs* on the island formed their own separate colonial community. This inevitably led to antagonism between the locals and the colonists, and Athens dealt with this problem in 166 BC by deporting all of the native Delians, who were never to return.

Its status as a free port under Athens soon made Delos one of the most important commercial and financial centres of the Roman world. The prosperity of the Delians greatly increased after the destruction of Corinth and Carthage by Rome in 146 BC, when, as Strabo writes, 'the importers changed their business to Delos ..., which could both admit and turn away ten thousand slaves on the same day'.

Delos reached the height of its prosperity *c.* 100 BC, when its population was an estimated 25,000, a very diverse mixture that included not only Greeks but large numbers of Italians, Syrians, Lebanese and Egyptians as well as a sizeable Jewish com-munity. It was at this time that the worship of Egyptian and other Middle

Eastern deities spread to Delos, as evidenced by sanctuaries of those foreign gods that have been excavated on the island, along with those of the deities of the Greek pantheon who were worshipped there besides Apollo.

Delos was ruined by the Mithraditic Wars, and it never recovered from the two attacks that were made upon it by the Pontic fleet in the second quarter of the first century BC. Although Pausanias writes that Delos was virtually deserted in his time, the mid-second century AD, archaeologists have discovered the remains of several churches on the island dating from the early Byzantine period. An inscription on one of the Byzantine houses, written in faulty Greek, invokes the new god who succeeded Apollo: 'O Lord our Christ, with all the angels help the mistress of this house. O Christ, help those who eat at this table, and the mistress of this table.'

At the beginning of the Latin period the island, then known as Sdiles, was part of the Ghisi principality, along with Rhenea. Then, early in the fourteenth century, Delos was occupied and fortified by the Knights Hospitallers of St John of Jerusalem, probably soon after they conquered Rhodes in 1310. But the Knights do not seem to have maintained their garrison in Delos for long, since there is no mention of it in later chronicles, and when the Venetian admiral Mocenigo stopped here in 1472 he found the island quite deserted.

During the next three centuries a few European scholars visited Delos to study its antiquities, some of which they carried away. The first systematic excavation of Delos was begun in 1873 by the French School in Athens, which, with some interruptions, has continued its work to the present day. The objects found in the earlier excavation were deposited at the museum on Mykonos, but now all but the most important sculptures, which are in the National Archaeological Museum in Athens, are exhibited in a museum on Delos organised by the French School.

The excavations of the French School have revealed that the first settlement on Delos was established on Mount Kythnos in the Early Cycladic period. This settlement remained inhabited until the Late Cycladic period, when it was abandoned in favour of a new location on more level ground to the north-west, on what would later be the site of the temples of both Apollo and Artemis. Many finds from the Mycenaean period were made under the Artemision, the Temple of Artemis, and it is evident that the second site was inhabited continuously from then through the late Roman period, with some occupation continuing on into the early Byzantine era.

The boat from Mykonos docks at a mole made up of debris from the archaeological site, whose entrance is near the foot of the pier. The artificial mole bisects the ancient harbour of Delos, of which the southern part was the Commercial Port and the northern the Sacred Harbour, where the *theoria* landed at times of festival.

At the foot of the pier are the remains of the Agora of the Compitaliasti, dated *c.* 150 BC. The Compitaliasti were members of Roman guilds, most of them freedmen and slaves from Sicily and southern Italy who worked for the wealthy Italians in the port of Delos. They took their name from the fact that they were worshippers of the Lares Compitales, divinities of the crossroads.

Beyond this area is the beginning of an ancient avenue known as the Sacred Way, the road taken by the procession of pilgrims heading for the sanctuary of Apollo. The long structure that forms the east side of the Sacred Way is known as the South Portico. A passage led through the South Portico into the Agora of the Delians, dating from the second century BC. Because of its close proximity to the Commercial Port, it is possible that the Agora of the Delians may have been the principal slave market on Delos.

The structure that forms the west side of the Sacred Way is the Stoa of Philip V of Macedon (r. 221–179 BC). The stoa, which was of grey marble, had a portico of 16 columns, of which only one remains.

At the northern end of the Sacred Way was the Propylaea, the monumental entryway to the Hieron (Sanctuary) of Apollo. The ruins here are all that remain of a gateway erected by the Athenians in the mid-second century BC, a structure which had three portals framed by four Doric columns, all standing on a four-stepped platform.

Immediately inside the Propylaea on the west are the remains of one of the oldest structures within the Hieron of Apollo, the Oikos (House) of the Naxians. This edifice was erected *c.* 600 BC, when Naxos was the dominant state in the Cycladic *thalassocracy*.

Behind the Oikos of the Naxians are the foundations of a small temple thought to date from the Mycenaean period. This is the oldest sanctuary on Delos, and it seems to have been the object of veneration throughout antiquity. It has been suggested that this may have been a shrine of the ancient Cycladic fertility goddess, perhaps worshipped here as Eilithyia, who served as midwife when Leto gave birth to Apollo.

On the east side of the Sacred Way beyond the Oikos of the Naxians there are the ruins of three temples. The first and largest of these is the great Temple of Apollo, begun in 477 BC but not completed until the third century BC. Just behind this to the north is the Temple of the Athenians, built in the years 425–417 BC. The third and northernmost of the three temples is known as the Porinos Naos, thought to have been erected by Peisistratus of Athens *c.* 540 BC; this was dedicated to Apollo and served as the treasury of the Delian League in the years 477–454 BC.

The right side of the Sacred Way near its northern end is formed by the first of five structures that fan out to the north and east of the Porinos Naos and the Temple of the Athenians. These buildings, which probably date from the second quarter of the sixth century BC, are usually called the Treasuries, because they are similar in plan to structures that served that purpose at Delphi and Olympia. The area just to the south of the first of these two buildings is believed to be the site of a Mycenaean palace.

South-east of the Temple of Apollo there are the ruins of a long and narrow structure known as the Sanctuary of the Bulls, dated to the early Hellenistic period The name comes from the *boucrania*, the carved figures of the head and shoulders of a bull, that flank its northern entryway.

To the west of the Sanctuary of the Bulls are the remains of the Bouleterion, or Council House, and the Prytaneion, or Senate, the former dated to the sixth century BC and the latter to the fifth or fourth century BC.

Inside the south-west corner of the Hieron of Apollo are the fragmentary ruins of the Stoa of the Naxians, erected *c*. 550–540 BC. Beyond this, on the west side of the Hieron of Apollo, there are the remains of two contiguous structures that have been identified, respectively, as the Oikos of the Andrians and the Hieropoion, the latter being the meeting place of the Hieropoio, or Ministers of Sacrifice; both of these date to *c*. 550–540 BC and were probably erected by Peisistratus.

The left side of the Sacred Way along the northern part of its course is bordered by the remains of an Ionic edifice on a high granite base, with Ionic porticoes to the east and north. This is the Artemision, whose sacred precinct formed a separate enclosure within the Hieron of Apollo. The present structure dates from *c*. 179 BC, rebuilt on the site of an archaic temple of Artemis dating from the seventh century BC. The archaic temple in turn seems to have been erected on the site of a Mycenaean sanctuary, perhaps the original shrine of the Cycladic fertility goddess.

Beyond the northern stoa of the Artemision there are the ruins of the Ecclesiasterion, the meeting place of the Ecclesia, or general assembly of the Delians. The ruins are a palimpsest of different structures ranging from the fifth century BC to the Roman era. Just to the west of the Ecclesiasterion there are the ruins of a building of the fifth century BC, identified as the Thesmophoreion, a shrine dedicated to Demeter and Persephone.

The northern boundary of the Hieron of Apollo is formed by the Stoa of Antigonus. A fragmentary inscription identifies the founder as the Macedonian king Antigonus II Gonatus (r. 277–239 BC). North of the stoa are the remains of the Portico of Poseidon, erected *c*. 208 BC as an exchange for the merchants and bankers of Delos. East of the portico is the Dodecatheion, the Sanctuary of the Twelve Gods, built at the beginning of the third century BC.

Eastward of the Dodecatheion is the Agora of the Italians, the largest building complex on Delos, a rectangular area measuring 34 by 22 metres, originally bordered by a peristyle of 112 columns, constructed near the end of the second century BC. The most notable of its extant remains is an archaic *kouros* by the Naxian sculptors Dionysios and Timarchide, now toppled from its pedestal. Outside the south-west corner of the *agora* are the remains of the Letoon, or shrine of Leto, dating from the mid-sixth century BC.

North of the *agora* is the dried-up bed of the Sacred Lake, where the sacred swans and geese of Apollo swam. A palm tree sprouting from the centre of the lake bed is a reminder that this is where Leto is supposed to have given birth to Apollo. The legendary tree is mentioned in the *Odyssey*, where Odysseus compares Nausicca's beauty to that of 'a young palm tree which I saw when I was in Delos growing close to the altar of Apollo'.

The famous Terrace of the Lions is on the west side of the Sacred Lake. This is a promenade 50 metres long flanked by the marble figures of a group of lions erected by the Naxians in the second half of the seventh century BC. One of the lions was removed by the Venetians during the period when they controlled the Cyclades, and now stands outside the Arsenale in Venice.

Above the terrace on a low hill are the ruins of a building complex, dated *c.* 110 BC, that housed the Poseiodoniasts of Berytos. This was a brotherhood of merchants and shipowners from Berytos, the modern Beirut, who here worshipped the god Baal under his Greek guise as Poseidon.

Just to the north of the Sacred Lake there are two structures known as the House on the Lake and the Granite Palaestra. The House on the Lake was originally a *palaestra*, a gymnasium where young men engaged in wrestling, with inner chambers used as exercise rooms and baths. The Granite Palaestra served the same purpose. Both structures date from the mid-second century BC.

East of the *palaestra* there are the foundations of a structure known as the Archigesion. This was a shrine devoted to the worship of Anios, the first King of Delos, who was also chief priest of the cult of his father Apollo.

North-east of the Archigesion is an area that served as the sports centre of ancient Delos, including a gymnasium and a stadium, both dating from the third century BC. These would have been used in the athletic competitions of the Delian Games.

East of the stadium on the shore of the island there is an isolated structure unearthed in 1912. This has been identified as a synagogue, believed to date from soon after 88 BC, as evidenced by its use of marble from the nearby gymnasium, which would have been destroyed in the First Mithridatic War. The Jewish community on Delos seems to have been established late in the second century BC, when large numbers of merchants moved here from Syria and the Lebanon.

Mount Kynthos dominates the south-east quarter of the archaeological site. At the foot of the hill on its north-west side is the House of the Herms, a typical Delian dwelling of the Hellenistic period, dated c. 100 BC. The house takes its name from the *herms* found there, roadside monuments decorated with an abstract representation of the god Hermes, representing only his head and genitals.

The road ascending the west slope of the hill passes the remains of numerous sanctuaries, dedicated to both Middle Eastern as well as Graeco-Roman deities. The largest of the shrines on Mount Kynthos is the Sanctuary of the Foreign Gods. An inscription records that this was founded in 128 BC by a Syrian merchant named Archaeus, who received permission to erect a temple to his native deities, the god Ahad and his divine mistress Atargatis. The most impressive part of this sanctuary is its large theatre, where an audience of some 500 devotees gathered for the orgiastic rites of the cult, which apparently shocked even the hedonistic Greeks of the Roman era.

On the summit of Mount Kynthos there was a sanctuary of Kynthian Zeus and Athena as well as shrines of Apollo and Artemis. Other shrines and altars are scattered around the summit, including a sanctuary dedicated to the Gods of Ascalon, the Phoenician town where Aphrodite had her first known temple. Archaeological excavations have revealed that the summit of Mount Kynthos was continually inhabited throughout the Early and Middle Cycladic periods, after which it was abandoned for a new site in what became the Hieron of Apollo. According to mythology, it was from this summit that Zeus watched the birth of his son Apollo, as Leto bore him beneath the palm tree on the shore of the Sacred Lake.

The main residential area of ancient Delos was situated in the south-west quarter of the archaeological site with many luxuriant villas owned by wealthy merchants and shipowners. The best-preserved of these are the House of the Dolphins and the House of the Masques. Both of them date from the latter half of the second century BC, each taking its name from the most notable design in its peristyle hall, the columns of which have been reerected.

The theatre of Delos is cut into the natural slope of the hillside. It could seat about 5,000 spectators, who came to watch the theatrical productions performed during the Delian Games. In front of the theatre there is a large cistern with a series of superbly constructed arches supporting its substructure. Just to the south of the cistern there is a group of three sanctuaries, the first of them dedicated to Apollo and Artemis, the second to Dionysos, and the third to Hekate, the Goddess of Night.

South of the pier is the former Commercial Quarter, where the ruins of ancient warehouses stand along the shore, along with those of several sanctuaries. The most notable of these is the Asklepion, or shrine of Asklepios, the god of healing, dated c. 300 BC.

The most numerous exhibits in the Archaeological Museum are archaic *kouori* and *korai*, monumental statues of young men and women personifying Apollo and Artemis, which would have stood in either the Hieron of Apollo or the Artemision. There are also a number of ancient tombstones with funerary reliefs; and numerous *herms*, along with marble statuettes, terracotta figurines and theatrical masques, articles of furniture and household objects, pottery, jewellery, stone sundials, and fragments of reliefs and frescoes from Delian houses.

When I first visited Delos in the early 1960s there were very few tourists, and so I had the site pretty much to myself. After a day of wandering among the ruins I sat down on the pier and waited for the *caique* to take me back to Mykonos, recalling the lines that Antipater of Thessalonica wrote early in the first century AD, when the other isles of the Cyclades were facing the same devastation and loss of population that Delos had experienced.

> Deserted islands, broken sherds of land
> Held in by the Aegean's belts of noise,
> You have copied Siphnos and the dry Cyclades –
> Their wretched loss of an archaic glory.
> Or Delos, brilliant once, taught you her way,
> The first to meet the god of desolation.

Mykonos: population 9,660; area 86 sq km; Mt. Profitis Ilias Vorniotis (372 m); ferries from Piraeus (94 mi) and Rafina (71 mi); airport; hotels in Chora, Agios Ioannis, Elia Beach, Agios Stephanos, Ornos, Platys Yialos, Tourlos, Psarou Beach, Ftelia, Kalo Livadi and Agios Sostis.

Delos: no permanent population; area 3.4 sq km; Mt. Kythnos (112 m); boats from Mykonos.

ten
Syros

My first impression of Syros, from the deck of the *Despina* in June 1962, was that it was utterly barren and rock-bound. As we passed along the north-eastern shore of the island, approaching the port at Ermoupolis, there was not a tree nor terraced farm or vineyard in sight on the tawny mountains that plunge into the sea without intervening strands. But apparently it wasn't always like this. In Book XV of the *Odyssey* the faithful swineherd Eumaios praises the abundance of the island, his birthplace, which he describes to Odysseus as being 'good for cattle and good for sheep, full of vineyards, and wheat raising'.

Syros is one of the smaller inhabited isles of the Cyclades, with an area of 84 square kilometres, only one-fifth the size of Naxos. But it has a population of 22,220, the largest in the archipelago, due to its role as the hub of the Cyclades. Ermoupolis is both the capital and by far the most important port of the Cyclades, with connections to other parts of the archipelago and other islands in the Aegean, as well as an air service from Athens.

The port of Ermoupolis is protected by a long breakwater to the east, and only after the ferry rounds this does the town come into view, suddenly and dramatically, with its tiered houses rising up the slopes of two hills, both of them crowned with churches. On the western hill is the Catholic church of Agios Yiorgios, which surmounts Ano Syra, the medieval Latin town, and on the eastern is the Greek Orthodox church of the Anastasis (Resurrection), which crowns the Vrontado hill, marking the top of Ermoupolis, the new town that came into being during the Greek War of Independence.

Syros was in antiquity one of the least significant of the Cyclades, and it is not mentioned by Herodotus, Thucydides or Pausanias. Strabo refers to it only as one of the Cyclades, particularly as the birthplace of Pherecydes, one of the earliest known Greek philosophers. According to tradition, Pherecydes was born early in the sixth century BC in Syros, where he founded a school of philosophy, his most renowned student being Pythagoras of Samos. Ancient sources say that Pherecydes was the first to talk about the immortality and transmigration of souls, concepts generally attributed to both Pythagoras and Plato. He was also one of the first Greek astronomers, and is traditionally credited with the invention of the sundial. Diodorus Siculus, writing in the first century BC, is the source for the strange story that Pherecydes died on Delos after being consumed by lice, and that before he passed away he was visited there by his old student Pythagoras.

During the medieval Byzantine era the island was known as Souda, which the Latins changed to Lasouda, a name that survived up until the fifteenth century.

Throughout the Latin period the island was ruled by the Dukes of Naxos or their heirs, who when in residence here styled themselves as 'Barons of Lasouda'. One of the first to hold this title was Guglielmo Sanudo, who succeeded his father Marco Sanudo as Duke of Naxos in 1303. While he was still ruling as baron on Syros, Guglielmo became involved in hostilities with Giorgio I Ghisi, lord of Tinos, who put Syros under siege before the Venetians intervened to settle the conflict. The dispute concerned a donkey that had been stolen from the Ghisi estates on Tinos by corsairs, who then sold the beast to Guglielmo Sanudo, and so the ensuing conflict came to be known as the War of the Ass.

Syros is the most Catholic of all the Greek isles, a characteristic that dates back to the Latin era in its history. This was reinforced

when a community of Capuchin monks settled on the island in
1633, followed a century later by the Jesuits. From then on Syros
became the centre of Roman Catholicism in the Cyclades. The
Catholics on Syros appealed to the French to save them from
the Turks, and in 1640 King Louis XIII responded by putting the
island under his special protection. This brought Syros into more
direct association with Europe than any of the other Cyclades,
which were cut off from Western civilisation through most
of the *Turkokrateia*. During the eighteenth century there were
6,000 Greek Catholics living on Syros and only 12 Greek
Orthodox families.

Tournefort was impressed with the industriousness of the
Syrans, though he complained that this kept him awake for they
worked both night and day: '...there's no sleeping in the island,
not in the night time, because of the universal Din made by the
Hand-Mills each man works at to grind his Corn; nor in the day-
time, because of the rumbling made by the Wheels for the spinning
of Cotton.'

The island was occupied by the Russians during the Russo–
Turkish war of 1770–1774, which allowed Greek mariners to sail
under the protection of the Russian flag and thus began the
development of the merchant marine in Greece. Five years later
Sultan Abdul Hamit I gave Syros and Andros to his favourite niece,
who granted special privileges to the islanders and allowed them
to govern themselves without Turkish interference, a status that
lasted until her death in 1803. Thus by the end of the *Turkokrateia*
Syros was beginning to emerge as a shipping and commercial
centre, a development that would be accelerated by the outbreak
of the Greek War of Independence.

Some forty thousand refugees arrived on Syros during the first
years of the war, the largest wave of them being the survivors of
the Turkish massacres on Chios in 1822 and Psara in 1824. By that
time the people of Syros had declared common cause with the
revolutionary government. The first Greek governor, Alexandros
Axiotis, arrived on Syros in July 1823, when he created a court of

law, organised a police force and appointed a harbour master. Some of the first cases in the court involved disputes between the refugees, who were mostly Greek Orthodox, and the established residents of Ano Syra, who were predominantly Roman Catholic. Municipal archives record that on 21 January 1824 the refugees petitioned Axiotis for permission 'to build a church here, financed by individual contributions, in which they can discharge their bounden Christian duty...'. Axiotis records the difficulties he encountered in finding and purchasing a suitable site, 'for the native inhabitants of the island were at that time unwilling to give even a square foot of land to the new settlers, whatever sum of money they were offered, – and especially when the land was to be used as a church of the Eastern Creed'. But a site was eventually found and purchased and 'within the same year, with the aid of further financial contributions, the walls were raised, the roof set in position, the various columns and the altar built, and the divine liturgy was performed on the altar before the end of the year'. The church was dedicated to the Metamorphosis, the Transfiguration – a prophetic name, for in a public meeting there in 1826 the new city of Ermoupolis was created out of the former shanty town of the refugees. The new city was named for Hermes, the patron of commerce, for its founders hoped that it would be the commercial centre of the Aegean.

By 1828 Ermoupolis was a fully established city with a population of 13,805, and five years later it was designated capital of the Cyclades. During the first quarter-century after independence Ermoupolis became the principal port in Greece, for its large harbour was on the main trade routes between western Europe, the Levant and the Black Sea.

Another wave of refugees arrived in 1866, when the Greeks on Crete rose in revolt against the Turks once again. Shiploads of Cretan refugees landed in Syros and many of them settled in Ermoupolis. Still more arrived from Asia Minor after the Graeco–Turkish war of 1919–1922 and in the population exchange that followed, when more than a million Greeks were moved from Turkey to Greece, a great many of them passing through Ermoupolis in their diaspora.

As capital of the Cyclades, Ermoupolis became the first planned town in the archipelago. Its public buildings were built in the same neoclassical style as those in the new Athens, some of them designed by the same architects, both Greek and European, who were then working for King Otho.

Ermoupolis became the seat for both the Greek Orthodox and Roman Catholic archbishoprics of the Cyclades, whose cathedrals and new churches were also built in the neoclassical style. The Greek Orthodox cathedral is the church of the Metamorphosis, built in the years 1824–1831. The Roman Catholic cathedral, dedicated to the Panagia Evangelistria, was completed in 1829, erected on the site of successive earlier churches that appear in prints depicting Ano Syros. Also on the summit of Ano Syros is the monastery of the Capuchins, built in 1633 by Louis XIII of France; the Jesuit monastery, founded in 1747 around the sixteenth-century church of Our Lady of Karmilou; and the Catholic convent school of the Ursilines, established in 1751.

Vrontado, the picturesque quarter on the eastern hill, is crowned by the Byzantine church of the Anastasis, or Resurrection. In the old days the Easter service was held early on the morning of Easter Sunday, but now the liturgy is performed on Saturday night. At the climax of the service the sanctuary doors swing open and the presiding priest appears with a lighted candle and chants: 'Come ye, partake of the never-setting Light and glorify Christ who is risen from the dead.' The congregation crowd round to light their candles from the taper of the priest, who leads a procession to the courtyard, where he reads the Gospel passage describing the Resurrection. He then proclaims *'Christos anesti'*, 'Christ has risen!', to which the congregation respond *'Alithos anesti'*, 'He has in truth risen', as they exchange the kiss of Resurrection. Everyone then carries their lighted candle home, trying to keep the flame burning so they can mark the sign of the cross above the doorway of their house, which will bring them good luck in the coming year. Many go on to celebrate at the tavernas on the slopes of the Vrontada hill, the lambent flames of their candles tracing out what appear to be streams of glittering stars when seen from the lower town.

The most notable of the neoclassical Greek Orthodox churches built in Ermoupolis during the first century of its existence are the Koimisis tis Theotokou (1828–1850), Agios Yiorgios (1839), Agios Nikolaos (1848–1870), Agia Anastasia (1873–1916) and the Taxiarchis (1890–1908).

There are a dozen other extant civil buildings of this period, all of them in the neoclassical style. The most remarkable of these are the Apollo Theatre, an opera house built in 1861–1862 as a scaled-down copy of La Scala in Milan, and the Town Hall, begun in 1876 and completed in 1908. In front of the Town Hall there is a statue of Admiral Andreas Miaoulis (1768–1835), one of the leaders in the Greek War of Independence.

The Town Hall is now the Nomarcheion, headquarters of the Nomarch, or governor, of the Cyclades. Designed in the neo-classical style by the German architect Ernst Ziller, it forms the upper side of the Plateia Miaoulis, a vast square measuring some 125 by 75 metres, its grandiose dimensions a reminder that in the early Greek Kingdom Ermoupolis was the second most important city in Greece after Athens, which it surpassed in its industry and commerce. The relative importance of the town is now much less than it was a century ago, but it is still the administrative, religious and economic centre of the Cyclades, as well as being the focal point of most of the ferry lines that thread their way through the archipelago. The square is particularly lively on Sunday evenings, when it is thronged with strollers, the arcaded cafés full and bubbling with animated conversation, and the town band playing from a bandstand adorned with figures of the Seven Muses.

There are a number of elegant neoclassical mansions in Ermoupolis dating from the first half-century of the Greek Kingdom, some of them clustered around the Town Hall and others in the Vaporia quarter, so called because the first houses there were built by retired captains of steamships, in Greek, *vaporia*. Many of these houses were decorated with murals painted by both Greek and European artists, while sculptors were hired to create the public statues that commemorate some of the renowned figures in the early history of Ermoupolis. There are also many old houses of the *laika* (folk) type in the more traditional Cycladic style.

Ermoupolis is most famous today for its *loukomia*, or Turkish delight, and all ferries arriving in the port are immediately boarded by peddlers hawking this delicious sweet, which was brought to Syros by refugees from Asia Minor.

There is little left to be seen of ancient Syros other than the objects exhibited in the Archaeological Musum. The museum's collection includes artefacts from three Early Cycladic sites on Syros. There is another museum devoted to the popular Greek composer and musician Markos Vamvakaris (1905–1972), one of those who popularised the *rebetika* songs that came to Greece with the refugees from Smyrna in 1923. More than a score of recordings have been made of his songs and he is honoured with a commemorative bust in the little *plateia* that bears his name in Ano Syros.

Observations by early travellers and discoveries of scattered antiquities indicate that Ermoupolis occupies the site of the principal city of ancient Syros, whose citadel was on the peak of Ano Syros. Four seats from an ancient theatre can still be seen in the basement of a house at 18 Odos Klisthenous, a short distance in from the south-western arc of the port, and an ancient relief is displayed on the wall of the church of the Metamorphosis, north-west of Plateia Miaoulis. A font within the church is made from the base of a monument to Hadrian; the statue of the emperor that it once supported was carried off by the Russians during their occupation of the Cyclades in 1770–1774.

A short stretch of the defence-wall of the ancient city survives on Katelymata hill, on the east side of the new gymnasium. The walls of the lower city, now vanished, circled around the present port, with gates opening out to the coast on the south-west and the south-east, the latter now occupied by the Vaporia quarter. There were originally seven gates in the walls, two of which have survived in the form of arched passageways through the local houses.

A number of stepped streets lead upwards from the port to Ano Syros, also known as Kastro, which is dominated by the Catholic cathedral of the Evangelistria and the Capuchin monastery. One of the streets leading up to Ano Syros passes the Greek Orthodox church of Agios Yiorgios, whose tall campanile is a landmark of the quarter known as Neapolis, the 'New City'. Agios Yiorgios was founded to be the centre of a new parish on the outskirts of Ermoupolis, and also to serve as the funerary chapel of a new Orthodox cemetery, for the old burial ground down by the port was needed for a building site. The cemetery at Neapolis is a veritable museum of neoclassical funerary sculpture, its most elaborate monuments being in the form of classical Greek temples adorned with statues of mourning angels along with busts and reliefs of the deceased. A section of the burial ground serves as the British Military Cemetery, shaded by a copse of pepper trees. Buried here are 108 British and Allied servicemen, more than half of them killed when the British troopship *Arcadia* was torpedoed and sank in the Aegean on 19 April 1917.

The oldest churches and monasteries on Syros are in the centre of the island, west and south of Ermoupolis. To the west is the convent of Agia Barbara, once an orphanage for girls, where the nuns run a weaving school that makes local handiworks for sale. A short way to the south of Agia Barbara is the old village of Episkopia, whose name indicates that it may have been the original seat of the Orthodox bishopric of Syros. The village church of Profitis Ilias, the oldest on the island, is believed to date back to the medieval Byzantine era. South-east of Episkopia is the Faneromeni monastery, where both the Orthodox and Catholics celebrate *paneyeria* on 24 September.

There is a succession of sand beaches along the west and south coast, the largest and most popular being Delfini. The fishing village of Kini also has two good beaches around a semicircular bay. The beach at Galissas has the island's two campsites, while the one at Armeos is the only one set aside for nudists. A short way south of Armeos, at Agia Pakou, is what is believed to be the ancient city of Galissas, now apparently vanished.

The popular beach at Finikas is on a huge bay at the south-western end of the island. The name Finikas has led to the suggestion that this was the site of a Phoenician settlement, but the only basis for this is found in the *Odyssey*, where Eumaeus tells Odysseus that as a child he was kidnapped by Phoenician pirates: 'There came Phoenician men, famous seafarers, gnawers/at other people's goods, with countless pretty things stored in their black ship.'

At the southern end of the same bay is the resort village of Poseidonia, formerly known as Dellagrazia. This became popular in the late nineteenth century, and in 1885 the island's first paved road was laid out from Ermoupolis to Dellagrazia, where wealthy Syrans erected the sumptuous Italianate mansions that still adorn the village.

There are two more beaches along the south coast at Megas Yialos and Vari, and a short way east of Vari, on the Chontra headland, archaeologists have unearthed a Cycladic settlement dating from the fourth millennium BC.

The more sparsely settled northern half of Syros is dominated by Mount Pyrgos, the highest peak on the island, 442 metres above sea level. The old farmhouses in this region, known as Apano Mera, are in a traditional style that probably has not changed since antiquity, in contrast with the modern villas one sees in southern Syros. At Syringas, north of Mount Pyrgos, there is a holy well whose healing water is sold throughout Greece.

The northern coast is most easily explored by excursion boats from Kini. On the north-west coast at Agios Loukas archaeologists have excavated an Early Cycladic burial ground, part of a settlement that seems to have been inhabited until the end of the Bronze Age.

There is a beautiful sand beach at Ormos Grammaton, a secluded bay at the north-westernmost end of the island. The bay takes its name (in Greek, *grammata* means 'letters') from the numerous inscriptions that have been carved on the marble outcropping of the promontory to its north. Bent writes of these inscriptions, having travelled there on horseback from Ermoupolis, remarking: 'A wilder, bleaker ride I never had, even in the Cyclades.'

> This tongue of marble is in three places covered with very neatly cut inscriptions placed on flat spaces of marble which slope down to the water's edge. Some of them are very old, but most date from the Roman and Byzantine epochs; for the most part they are prayers for good voyages and thanksgivings for safety made by those anchoring in this little bay in time of tempest, both for themselves and their friends... There are about 100 of these, affording a curious collection of names, occupations and countries... showing what a popular place of resort once was Grammata Bay, now lost almost to the world, for hardly anyone in Syra had heard of it, and if he had heard of it he would never think of riding four hours to see such a sight.

Boats from Kini round Cape Diapori to cruise along the northeast coast of the island, where there is another remote beach at Sykama. Farther to the south along the coast, at Kastri, excavations have unearthed one of the earliest fortified settlements in the Cyclades, dating to the third millennium BC. At Chalandriani the Greek archaeologist Christos Tsountas unearthed a large Cycladic burial site dated to *c.* 2700 BC.

An interesting hike takes you in a looping clockwise itinerary north from Ermoupolis through the villages of Mitikas and Platys Vouni, returning along the shore road. A short way south of Platys Vouni, there is a double cave known as Spilia tou Ferikidou. Legend has it that this is the home of Pherecydes, the philosopher who is said to have been the first prose writer.

The shore road back to Ermoupolis passes the pretty seaside chapel of Agios Dimitrios. Two *paneyeria* are celebrated here, first on the last Sunday in May to celebrate the finding of the saint's icon, and the second on 26 October to celebrate his name-day. On the feast day of St Dimitrios, which in the old calendar marks the beginning of winter, it is the custom to open and taste the barrels of new wine, an occasion of much drinking and revelry. The following day goat-herders drive their flocks down from the hills to their folds on the plains, while fisherman pull up their boats on the shore and prepare for the storms that follow after the Little Summer of Saint Dimitrios.

And so the year passes on Syros and the other isles of the Cyclades.

Syros: population 22,220; area 84 sq km; Mt. Pyrgos (442 m); ferries from Piraeus (76 mi); airport; hotels in Ermoupolis, Galissas, Azolimnos, Kini, Finikas and Megas Yialos.

eleven
Paros and Antiparos

T he Greek poet George Seferis thought that Paros was the loveliest of all the Cyclades, and he felt that the streets and squares of Paroikia, its port and capital, were arranged as harmoniously as a musical composition. I thought of this when I first approached Paros on the *Despina* in June of 1962, the houses and churches of Paroikia coming into focus as we entered its large bay on the western coast of the island, the striking forms of the white Cycladic cubes revealing themselves around the periphery of the harbour.

Though Delos was the ancient spiritual focus of the Cyclades, the geometrical centre of the archipelago is Paros, midway east –west between Milos and Amorgos and about halfway between Andros and Santorini north–south. Arriving in Paros, I felt that I was now in the heart of the Cyclades.

During the classical period Paros was the wealthiest of the Cyclades, as evidenced by the fact that the tax levied on it in the Delian League was twice that of Naxos and Melos, the next most prosperous isles. The principal source of this wealth was Parian marble, much sought after by sculptors and architects and used for the reliefs on the Parthenon in Athens as well as for the famed Venus de Milo. Two of the renowned sculptors of the Archaic period were from Paros, namely Agorakritos and Scopas. A colossal marble head of Nemesis by Agorakritos is preserved in the British Museum.

Scopas worked on two of the seven wonders of the ancient world, the Mausoleum at Halicarnassos and the Temple of Artemis at Ephesos, both of which were adorned with his reliefs.

The prosperity of Paros continued throughout the Hellenistic period, when the island's population reached an estimated 150,000, more than ten times its present number, many of them probably slaves who worked in the marble quarries. But a sharp decline began soon after the conquest of Greece by Rome, when Italian merchants took over the marble quarries and cut down all of the island's trees for shipbuilding, leaving Paros poor and denuded, beginning a period of poverty that was to last for many centuries.

The fortunes of Paros revived after the Latin Duchy of the Archipelago began in 1210. Marco Sanudo ruled directly over Naxos and Paros, as did his successors in the Sanudi dynasty. When Francesco Crispo became Duke of Naxos in 1383 he awarded Paros as a sub-fief to the Duchess Francesca, widow of the late Duke Niccolo III. The duchess then married a nobleman from the Veronese family of Sommaripa, whose descendants ruled Paros and Andros until the latter years of the Latin period.

The Sommaripa line on Paros became extinct *c.* 1524, when the last duke of that name died without leaving a male heir. The title passed in turn to his two surviving sisters, first to Fiorenza Venier, and then on her death to Cecilia Sagredo, whose husband Bernardo was fated to be the last Latin ruler on Paros. Bernardo's rule ended in 1537, when he died defending Paros against Barbarossa, who enslaved virtually all of the surviving inhabitants of the island. An old Parian folk song grieves over Barbarossa's raid, in which Paros suffered far more than any other island in the archipelago.

> All the twelve islands are at peace
> And hapless Paros stands besieged.
> All those who know her, weep and grieve for her,
> And no one weeps more than Our Lady.
> 'Paros, fragrant apple tree,
> Apple of paradise,
> Paros, why does this Barbarossa vent his rage on you?'

One of those captured by Barbarossa was a 12-year-old girl named Cecelia Venier-Baffo, the illegitimate child of a Graeco-Venetian couple of noble lineage. She was brought to Istanbul, where she was given the Turkish name of Nurbanu and presented to Selim II, son of Süleyman the Magnificent, who succeeded his father as sultan in 1566 and ruled until 1574. Nurbanu bore Selim four children, including the future Sultan Murat III (r. 1574–1595). She was the power behind the throne during the reign of Selim and through the first eight years of Murat's reign, until she passed away in 1582. When Nurbanu died the Venetian ambassador sent word to the Doge, remarking: 'All universally admit that she was a woman of the utmost goodness, courage and wisdom.'

Paros was eventually resettled by those who had survived Barbarossa's raid, but they were few in number and through the first two centuries of the *Turkokrateia* the island was little more than a nest of pirates. The renowned French pirate Hugues Creveliers, whose buccaneering fleet operated out of the Parian port of Naoussa in the 1570s, was the prototype for the principal character in Byron's *Corsair*. After Tournefort's visit to Paros in 1700 he noted that 'the greatest part of the Inhabitants are French and Maltese Corsairs, who are neither Greeks or Latins'.

Diplomatic ties between France and the Ottoman Empire began in 1536, when Francis I sent an embassy to the court of Süleyman the Magnificent. This alliance gave the French kings the opportunity to protect the Cyclades from Turkish oppression. French missionaries, originally based in Syros, came to Paros and founded Catholic churches, monasteries and convent schools. But despite this the Parians remained staunchly Orthodox, except for the Catholic descendants of the Latin aristocracy, and during the latter part of the seventeenth century the Greeks built more than a score of churches and monasteries on the island.

The most renowned Greek to emerge from Paros during the *Turkokrateia* was Nikolaos Mavroyennis (1738–1789), who in the years 1786–1789 served as Hospodar, or governor, of Moldavia and Wallachia under the aegis of the Ottoman sultan. His niece

Mando Mavroyennis, the heroine of Mykonos, spent the last years of her life in Paros, where she died in 1838.

The principal monument of Paroikia is the cathedral of the Panagia Ekatontapyliani, Our Lady of the Hundred Gates. Parians refer to it simply as the Panagia, for its fame as a shrine of the Virgin is surpassed only by that of the Evangelistria on Tinos, and on the feast day of the Assumption the Ekatontapyliani also draws thousands of pilgrims from all over Greece. The name of the cathedral is probably a corruption of 'katopoliani', meaning 'below the town', referring to it in opposition to Kastro, the Upper Town, which would have comprised virtually all of Paroikia when the church was erected, early in the reign of Justinian (r. 527–565).

The church was designed by Isidorus of Miletos, who in 532 was appointed by Justinian to be one of the two architects of the great church of Hagia Sophia in Constantinople. While building the Ekatontapyliani, Isidorus was assisted by a Parian architect named Ignatius, who is supposed to have carried the work through to completion after his master returned to Constantinople.

The church is cruciform in plan, with the transepts crossing the nave under the hemispherical dome, which is carried on arches that spring from four huge piers resting in the corners of a square. The present dome was constructed after the original cupola was destroyed by an earthquake in 1507. The columns of the aisle arcade are ancient, with superb Byzantine capitals carved in low relief. The iconostasis, divided into five spaces by four marble columns carrying an entablature, is adorned with beautifully carved and gilded woodwork. The panel to the left of the central door frames the sacred icon of the Panagia, of which all but the Virgin's face is obscured by silver plating donated in 1788 by Nikolaos Mavroyennis. This icon, which is believed to date from the twelfth century, is the object of great veneration, and on the two principal feast days of the Panagia, 28 March and 15 August, it is carried in procession through the streets of Paroikia.

The altar is a slab of white marble supported by two pieces of ancient columns. The four columns supporting the massive marble ciborium have finely carved melon capitals, which carry a dome nearly two metres in diameter carved from a single piece of marble. Beneath the altar there is an *agiasma*, whose healing waters are dispensed to pilgrims during the Virgin's two feast days. The semicircular apse has eight tiers of seats for the clergy, with a stone episcopal throne approached by a flight of eight steps. There are frescoes high on the wall of the *bema*, but these can best be viewed from the gallery of the church.

The apse is flanked by two *parekklesia*, or side chapels. The one on the right serves as the sacristy, while the one on the left is dedicated to Agios Nikolaos. The domed nave of the latter chapel, which dates from the early Byzantine period, is flanked by two colonnades, each with three ancient monoliths of Parian marble crowned with elaborate capitals; the *iconostasis* dates from 1611.

The south transept contains the tomb of Agia Theoktisti, the patron saint of Paros, whose relics are exhibited on her feast day, 9 November. The south wing of the transept houses three chapels, dedicated, respectively, to Agios Philippos, the Holy Spirit, and Agioi Anargyroi (SS Cosmas and Damian). There is also another *agiasma*, beneath which there is an ancient crypt.

The original baptistery, dedicated to Agios Ioannis Prodromos, is attached to the south side of the church. A stairway in front of the baptistery leads to the gallery of the church, which commands a good view of the mosaics on the wall of the *bema*. These paintings form an iconographic cycle known as the Akathistos, depicting 24 scenes from the life of the Virgin Mary. Each painting is associated with one of the Akathistos Hymns, 24 songs in praise of Mary, the unwedded bride and God-bearer, each beginning with one of the letters of the Greek alphabet.

The Archaeological Museum is down the street on the right side of the church. The most important exhibit in the museum is a fragment of the famous Parian Chronicle. This an inscription recording the principal events in ancient Greek history from the reign of the legendary King Kekrops of Athens down to 264 BC, a record probably carved soon after the latter date. A large part of this inscription was discovered in 1627, built into the defence-walls of the Latin Kastro in Paroikia, and this is exhibited as part of the Arundel Marbles in Oxford's Ashmolean Museum, while the fragment on show in the Paros museum was discovered in 1897. Two other exhibits of particular interest, both in the courtyard, concern the poet Archilochus. One of these is a plaque, dated *c.* 250 BC, with a biography of the poet; the second is a capital of the sixth century BC, found in a shrine dedicated to Archilochus outside Paroikia.

A flight of steps leads up from the *paralia* to Kastro, the medieval Latin fortress. The principal monument here, besides the remains of the fortress itself, is the church of Agioi Konstantinos and Eleni, built in 1689. This stands on the site of an ancient temple of Apollo, dated *c.* 600 BC, fragments of which are built into the façade of the church. Nearby in Kastro there is a double church dating from 1752, with one chapel dedicated to Agios Ioannis Prodromos and the other to Agios Stylianos, the latter adorned with a beautifully carved *iconostasis* and some interesting old icons. Another chapel in Kastro is Agia Anna, which is built up against a tower of the Latin fortress, with ancient architectural members incorporated in its structure.

The churches in the lower town that can be dated definitely are Evangelistria and Profitis Ilias (1612), Agios Yiorgios (1619), Agios Artemios (1632), Taxiarchis (1633), Gennesis tis Theotokou (Birth of the Virgin) (1636), Agia Kyriaki (1638), Eisodia tis Theotokou (Presentation of the Virgin) and Agia Paraskevi (1645), Agios Phanourios and Evangelistria (1645), Agioi Anargyroi (1666), Agios Nikolaos (1667), Treis Hierarchi (1695), Agios Athanasios (1695), Agios Ioannis Prodromos (1752), Virgin of Bethlehem (1775) and Agios Nikolaos (1823), the latter being the first church to be built in Paroikia after the beginning of the War of Independence.

There are also a number of picturesque old Cycladic houses in Paroikia, as well as three baroque street fountains built in 1777 by Nikolaos Mavroyennis. All of the fountains are inscribed with the founder's name and the date, and one also bears a verse, which can be translated thus: 'I am a goodly spring and furnish water, neither stagnant nor in floods, but like the loom I murmur, gurgle and say, "Come, good folk, every one, take drink but be sparing of me"'.

Bent, in his description of Paroikia, writes of the unusual names of some of the chapels in the vicinity of the town.

> The valleys and hills around the town are dotted with tiny white churches...; there is one dedicated to St John the Rainy, another to Our Lady of the Lake, another to Our Lady of the Unwholesome Place, another to St George of the Gooseberry, a rare fruit in the East, and, most extraordinary name of all, there is a church dedicated to the Drunken St George. Here, I thought, must be a true descendant of Bacchus; an instance of how the Greeks still love to deify the coarser passions; and on enquiry I was told that on 3 November, the day of the anniversary of St George's death, the Pariotes usually tap their new made wine and get drunk; they have a dance and a scene of revelry in front of this church, which is hallowed by the presence of the priests.

The monastery of Agioi Anargyroi is the most prominent landmark visible to the traveller approaching Paroikia by sea, looming high up on the mountainside above the town. According to tradition, the monastery was founded by a Greek merchant named Pavlakis Iordanis who fled Constantinople before it fell to the Turks in 1453. It seems that when Iordanis arrived on Paros his only possession was a fighting cock, which supported him by winning all of its matches. But then in one of its matches it killed the gamecock of a Venetian aristocrat, who in his anger wrung its neck. Iordanis immediately cut the Venetian's throat and then fled into the mountains above Paroikia, where he eventually built this monastery.

The present structure dates from 1660, and is a typical Cycladic *pyrgos*-monastery, with massive buttresses on the seaward side. Agioi Anargyroi is now uninhabited, but its *katholikon* is open for its *paneyeria*, 8 May and 25 September, on the eve of which kerosene lamps are lighted along the ramparts so that the monastery can be seen from Paroikia.

There are several sites one can see on excursions to the south of Paroikia, as well as to Delphini beach and the beaches at Parasporos and Agia Eirene.

The first of the sites south of Paroikia is a shrine of Asklepios, of which there remains only a few scattered column drums and some other architectural fragments. The sacred spring of the shrine is still flowing, and Pariotes consider its waters to be medicinal.

About five kilometres south of the town is the convent known as Christos sto Dassos, Christ of the Wood. This was founded in 1792 by the Mavroyennis family, at first housing a community of monks; then in 1805 it was converted into a convent. It is noted as the burial place of Agios Arsenios (1800–1877), one of the most recent saints in the Greek Orthodox Church, canonised only in 1967. Arsenios was celebrated as a miracle-worker even in his own lifetime, particularly when he was credited with bringing rain to the island after a long drought. Pariotes tell the story of how a delegation of farmers sought him out in the monastery of Agios Yiorgios high on the slopes of Mount Profitis Ilias, asking him to intercede with God to bring them rain. When Arsenios heard their request he said to them, 'If you truly have faith, why have none of you brought umbrellas?'

About a kilometre farther south is Petaloudes, the Valley of the Butterflies, within the grounds of an old Venetian estate, lush with flower gardens, groves of fruit trees, and colonnades of spectral cypresses. This is one of the loveliest spots on Paros, particularly in the spring, when the vale is filled with the brilliant swarms of butterflies from which it takes its name.

Further south there is a ruined Venetian tower known as the Alisafis Pyrgos. An inscription on the wall of the tower records the name of its builder, Ioakovos Alisafis, and the date, 1626. Local legend has it that the last of the Alisafis to dwell here were 12 brothers and their beautiful sister, who were besieged by Algerian pirates. When the water supply of the *pyrgos* was cut off the brothers killed their sister rather than let her fall into the hands of the pirates, and then they themselves fought to their death rather than surrender.

North of Paroikia there are several beaches around the two coves of the bay. At Livadia, on the first cove beyond Paroikia, a path leads to the summit of a hill to an ancient site known as the Delion, where there are the scant remains of a shrine of Delian Apollo. The sanctuaries of Apollo here and on Naxos form the base of an isosceles triangle, whose apex is the shrine of Apollo on Delos, and in ancient times fires were lit at the three sites to signal the beginning of the god's festival.

A short way outside Paroikia the Naoussa road passes an archaeological site known as Trias Ekklesias, or Three Churches. The name comes from the three chapels that once stood there, all dating from the seventeenth century. These chapels were built from the ruins of a seventh-century church, which in turn was constructed from the remains of an ancient structure believed to have been a *heroon*, or shrine dedicated to a hero, in this case the poet Archilochus. The *heroon* has been dated to the sixth century BC from an inscribed capital of that date bearing a dedication to Archilochus, now in the Archaeological Museum in Paros.

About two kilometres farther along one can see to the left a two-peaked hill named Kounades. One of the peaks is crowned with a chapel of Profitis Ilias, built on the site of a shrine of Zeus Hypatios. No trace remains of this shrine, nor of the temples of Aphrodite and Eilithyia which in times past were identified in this area. Below the summit there is a ruined monastery of Agios Ioannis Prodromos, dating from 1590.

Some four kilometres out of Paroikia a track on the left leads off to Moni Agios Michaelis Taxiarchis, a small monastery established in 1587, with a *katholikon* dated 1609. The monastery is now abandoned, but the church is still used on special occasions.

Halfway between Paroikia and Naoussa a dirt road leads to Moni Longovardas, the largest monastery on Paros, which towers on the hillside above like a medieval fortress. (Women visitors are not permitted in the monastery.) Founded in 1638, the monastery is dedicated to the Panagia Zoodochos Pigi, but it has long been known as Longovardas, a name of unknown origin. The *katholikon* has frescoes dating from 1657, with one iconographical series depicting the Akathistos Cycle and the other the Twelve Feasts of the Life of Christ, while the icons on the *iconostasis* are works by Cretan artists of the nineteenth century. The monastery has a good library with a number of rare old works, and it has a small but interesting collection of post-Byzantine icons. Some of the monks paint icons, which are sold to churches and monasteries elsewhere in Greece.

Naoussa is set at the inner end of the great gulf that cuts deeply into the northern end of the island. The village is flanked by excellent beaches, with Kolimbithres on the west side of the bay and on the east Santa Maria and Langeri. These beaches and the superb setting of Naoussa have made it an internationally famous resort, but despite this the village retains something of its original Cycladic character.

Naoussa is one of the most historic ports in the Cyclades. Its harbour has been used by warships and corsairs since antiquity, one notable occasion being when the Russian fleet anchored here during the Russo–Turkish War of 1768–1774. Each year on 23 August the people of Naoussa celebrate a victory over the Turks in the War of Independence, climaxed in the evening with a torchlit sail-by of *caiques* around the harbour under a barrage of fireworks.

All that remains of the Venetian fortress of Naoussa is a ruined defence-tower at the end of the breakwater. But the core of the village of the Latin period survives in the quarter by the seaside *plateia*, a labyrinth entered through an arched passageway that was once the main gateway of the medieval town.

The two oldest churches in Naoussa are Agios Ioannis Theologos and Agios Nikolaos Mostratou, both of them eighteenth-century chapels with interesting icons by local artists. Agios Nikolaos also has a fascinating collection of ex-votos representing ships of all kinds and dates, dedicated to the church by mariners in thanksgiving to the saint for having saved them from the perils of the sea.

The local graveyard is also worth a visit, for many of the tombstones are carved with representations of galleons, anchors and other symbols of the maritime trades of the deceased.

Caiques sail out from Naoussa to the beaches around the bay, and on the headland that forms the western horn of the bay is Akri Tourkos, the Cape of the Turk, which is surmounted by the seventeenth-century monastery of Agios Ioannis Prodromos.

The main road on Paros crosses from Paroika to the eastern shore, with turn-offs to villages and monasteries along the way. Some 3.5 kilometres out of Paroikia there is a track leading south to the convent at Thapsana. The convent, which is dedicated to the Theotokou Myrtidiotissa, Mother of God, Our Lady of the Myrtles, was founded in 1929 on the ruins of a monastery built in the sixteenth century by monks from Chios. There are now some thirty nuns in the convent, where only women visitors are permitted, and then only if clothed modestly.

The track continues south to ascend Mount Agioi Pantes (All the Saints), the highest peak on Paros, 777 metres above sea level. On the peak, which is surmounted by a military communications post, off-limits to the public, there are two chapels, one dedicated to Agios Profitis Ilias and another to Agioi Pantes. The latter church, a modern construction, has at its entrance a marble plaque with an inscription beginning with these lines: 'This house of God and these pillars of Heaven are not to me a fearful place.'

Just beyond the village of Marathi – named for the fertile valley below – there is a complex of deserted buildings, erected in 1844 by a French company that cut marble from the ancient quarries of Paros for Napoleon's tomb in Paris. The ancient quarries, consisting of three deep shafts at the base of a hill, are some 200 metres to the left of the road. They were the source of the famous Parian marble so prized by sculptors in the ancient world. The sparkling white stone was known as *lychnites*, or 'won by lamplight', since the slaves who quarried it deep inside the shafts had to use lanterns while they worked. Down in the central shaft of the quarry there is a relief dated to the fourth century BC, representing the Wedding of the Nymphs, now much damaged by vandals.

South of Marathi there is an abandoned monastery dedicated to Agios Minas. The monastery was founded in 1594, but the present building is for the most part due to a reconstruction in the seventeenth century, with numerous ancient architectural fragments built into its walls.

The next turn-off leads eastward to Kostos, an old fortified village set in the midst of an olive grove. The village church, dedicated to Our Lady of the Passions, was founded in the seventeenth century. The church has a finely carved wooden *iconostasis* and some interesting icons, including one of the Virgin dated 1696.

The road now heads south towards Lefkes, passing on the left Moni Agios Ioannis Theologos, founded in 1656. The road then passes the hamlet of Apati, where to the left there is an old fountain-house known as Afentiko Pigadi, the Well of the Master.

The very pretty village of Lefkes is by far the largest community in the interior of the island, with a population of some 500. During the *Turkokrateia* it was the capital of Paros, serving as a refuge for islanders fleeing from Paroikia and Naoussa because of corsair raids.

The principal church in Lefkes is Agia Triada, a pseudo-Renaissance edifice erected in 1830. The oldest church in the village is Agia Paraskevi, founded in the fifteenth century. Next to the church is the old Zoumis mansion, once the Ottoman consulate. Other old churches in the village are Agia Barbara, dated 1618, while Agia Theodosis and Agios Sotiris (the Holy Saviour) date from later in the seventeenth century. The church of Agios Spyridon has classical marbles built into its façade, indicating that it was erected on the site of an ancient edifice. Large blocks from an ancient structure are also built into a Byzantine fountain called Paleoaterno, which is at the bottom of the street below Agios Spyridon.

The little museum in the village *plateia* has a small but interesting collection of local folk arts. On the ridge above Lefkes there is a picturesque line of windmills, which at harvest time still operate to grind grain for local farmers, while in the village itself there is a working olive press.

Bent's guide in Lefkes was the *demarch*, who told him stories about local superstitions, including the belief that children born between Christmas and Epiphany are liable to become *kalkagari*, or hobgoblins.

> 'We know of several *Kalkagari* in Leukis,' said the demarch solemnly, 'children who have been born at this unlucky epoch.' And then he told stories of how these unfortunate youngsters would walk in their sleep and torment their friends. 'We know of them,' he concluded, 'but we do not talk of them; for their parents do not like to have the fact alluded to. The only way of averting the disaster is to place a blessed palm branch (*vaia*) over the door at the time of birth.'

There are two old monasteries that can be reached by the secondary road leading south from Lefkes. The first of these is Agios Ioannis Kaparo, which is under the sheer eastern face of Mount Profitis Ilias. The monastery dates from sometime before 1646, when it was rebuilt. The second monastery, Agios Yiorgios, is farther south on the eastern slope of Mount Stroumboulas, the second-highest peak (630 m) on the island. Agios Yiorgios was founded in the seventeenth century, and its most famous resident was St Arsenios of Paros. Still farther to the south is the Kalambaki Cave, which should be explored only by experienced speleologists.

The main road cutting across the waist of the island continues eastward from Lefkes, passing through the villages of Prodromos and Marpissa, with a deviation to Marmara, before finally reaching the sea at Piso Livadi. Those making the trip on foot would be well advised to take the old Byzantine road, a well-paved stone path that originally extended all the way across the island from Paroikia to Piso Livadi.

Prodromos is named for its seventeenth-century church, dedicated to St John the Forerunner. In times past the village was called Dragoulas, a corruption of Tragoulos, which took its name from an ancient shrine of Apollo Tragos, the Goat God. The shrine has vanished, but the ancient architectural fragments built into the walls of the village houses may have been parts of its structure. The entrance to the village is particularly picturesque, as the road passes through an archway between a pair of chapels, both dating from 1687. There are two abandoned seventeenth-century monasteries in the near vicinity of the village, one dedicated to Agios Pandeleimon and the other to Konda Panagia, Our Lady Nearby.

Marmara takes its name from the large number of architectural fragments of marble (in Greek, '*marmara*') found in and around the village. These fragments range in date from the Graeco–Roman age through the Byzantine and Latin eras, and many of them have been reused in the local churches and houses. Several old houses have over their doorways marble coats of arms of the former Latin aristocracy. A number of marbles of the Classical period are collected in the courtyard of the village church, dedicated to St John and the Dormition of the Virgin, which was built before 1639. Carved marble fragments of the Byzantine period are built into the church of Agia Savvas, dated 1608, which is on the road between Marmara and the beach at Molos. Farther along this road there is another seventeenth-century church, dedicated to Pera Panagia, Our Lady Beyond, whose courtyard has a number of Byzantine marble fragments.

The village of Marpissa takes its name from the goddess Marpessa, a granddaughter of Ares who married the hero Idas, whose exploits include sailing with Jason in search of the Golden Fleece and killing the Boar of Calydon.

Beginning at the windmills above Marpissa, a path leads out to Akri Kefalos, the easternmost cape of Paros. En route, you pass the ruined sixteenth-century Venetian monastery of Agios Antonios. The cape itself is dominated by the ruins of the fortress of Kefalo, built late in the fourteenth century by Niccolo Sommaripa, Duke of Paros. Bernardo Sagredo, the last Duke of Paros, fought to the death defending this fortress against the Turks in 1537. Now, all that remains are some fragments of the fortress walls and several chapels, all in utter ruins except for one dedicated to the Dormition of the Virgin, dated by an inscription to 1410.

From Marpissa one can drive all the way around the southern coast of the island on the way back to Paroikia, with detours down to the beaches at Piso Livadi, Chrisi Akti, Pounda, Mezada, Glyfa, Alyki and Voutakos, as well as inland to a number of old monasteries.

The beach at Glyfa on the south coast is bounded to its east by a promontory known as Pirgaki, which takes its name from a ruined Hellenistic *pyrgos*, where archaeologists have excavated tombs from a Bronze Age settlement.

Above the beach at Glyfa there is a small fortified monastery dedicated to Agios Ioannis Spiliotis, St John of the Cave, so called because its *katholikon* is built inside a grotto in the hillside. At the entrance there is a marble stele with an inscription in classical Greek, and inside the chapel there is an ancient marble column now used as a candelabrum. These antiquities have led to the suggestion that the church is built on the site of a temple of Artemis. The church celebrates a *paneyeri* on 8 May, the feast day of St John the Theologian. Legend has it that during the *Turkokrateia* the local villagers once took refuge here during a corsair raid and were saved by a miracle. St John turned the door of the church to stone so that the pirates could not make their way in, and he opened up a tunnel into the hill so that the villagers could escape, as an old woman told me one day, blessing herself repeatedly.

A road leads inland from Angeria to the monastery of Agioi Theodoroi, founded in the seventeenth century and completely rebuilt in 1928. Agioi Theodoroi is now a convent inhabited by some two dozen nuns. The nuns, when not at their devotions, work at their looms making bedspreads, tapestries, embroideries and carpets, all on commissions from their customers, who supply the materials.

A track looping north from Agioi Theodoroi leads to the monastery of the Analypsis (Ascension), where a few monks support themselves by the sale of honey from their beehives. The monks here, as well as the nuns at Agioi Theodoroi, are known as *palaeomerologites*, or 'old calenderites', since they observe their holy days according to the old calendar.

The main road north from Angeria to Paroikia passes the Paros airfield, after which there is a turn-off on the right for the village of Kambi. The road continues beyond Kambi to the fortified monastery of Agios Haralambos and then on to Dafnes, a hamlet set among gardens and vineyards under the western slope of Mount Agioi Pantes.

Three kilometres beyond the Kambi road there is a turn-off on the left to Pounda, from where there is a ferry service across the narrowest part of the strait between Paros and Antiparos. There is also a ferry service to Antiparos from Paroikia.

***

Ferries cross to the village of Antiparos, which rests near the northern tip of the island. Most of the 1,057 inhabitants of the island of Antiparos live in the village, which has a number of hotels and restaurants, for tourists are now spending holidays there rather than just coming on a day trip to see its famous cave.

Antiparos was ruled by the Dukes of Naxos from 1207 until 1440, when Crusino I Sommaripa became Duke of Paros and gave the island to his son-in-law Giovanni Loredano. Loredano rebuilt the fortress that protected the village of Antiparos, and he brought in Venetian colonists to resettle the island, which had been virtually abandoned because of raids by Turkish corsairs. But the Turks struck again in 1470, and after that raid a traveller reported that there were only about a hundred people left on the island. Loredano's descendants continued to hold Antiparos up until a few years before Barbarossa's raid, when the island was ruled for a time by the Quirini.

The principal monument in the village is the cathedral, a large domed edifice near the *plateia*; this is dedicated to Agios Nikolaos and dates from the seventeenth century. Two other village churches are the Evangelismos, built in 1660, and Agios Athanasios, which also appears to date from the mid-seventeenth century. There are still a number of old Cycladic houses in the back streets of the village, and even a few mansions dating from Ottoman times. The oldest house appears to be one with a marble plaque bearing the coat of arms of the Loredano family and the date 1611. Little remains of the Latin Kastro other than the foundations of a tower on a hill to the south of the village.

The great cave of Antiparos is some 6.5 kilometres south of the village along the east coast of the island. One can proceed there either by bus or by boat, with donkeys available to take visitors up the last stretch to the cavern entrance, which is on the hill of Agios Ioannis. Just inside the overhanging shelf of rock at the mouth of the cave there is a chapel dedicated to Agios Ioannis Spiliotes, dated 1774.

In the past one had to descend into the lower depths of the cave, 50 metres below, by a series of ropes and ladders, but now a flight of 400 cement steps makes the descent much easier. The stairway leads to a series of three chambers, the second of which is known as the Cathedral and the third as the Royal Hall. The Cathedral is so named because it is some 40 metres high; an enormous stalagmite at its south-west corner, which Bent estimated to be 24 feet high and 20 feet in diameter at the base, is known as the Altar. An inscription in Latin on the base of the stalagmite commemorates its use as an altar in the celebration of a Roman Catholic Mass in the cave at Christmas 1673. The Mass referred to in the inscription was part of a three-day extravaganza held by the Marquis de Nointel, French ambassador to the Sublime Porte, accompanied by an entourage of some five hundred followers, who, according to Bent, included 'his domestics, merchants, corsairs, timid natives who were bribed by largesses – any, in fact, who were willing to follow him'.

> It must have been a most impressive sight, that midnight mass in the bowels of the earth. A hundred torches of yellow wax and four hundred lamps burning day and night illuminated the place, and men posted in every available

space, on stalactites [actually stalagmites] and in crevices all the way to the entrance, gave notice by the waving of handkerchief one to the other at the moment of the elevation of the host, and at the given moment explosives were let off at the entrance of the cavern, and trumpets sounded, to herald the event to the world.

Other visitors to the cave included Tournefort, King Otho of Greece, and also Byron, who carved his name into the walls. Beyond the cave is the bay of Agios Yiorgios on the south-western shore of the island, where there is anchorage for fisherman and a beach with a taverna. The beach looks out across a narrow strait to the uninhabited islet of Despotiko, where goatherds graze their flocks during the summer.

A short way inland from Agios Yiorgios a track leads upward to the summit of Mount Profitis Ilias, the highest peak on Antiparos, at an altitude of 306 metres, from where there is a sweeping view of Paros and the south-western Cyclades.

Here one might recall the words that Archilochus wrote as a farewell to his native island, perhaps before the expedition to Thasos in which he lost his life: 'Goodbye to Paros, the figs and the seafaring life.'

Antiparos: population 1,057; area 35 sq km; Mt. Profitis Ilias (306 m); boats from Paros; hotel in Antiparos village.

Paros: population 12,783; area 197 sq km; Mt. Agioi Pantes (777 m); ferries from Piraeus (95 mi) and Rafina (71 mi); airport; hotels in Paroikia, Naoussa, Santa Maria, Piso Livadi, New Golden Beach, Parasporos, Drios, Asteras and Pounda.

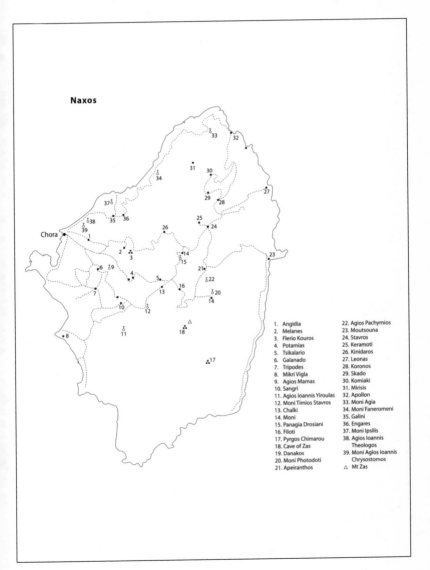

Naxos

Chora

1. Angidia
2. Melanes
3. Flerio Kouros
4. Potamias
5. Tsikalario
6. Galanado
7. Tripodes
8. Mikri Vigla
9. Agios Mamas
10. Sangri
11. Agios Ioannis Yiroulas
12. Moni Timios Stavros
13. Chalki
14. Moni
15. Panagia Drosiani
16. Filoti
17. Pyrgos Chimarou
18. Cave of Zas
19. Danakos
20. Moni Photodoti
21. Apeiranthos

22. Agios Pachymios
23. Moutsouna
24. Stavros
25. Keramoti
26. Kinidaros
27. Leonas
28. Koronos
29. Skado
30. Komiaki
31. Mirisis
32. Apollon
33. Moni Agia
34. Moni Faneromeni
35. Galini
36. Engares
37. Moni Ipsilis
38. Agios Ioannis Theologos
39. Moni Agios Ioannis Chrysostomos
△ Mt Zas

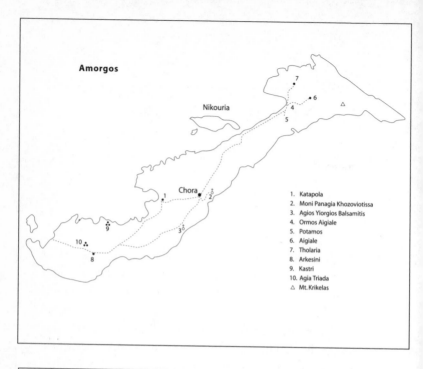

Amorgos

Nikouria

Chora

7

6

4

5

△

1. Katapola
2. Moni Panagia Khozoviotissa
3. Agios Yiorgios Balsamitis
4. Ormos Aigiale
5. Potamos
6. Aigiale
7. Tholaria
8. Arkesini
9. Kastri
10. Agia Triada
△ Mt. Krikelas

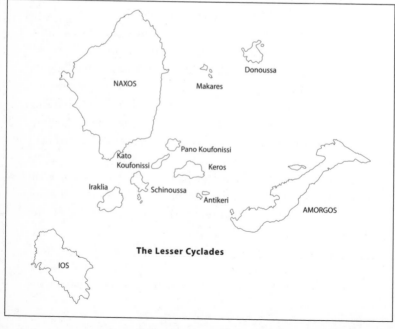

NAXOS

Makares

Donoussa

Pano Koufonissi

Kato
Koufonissi

Keros

Iraklia

Schinoussa

Antikeri

AMORGOS

IOS

The Lesser Cyclades

twelve
Naxos

Naxos has always been associated with the legend of Ariadne, abandoned there by Theseus and then found by Dionysos, who had come to the island in his youth after he escaped from the pirates who had kidnapped him. Another legend tells of how Dionysos was reared on Naxos by the nymphs who lived in the mountainous interior of the island, where their cult survived up until relatively recently, as did that of Ariadne.

Naxos, the largest of the Cyclades, is the quintessential Greek island, famed since antiquity for its beauty and abundance. Herodotus called Naxos 'the richest island in the Aegean'. It is by far the most fertile of the Cyclades, growing more vegetables, fruit, grain and olives than are needed on the island, and exporting the surplus. The principal crop is the potato, which is grown mostly in the Livadi, the coastal plain inland from the Chora. Another export is marble, which even in ancient times was quarried here in larger quantities than on Paros.

Naxos was the most important island in the Cyclades up until the beginning of the Classical period but after the abortive attempt of the Naxians to withdraw from the Delian League in 470 BC the island lost its primacy in the archipelago.

Naxos came into prominence again in 1210, when Marco I Sanudo made it the capital of the Duchy of the Archipelago, building a fortress known as Kastro on the acropolis of Chora, the port and capital of the island. His dynasty lasted until 1383, when it was supplanted by that of the Crispi, who ruled until the beginning of the *Turkokrateia*.

When Barbarossa ravaged Paros in 1537 Duke Giovanni IV Crispo came to an agreement with the Turkish admiral, allowing the Turks to take all the booty they could carry, and promising to pay an annual tribute of 5,000 gold ducats, the first instalment to be paid immediately. Thus Naxos escaped the fate of Paros, but the days of Latin rule were numbered.

The Duchy of the Archipelago lingered on until 1566, when the last of the Crispi dynasty, Giacomo IV, was imprisoned in Istanbul by Sultan Selim II. The sultan then appointed as Duke of Naxos his intimate friend and financial advisor Joseph Nasi, a Portuguese Jew who had moved to Istanbul. Nasi himself never made an appearance on Naxos, governing there through his agent, a Spanish Jew named Francesco Coronello. In 1571 the Venetians made an abortive attempt to restore Giacomo IV, who had been languishing in prison for five years, but the Turks ousted him and he died soon afterwards. Joseph Nasi himself continued his absentee rule as Duke of Naxos until his death in 1576, after which the island came under the direct rule of the Sublime Porte.

During the two and a half centuries of Ottoman rule Naxos was never really occupied by the Turks. The Turkish government sent a Cadi, or Judge, who merely administered the sultan's laws and saw to it that the yearly head tax on Christians was paid.

The most prominent landmark for ships approaching Chora is the colossal marble gateway on the little islet to its north, which in modern times has been connected to the *paralia* of the town by a causeway. The islet is known locally as Palatia, from the legend that the gateway was the entrance to the palace of Ariadne, whose cult on Naxos was intertwined with that of Artemis.

The gateway on the islet was actually the western portal of a temple erected in the third quarter of the sixth century BC by the tyrant Lygdamis, but which was never finished. All that remains today are the platform of the temple, some scattered columns and architectural fragments, and the western portal, made from five massive blocks of Naxian marble. In the past it was generally assumed that the temple was dedicated to Dionysos, because of the wine god's mythical association with Naxos and his romance with Ariadne. But now archaeologists have identified it as a temple of Delian Apollo, whose birthplace on Delos can be seen from Palatia on a clear day.

The most familiar landmark in the harbour is the Panagia Myrtidiotisa, Our Lady of the Myrtles, a picturesque chapel standing on a tiny islet off the foot of the pier in the centre of the port. The islet is actually part of the original mole that Marco Sanudo built in 1207. The chapel is only open on the feast day of the Myrtidiotisa, 25 September, when everyone makes a little pilgrimage to the islet, for Our Lady of the Myrtles is revered as the protectress of Naxos.

The bronze statue on the *paralia* is a monument to Petros Protopapadakis (1860–1922), a native of the Naxian village of Apeiranthos. Protopapadakis served as prime minister for a short time in 1922, at the end of the Graeco–Turkish War. He and five other members of his government were executed by a military junta after their government was overthrown in the autumn of 1922.

The Catholic church of Agios Antonios stands at the north end of the *paralia*, near the causeway to Palatia. The church was founded before 1440 by the dowager duchess Francesca Crispo, wife of Giovanni II and mother of Giovanni III. In 1452 the duchess bestowed the church on the Knights Hospitallers of St John, since her late husband had been a commander of the order.

The daily life of Chora centres on the *plateia*, the arcaded square just off the *paralia* by the old Venetian mole. The alley leading off from the *paralia* to the right was once the main street between the port and the upper town, but in the late 1950s it was hemmed in by the modern buildings erected along the seafront.

At the end of this street a narrow alley to the left leads to the church of Agios Profitis Ilias, built *c.* 1440 by the duchess Francesca Crispo. The church possesses two icons by Angelo the Cretan, a teacher of El Greco. On the façade of the church a stone tablet displays the imperial monogram of the Palaeologi, the last dynasty to rule over the Byzantine Empire (1259–1453). The monogram consists of the letter B (for *Basileos*, or King), repeated four times, signifying the motto of the dynasty: 'King of Kings, who King it over Kings.' A branch of the Palaeologos family has lived on Naxos since the days of Byzantium, and a few of them are still in residence today.

There are 20 churches in Chora that date in foundation to Byzantine times, though nearly all have been heavily rebuilt in the past century or so. Perhaps the oldest of these is Agios Yiorgios stin Grotta, which is just a short distance in from the Catholic church of Agios Antonios on the *paralia*. Grotta is the name of the ancient quarter in which it stands, where archaeologists have unearthed a burial ground of the Early Cycladic period.

The largest church in Chora is the Metropolitan Cathedral, which is dedicated to Agios Nikodemos and Agios Nektarios. The cathedral was built during the years 1780–1787 on the site of an earlier church of the Zoodochos Pigi, whose dedication is perpetuated in a side chapel. According to tradition, the Gospel used in the cathedral was presented to the church by Catherine the Great. The outer courtyard of the cathedral occupies the site of the ancient *agora* of Naxos, sections of which have been excavated and now form an attractive archaeological site and museum.

The oldest and most picturesque quarter of the lower town is the Borgo, which is situated just inside the *plateia* and the northernmost stretch of the *paralia*. The Borgo is a labyrinth of narrow alleyways and stepped streets below Kastro, its arched passages sometimes burrowing through the maze of Cycladic houses in what the Venetians call *sottoporticos*, probably taking its present form when Marco Sanudo established his capital on Naxos.

The main entrance to the Borgo is Kato Porto tou Yialou, the Lower Shore Gate, a marble portal at the upper right-hand corner of the *plateia*. The narrow alleyway leading off to the left through the gateway is Odos Agios Nikodemos, named after the patron saint of Naxos, who was born in 1749 in a house that still stands a short way down the left side of the street. The feast day of Agios Nikodemos is 14 July, a public holiday celebrated by a parade and other festivities in Chora.

The most direct way up to Kastro is via the stepped street that ascends to the right from Kato Porta tou Yialou. The street ends at the north gate of Kastro, which is dominated on its left by a splendid medieval tower. Known as the Glezos Pyrgos, this is the only one of the original seven towers of Marco Sanudo's fortress of 1207 to remain standing and in its original form, for the others were all rebuilt and converted into residences by the Latin aristocrats in Kastro. The north gate itself is also part of Marco Sanudo's original fortress.

The descendants of the Latin nobility still live on in Kastro today, their coats of arms displayed over the doorways of their towered mansions along the ramparts. Among the Latin families of noble lineage still living in Kastro are the Sommaripa, Barozzi and Dellarokka, the first two descended from rulers of Paros and Santorini and the third from the de la Roche dynasty who ruled as Dukes of Athens in the thirteenth century. The Dellarokka residence now houses the Venetian Museum.

The remains of the central tower of Marco Sanudo's fortress stands at the centre of Kastro. The tower, which has numerous marble columns and other ancient architectural fragments built into its rubble structure, now serves as the main cistern for Chora.

Just beyond the tower is the Roman Catholic cathedral, the Capella Casazza, built in the fourteenth century and heavily restored in the 1950s. On the pavement inside the church one can still make out several coats of arms of the noble families who once ruled Naxos and other isles of the Cyclades. The most precious possession of the church is a Byzantine icon of the Virgin.

At the south end of Kastro's ramparts is the former French Commercial School, one of the earliest educational institutions to be established in Ottoman Greece. It was founded by the Jesuits in 1627 as a free school for boys, both Catholic and Orthodox, and it had the unique distinction of having had its charter approved by both a pope, Urban IV, and a sultan, Murat IV. The Cretan writer Nikos Kazantzakis was a student at the French School for a few months in 1896, when he was 11 years old, and though his stay was brief he treasured the education he received there for having opened up new horizons for him. But his father feared that Nikos was being converted to Catholicism, and one night he appeared at the door of the school, threatening to burn it down unless they freed his son. As Kazantzakis writes of this incident in *Report to Greco*: "'My boy!' called my father, waving the lighted torch, "My boy, you papist dogs, or else it's fire and the axe!"'

The French School was eventually closed, and in 1972 the building was reopened as the Naxos Archaeological Museum, one of the finest local museums in Greece. The most fascinating exhibits are the marble figurines found in the 36 Bronze Age burial sites on Naxos, most of them representations of the Cycladic fertility goddess. Besides Cycladic figurines and pottery, there are also exhibits dating from the Mycenaean, Geometric, Archaic, Classical, Hellenistic and Roman periods, as well as some from the Byzantine and Latin eras, evidence of the continuous human occupation of Naxos over five millennia.

Next to the museum is the Ursiline Convent and its former girls' school, both founded in 1672. In its time the convent school was one of the finest institutions of its kind in Greece, but unfortunately it closed just a year after its third centennial, evidence of the waning influence of the Roman Catholic Church in the Aegean.

There is a tiny beach in Chora, on the shore of the causeway leading out to the Palatia islet, where the townspeople have always taken their *banyo* in late afternoon during the summer months. The nearest proper beach is Agios Yiorgios, which is just beyond the headland to the south of the port. There are much better beaches along the south-west shore of the island at Agios Prokopios and Agia Anna, served by a frequent boat service from the Chora. Farther along the south-west coast there are superb beaches at Plaka, Mikri Vigla, Kastraki and Agiasou.

Most visitors make their first tour of Naxos by taking the bus to Apollon, a tiny port at the northern end of the island. Those with their own transport can return along the coast road from Apollon to Chora.

There are a number of excursions than can be made from Chora into the interior of the island. The shorter excursions can be made entirely on foot along old mule trails leading inland from Chora, whereas on the longer treks one might take a morning bus out into the interior and then catch the last one back. Many of these mule trails are paved in marble, and were used long before the first roads were laid down in the mid-nineteenth century.

The closest village to the Chora is Angidia, set at the base of the first ridge east of the town, approached by a turn-off to the left from the main road. About halfway to Angidia on the right is the Catholic church of the Evangelismos, built in 1535 as the *katholikon* of a Venetian monastery known as the Fraros. On the hillside across the road from the church a dense growth of cactus almost completely obscures the ruins of a small classical temple, of which there remains only the *stylobate*, or platform, and a few column drums.

The road goes on to Angidia, with a turn-off to the right leading via a rough track to the Melanes Valley. Here the track links up with the road leading to the head of the Melanes Valley, while just below is the road to the Potamias. Off to the right of the Potamias road there is an old Venetian villa in the midst of its *perivoli*, or garden, a place still known as Aphendiko, 'the lord's domain'. This is where Marco III Dalle Carceri was assassinated in 1383, supposedly by the henchmen of Francesco Crispo, who then succeeded him as Duke of Naxos.

The walk to Angidia can be extended on into the Melanes Valley via the hamlet of Agios Thalaleos. At the head of the valley beyond Agios Thalaleos the resplendent Dellarokka Pyrgos stands as a landmark in Kouronochori. This is one of a constellation of four villages that together make up Melanes, the others being Miloi, Agioi Apostoloi, and Melanes itself. Bent describes Melanes as 'a spot of fairy-like beauty, buried in a narrow gorge, in a nest of olives, oranges, pomegranates, and cypresses'.

Kouronochori takes its name from the Flerio *kouros*, which is approached by a rough road that leads around above the village to the upper end of the Melanes valley. Down in the valley below there are the ruins of a Venetian chapel, all that is left of the Flerio monastery, from which the surrounding vale and the *kouros* take their name.

The *kouros*, some 5.5 metres in length, lies in a lovely *perivoli*, whose owner operates a rustic café for the visitors who come to see the colossal archaic statue in his garden. Like others of its type, the *kouros* here is an idealised representation of a young man personifying Apollo, intended to stand in a sanctuary of the god, probably on Delos. The form of the archaic youth is beautiful and finely carved, a strangely touching figure resting on his back with a stone pillow beneath his head, appearing as if he had fallen into an enchanted sleep, dreaming eternally in the dappled shade of the *perivoli*.

The Flerio *kouros* has been dated to the period 575–550 BC and classified on artistic grounds as one of the Tenea-Volomandra Group, so called for the superb *kouroi* of those names in the museums at Munich and Athens, respectively.

There is another *kouros* on the hilltop above the Flerio vale. This rarely visited *kouros* is almost identical with the one below, and its site is almost equally romantic. Naxian legend has it that these two *kouroi* are the petrified figures of Otus and Ephialtes, the twin giants who were slain by Apollo. Homer mentions them in Book XI of the *Odyssey*, where he writes: 'It was their ambition to pile Mount Ossa on Olympos and wooded Pelion on Ossa, so as to make a stairway up to heaven.' But Apollo 'destroyed them both before the down came curling on their cheeks and decked their chins with its fleecy mantle'.

There is a well-marked trail that leads from Flerio over the rocky hills to Ano Potamia. The trail ends at the church of Agios Ioannis Theologos, where a never-failing spring supplies all three villages in this paradisiacal valley, its water flowing down from Ano Potamia through the gardens and orchards of Mesi Potamia and Kato Potamia. Just opposite the fountain-house is the taverna of Ano Potamia, its courtyard surrounded by a flower garden, a fruit orchard and an olive grove, where you can take your ease in the shade of a giant plane tree after the long hike from the Chora.

Down in the valley there is a Venetian *pyrgos* that once belonged to the Coccos family, with an abandoned Byzantine chapel in its *perivoli*, now overgrown. Bent describes the *pyrgos* as being 'quite like a villa in Turcany, buried in olive and citron groves'.

A rough road leads from Ano Potamia to Chalki via the hamlets of Chimarros and Tsikalario. Tsikalario is at the foot of a rocky crag surmounted by the barely visible ruins of a medieval fortress. This is Apano Kastro, a castle built by Marco II Sanudo soon after he became Duke of Naxos in 1262. The site is a very ancient one, and a cemetery of the Geometric period has been excavated below the peak near Tsikalario, its site marked by a huge upright stone identical to the menhirs of Ireland and other northern European countries.

The first bus stop along the main road from Chora to Apollon is Galanado, which is one of a constellation of three hamlets set in the hills above the Livadi plain, the other two being Glinado and Agios Arsenios. The village church in Galanado is dedicated to the Exaltation of the Cross, whose *paneyeri* is celebrated on 14 September. On that day it was the custom for local farmers to bring to the church the seeds which they would use during the coming year. After the priest blessed these seeds each farmer mixed them with the rest of his grain, saying: 'Come Jesus and Mary, bring me wealth and good fortune.'

A secondary road leads south from Galanado to Tripodes, distinguished by the three windmills on the ridge that rises above it to the west. The village has recently reverted to its ancient name of Biblios, which is mentioned in Book XI of the *Odyssey* by Homer, who places the deaths of Opus and Ephialtes there.

A trail leads south-west from Tripodes through the region known as Plaka, which begins at the southern end of the Livadi plain. About halfway along this trail you come to the impressive ruins of an ancient structure known variously as Palaeopyrgos or Pyrgos Plakas, which appears to have been a Hellenistic watchtower.

A few hundred metres beyond the tower is the Byzantine church of Agios Mattheos, which appears to date from the eleventh or twelfth century. The church still has remnants of a mosaic pavement, and in its precincts there are fragments of classical columns and capitals. It would appear that the church was built on the site of an ancient temple, though the dedication and date of this sanctuary are unknown.

The road comes to an end at the beautiful beach of Plaka, which stretches for three kilometres from Agia Anna to Akri Parthenos, one of the western capes of Naxos. The rocky promontory on the southern side of Cape Parthenos is Mikri Vigla, where archaeologists have found evidence of a Mycenaean settlement. From Mikri Vigla another superb beach stretches off for more than a kilometre to Kastraki.

Just beyond Galanado the main road passes the Bellonia Pyrgos, a recently restored Venetian tower-house that was once the residence of the Catholic Archbishop of Naxos. On the grounds of the *pyrgos* there is a double church dating from the Latin period, with one chapel belonging to the Greek Orthodox and the other to the Roman Catholic faith, both of them dedicated to Agios Ioannis.

The main road now passes south of the lush vale of Drymalia with its three villages of Kato, Mesi and Ano Potamia. At the bottom of the valley, below the main road, is the Byzantine church of Agios Mamas. The church was built in the second half of the ninth century, and during the later Byzantine period it served as the seat of the Greek Orthodox Archbishop of the Cyclades. After the conquest of Naxos by Marco Sanudo the church was given over to the Roman Catholic archbishop, and from then on it was little used, for the great majority of the Greeks remained Orthodox in their faith. In the course of time Agios Mamas was abandoned and fell into ruins, but it has since been restored.

Farther along the main road the twin villages of Kato and Ano Sangri come into view, clustered at the upper end of a long and fertile valley that extends down to the south-western shore of the island. Off in the fields to the left of the main road there is a handsome old tower-house surrounded by a stand of cypresses. This *pyrgos* and its surrounding *perivoli* still belong to a local branch of the Palaeologos family, the last dynasty to rule Byzantium.

There are a number of interesting places to be seen in the region south of Ano and Kato Sangri. Both villages have Venetian tower-houses, the oldest being the Sommaripa Pyrgos in Ano Sangri. Ano Sangri is also the site of Moni Agios Eleftherios, one of the oldest monasteries on Naxos, probably dating from the Byzantine period.

The most interesting site in this region is Agios Ioannis Yiroulas, which is about half an hour's walk from Ano Sangri on a trail leading south from the village. Agios Ioannis is a small Byzantine chapel constructed on the site of an early Christian basilica, which was itself built on the *stylobate* of an ancient temple. Recent excavations revealed that the temple was erected in 530–520 BC and was dedicated to Demeter. Parts of the temple and its collonade have been re-erected to create a superb archaeological site with a small museum.

Beyond the turn-off to Ano and Kato Sangri the main road veers left around the steep eminence known as Profitis Ilias, crowned by a chapel to that saint. At the foot of the hill there is an abandoned but still well-preserved *pyrgos*-monastery dedicated to Timios Stavros, the True Cross, founded in the late seventeenth century. After the monastery was abandoned by its monks it reverted in 1834 to the new Greek state. Then in the late nineteenth century it was acquired by the Bazeos family, who still hold title to the pyrgos. Restoration of the pyrgos began in 2000, and today it serves as a cultural centre.

Once past Timios Stavros the main road enters the Tragaea, the richest and most beautiful region on the island, most of its villages barely visible among the olive groves that surround them and spread up onto the slopes of the Naxian mountains. Then the road crosses a narrow bridge and enters the serenity of the olive grove itself, passing on the right the hamlets of Damalas and Damarionas as it approaches Chalki, the main village of the Tragaea, which served as the capital of Naxos during the medieval Byzantine period.

Chalki is the best base for visiting the old churches and Venetian tower-houses of the Tragaea, where the village *kafenion* in the picturesque *plateia* is a convenient place to start and end explorations of a region that has always been the heart of Naxos.

The parish church of Chalki, the Panagia Protothrone, which is next to the bus stop, is dedicated to the Annunciation of the Virgin. The church has in recent years been the subject of intensive study, which has revealed five layers of paintings ranging from the early Byzantine era to the thirteenth century. An inscription at the base of the belfry records a reconstruction of the church in 1052.

A short way behind the Panagia Protothrone is the splendid Grazia Pyrgos, built at the beginning of the seventeenth century. Above the entryway is the coat of arms of the original owners of the *pyrgos*, the Barozzi – lords of Santorini and at various times rulers of several other islands in the Cyclades.

Several of the Byzantine churches in the Tragaea are in the olive groves just north of Chalki, and are best approached by the village street leading off in that direction. The street eventually becomes a path and leads directly to a chapel dedicated to Agia Marina, which has in its courtyard a holy well that is the principal source of water in this part of the Tragaea. The *paneyeri* of Agia Marina is celebrated here on 17 July, preceded by the *paranomi*, or prelude, a liturgy performed on the eve of the feast. The *paranomi* begins at sunset, when the people of Chalki walk to the chapel and thank Agia Marina for her gift of water, after which they return in procession to the village, their train of flickering candles winding its way through the olive groves at twilight.

A path leads from Agia Marina to the Byzantine church of Agios Yiorgios Diosoritis, which has several layers of frescoes, the earliest dating to the eleventh century, a total of 115 extant paintings.

The most beautiful of the Byzantine churches in the Tragaea is the Panagia Drosiani, the Virgin Fresh as Dew, which is in the olive groves just below Moni beside the Chalki road. The church seems to be part of the knoll on which it stands, for it is made from the undressed flat stones that are used for field walls throughout the olive groves. Three layers of wall paintings have been uncovered dating from the sixth century to the thirteenth. The paintings in the earliest layer are among the rare examples of Byzantine art prior to the Iconoclastic period.

The next bus stop on the main road beyond Chalki is Filoti, a large village overlooking the Tragaea from the north-west slope of Mount Zas, the highest peak in the Cyclades, 1,010 metres above sea level. Filoti is noted for its *paneyeri* of the Virgin in mid-August, when all of Naxos comes to celebrate a three-day festival that is truly a Dionysian revel.

Those who are prepared for a long and arduous hike might follow the road that leads south from Filoti to Pyrgos Chimarou and the south coast at Kalandros. Chimarou dates from the Hellenistic period and is the most impressive ancient *pyrgos* in the Cyclades, some seven metres in diameter and more than 20 metres high, built from large rectangular stone blocks carefully fitted together.

A trail heading off from the right side of the main road above Filoti leads to the great cave at Arghia, which is just under the sheer western face of Mount Zas at the head of a precipitous gorge. The entrance to the cave is a natural stone arch some ten metres wide and 2.5 metres high. This leads into the main chamber of the cave, one of the most spectacular in Greece, 115 metres long and 75 metres across at its widest point, its rock dome covering an area of more than 4,100 square metres without any internal support, looking like a vast subterranean cathedral. Obsidian tools found in the cave indicate that it was one of the first sites of human habitation on Naxos, dating back to the Neolithic period. Within a smaller inner chamber, opposite a huge boulder known as the Altar, there is an old cave sanctuary dedicated to the Panagia Zoodochos Pigi, where, according to Bent, 'a priest goes once a year in the summer time to hold a liturgy for the mountain shepherds'. The sanctuary is now abandoned, its life-giving spring having dried up in recent years, as have so many others on Mount Zas, the water table having dropped because of the enormous drain of tourism on the coast. Some years ago an old goatherd from Filoti told me that he no longer grazed his flock on the upper slopes of Zas as he and his forebears had since the beginning of time, for there was no longer enough water on the mountain.

Once past Filoti, the road climbs up the north-western slope of Zas and then turns northward along a ridge, with a breathtaking view out over the whole of the Tragaea and its surrounding mountains. At this point there is a turn-off on the right for Danakos, an isolated village on the north-east slope of Zas.

The ascent to the summit of Zas is best made from the Danakos road, where a trail leads off to the right from the chapel of Agia Marina. About 500 metres along the trail there is a spring of drinkable water, one of the few still flowing on the mountain. Nearby there is a marble block with an inscription in ancient Greek, stating that this is 'the mountain of Milesian Zeus'. The trail leads upward through olive groves and stands of holly oak, the way marked at intervals by old cairns and more recent red arrows. At the base of the conical summit one must leave the trail and climb upward along the steep rock face to the peak. The view is truly magnificent, and on the clearest days one can see all of the Cyclades, with Asia Minor off to the east, the Peloponnesos to the west, and the mountains of Crete to the south.

Danakos is a little hamlet nestling in a long gorge leading out to the eastern coast. The village church is dedicated to the Panagia Zoodochos Pigi, whose sacred spring is believed to have been an ancient shrine of Artemis.

A trail a few hundred metres long leads from Danakos to Moni Photodotis, the oldest and most impressive of the *pyrgos*-monasteries on the island. An inscription in the *katholikon* dates the church to 1497, but there is evidence that the monastery itself was founded in the Byzantine period. According to tradition, a monk returning to Photodotis from Constantinople in 1453 was the first to bring the news to Naxos that Byzantium had fallen to the Turks.

Beyond the Danakos turn-off the main road bends northward along a ridge, from which there is a magical view out over the whole of the Tragaea and its surrounding mountains. At the end of the ridge, at a chapel of Agios Ioannis Theologos, the road rises over a pass, and a view opens up over the north-eastern quarter of the island, revealing a succession of long and convoluted valleys extending down from the central ridge to the eastern coast.

Soon the conical peak of Mount Fanari looms above the road and just below it you finally see Apeiranthos, the most fascinating village on Naxos. Even at first sight Apeiranthos looks different from other Cycladic villages, for most of its houses are not whitewashed but have the stark grey shades of the rough stones from which they are built, looking as if they were part of the barren mountain itself. The Apeiranthians are different too, the descendants of Cretan refugees, described to Bent by other Naxiotes as 'a village of robbers'.

The principal entrance to Apeiranthos is at its eastern end, where a marble-paved street leads in past the village church of the Panagia Apeiranthissa, Our Lady of Apeiranthos. The church dates from the eighteenth century and is noted for its carved marble *iconostasis*, which has a number of interesting post-Byzantine icons.

The street leads in to the tiny *plateia*, which is dominated by the recently restored Zevgolis Pyrgos. Both this and the nearby Bardanis Pyrgos date from the Venetian period, as evidenced by the relief of the winged lion of St Mark that each of them has over its entryway, symbol of the Serene Republic of Venice.

There are several museums and other cultural institutions in the village. The Archaeological Museum has a collection of antiquities found locally, mostly pottery and other objects of the Early Cycladic period, the most interesting exhibits being a group of marble plaques with primitive carvings of scenes from everyday life in the Bronze Age, including a representation of three dancers. The Folklore Museum has a very interesting collection of objects used by Apeiranthians in their daily life, past and present, as well as re-creations of rooms in a typical Apeiranthos house. The Geological Museum is devoted to the local emery mining industry and the Art Gallery has works by noted Apeiaranthian artists. The library, founded in 1966 in memory of the local scholar Nikolaos N. Glezos, has an important collection of some 10,000 books.

The people of Apeiranthos are renowned for their distinctive form of folk poetry, the extemporaneous couplets which in Crete are called *mantinades*, known locally as *kotsakia*. These are recited or sung at weddings, baptisms and wakes, or even as greetings by those passing one another in the *plateia*, the theme depending on the time of day and the occasion, the quality of the *kotsakia* rising to the heights of lyric poetry when the occasion demands. One evening at a wedding in Apeiranthos we heard the groom's sister reciting a *kotsakia* to the bride, whose father had died just a few months before. 'If your father could see how happy you are tonight,' she sang, 'he would ask permission from Death to be at your side.'

The old trail to Danakos leads south from the lower end of Apeiranthos. After passing the chapel of Agios Vassilios the trail comes to the ruined Byzantine church of Agios Pachymios, which has an interesting tradition associated with it. Agios Pachymios was one of the founders of the monastic movement in Egypt, and in the Byzantine era he was venerated on Naxos in what was obviously the survival of an ancient fertility cult. The church of Agios Pachymios has a curious arched opening over the door, and in times past sick or emaciated babies were passed through this aperture as a symbolic rebirth which would make them healthier and fatter. This cult was still popular at the beginning of the Venetian period, and when Marco II Sanudo became Duke of Naxos in 1262 he attempted to end the superstitious practice. This only enraged the Greeks of Naxos, who rose up against the duke and besieged him in his fortress at Apano Kastro, until he finally relented and removed his ban on the cult of Agios Pachymios, which is still active, as I have been told in Apeiranthos.

Farther along, the trail comes to the Byzantine church of Agios Yiorgios, which has been dated by an inscription to 1252–1253, with fragments of its original wall paintings still visible.

Just beyond Apeiranthos there is a turn-off from the main road to the right for Moutsouna, a seaside hamlet that once served as a port for shipping the emery that was mined in the central mountains of Naxos.

The main road finally emerges from the shadow of Mount Fanari at the pass known as Stavros, the Cross. On the right at the crossroads there is a little chapel dedicated to Timios Stavros. This is a favourite stopping place for herdsmen and hikers, who often take shelter in the chapel from the winds that howl across this exposed pass from all quarters of the compass. Bent was led here by his guide Gabalas, a Cretan from Chalki, who did an impromptu dance at Stavros to demonstrate the wild motion of the winds.

> Presently we came to a particularly gusty spot. Gabalas informed us that this spot was called, as it justly deserved, 'the dancing-place of the winds' (*anemochoreftra*). 'And this is how they dance,' he said, as he went through some of the wild evolutions of the *syrtos* for our benefit, which has in it so much of the ancient Pyrrhic dance; and very funny he looked as he impersonated the antics of the winds on the mountain top.

Two secondary roads go off to the left at the Stavros crossroads, one leading to the isolated village of Keramoti and another to Moni, with a turn-off from the latter road leading to Kinidaros, site of the principal marble quarry on Naxos. The road to Moni passes through the deserted village of Sifones, abandoned by its inhabitants during the Second World War, when many of the islanders died of starvation. Sifones has never been resettled, but some of its former inhabitants return in the summer to look after their olive groves and vineyards.

Beyond Stavros the road makes a long bend to pass around the eastern slope of Mavrovouno, the Black Mountain, the second-highest peak in the Cyclades, with its summit 998 metres above sea level. Mavrovouno is the principal peak in the Koronis Mountains, named after one of the nymphs who are supposed to have raised Dionysos in a cave on Naxos. Local legend has identified the birthplace of Dionysos as Kako Spilion, the Bad Cave, a grotto on Mavrovouno, where a crude sanctuary with devotional oil lamps shows signs of recent use, indicating that local herders and farmers still consider this to be a sacred place.

The road makes a sharp bend as it approaches the mountain village of Koronos, passing two successive turn-offs to the right, the first leading to the monastery of the Panagia Argokilistria and the second to the tiny port of Leonas. Then the road passes in succession Koronos, Skado and Komiaki, three mountain villages famous for their wine and folk musicians.

Our favourite hike in the mountains of northern Naxos begins in Komiaki, from where a trail leads westward over a pass between two outlying peaks of Mount Koronis. Once over the pass the trail leads to the upper end of a steeply descending valley of astonishing fertility, approached by a stepped path paved in marble slabs. The path, which is said to have more than a thousand steps, leads down to the isolated hamlet of Mirisis, which in Greek means 'fragrant', an appropriate name for a place whose air is scented with thyme, rosemary, oregano and other aromatic plants. Mirisis is inhabited by people from Komiaki, who come down here in the summer months to tend their farms, orchards, olive groves and vineyards. They make their own bread, cheese and wine, slaughtering their sheep and goats for meat that they grill on a spit over a charcoal fire, drawing water from their wells and living entirely on the produce of their land, a way of life that has not changed since time immemorial.

Beyond Komiaki the main road descends in a series of hairpin turns and finally comes to an end at Apollon, a little port at the northern end of Naxos that has in recent years become a summer resort.

On the hillside above Apollon there is a huge archaic *kouros*. This is a partially completed statue of a youth, 10.5 metres in length, apparently hewn *in situ c.* 600 BC on the marble hillside, where it was abandoned when it broke before completion. The Apollon *kouros* looks as if he has a long beard, but this is merely a piece of uncut marble below his chin.

The secondary road back along the north-west coast from Apollon to Chora is not nearly as scenic as the main road through the mountains, but there are a number of interesting sites to be seen along the way.

About eight kilometres out of Apollon the road comes to the monastery of the Panagia, known locally as Moni Agia. The monastery was founded in 1717 by the Cocco family, who built several *pyrgoi* on Naxos in the seventeenth and eighteenth centuries. The Cocco were originally from Venice, but in time they became so Hellenised that they led the Greeks on Naxos in several bloody disputes with the Latin aristocracy. The monastery is no longer functioning, but the *paneyeri* of the Dormition of the Virgin is still celebrated here on 15 August.

This is the purest and most old-fashioned of the *paneyeria* on Naxos, without crowds or amplified music, just a few families who bring along their own food and drink and sleep rough in the courtyard of the monastery on the eve of the feast day, when they join with the village priest in the liturgy and then dance to the accompaniment of their own instruments.

About seven kilometres beyond the monastery a dirt road leads down to the little seaside resort of Abram. Then, after passing the tiny hamlet of Chilia Vryssi, you reach the abandoned Moni Faneromeni, a monastery, founded in the seventeenth century. The monastery was still inhabited when Bent rode this way, and he writes of the icon that was shown to him by the monks. 'They have in their possession the most miraculous picture on Naxos, which was found, they told me, in the ground by the sailors of a ship, who were fleeing from the fall of Constantinople in 1453, and who were attracted to this spot by a mysterious light.'

The shortest route back to town from the Engares Valley is by the old trail that begins at Galini, where the pretty blue-domed parish church, the Panagia Monasteriotissa, Our Lady of the Monastery, dates back to the Byzantine period.

The road then curves inland to Engares, the principal village on the north-western coast of the island. This is actually a constellation of five villages at the head of the only fertile valley on the north-west coast, the two largest being Engares itself and Galini, from where there is a dirt road leading down to the sea at the Amites beach. Near the end of this road is Moni Ipsilis, one of most impressive *pyrgos*-monasteries on the island. The monastery, which is dedicated to the Panagia Ipsilitera, Our Lady of the Higher Land, was founded in 1600 by Ioakovo Cocco, of the same aristocratic family who built the monastery at Agia.

The last stretch of the coast road, from Galini to Chora, passes only a few farm huts and a chapel dedicated to the Holy Cross. Some two kilometres before reaching the Chora there is a small chapel in a grotto high on the rocky cliff to the left. The chapel is dedicated to Agios Ioannis Theologos, and is thought to date from the twelfth century. According to tradition, the chapel was founded by monks from the monastery of St John the Theologian on Patmos, who are believed to have taken shelter in this grotto when they were shipwrecked on Naxos.

Just beyond this chapel is the convent of Agios Ioannis Chrysostomos, a handsome white *pyrgos* perched high on the hill that rises behind the Chora. The convent was founded in 1606 and rebuilt in 1757. It is the best-preserved of all the *pyrgos*-monasteries on Naxos, and at the time of our last visit there were still two nuns in residence.

My favourite excursion on Naxos is to a country taverna on the beach at Mikri Vigla, where most of the customers come by bus from Filoti to swim and have lunch there and whoop it up on weekends. The high point of the summer here is the *paneyeri* of Agia Paraskevi on 26 July, when the liturgy is held at the seaside chapel of the saint in Kastraki, followed by music and dancing at the taverna in Mikri Vigla. The songs are always *nisiotika tragoudia*, the traditional melodies of the Greek islands, most of them very old favourites, though every year the local composer Thanassis

Peristerakis writes a few new ones for Manolis Barbarakis, the renowned singer from Komiaki. One of these songs comes to mind whenever I think of Mikri Vigla, and its haunting refrain brings me back to Naxos on the wings of memory.

> The lute and the violin
> I long to hear again,
> To bring back the memory
> Of an old sweet song of love.

Naxos: population 17,646; area 389 sq km; Mt. Zas (1,010 m); ferries from Piraeus (103 mi) and Rafina (79 mi); airport; hotels in Chora, Agios Yiorgios, Agios Prokopios, Agia Anna, Agios Arsenios, Plaka, Orkos, Mikri Vigla, Kastraki, Galini-Engares.

thirteen
Amorgos and the
Lesser Cyclades

I first saw Amorgos from the deck of a ship in the early 1960s, the pale glow of dawn tinting the serried mountains of the elongated island, its shores still wreathed in the marine mist. There was no pier, and several rowboats had come out in the harbour to transport the passengers who would embark and disembark, but there were few of either, for Amorgos was then very much off the beaten track.

Amorgos is the easternmost of the Cyclades, 138 nautical miles from the Piraeus. In Bent's time it was the eastern limit of Greece in the Aegean, and he describes it as 'the remotest island of the Cycladic group, and the bulwark of the modern Greek Kingdom'.

The island is very long and narrow, measuring 33 kilometres from north-east to south-west, and only one to three kilometres in width. It has three mountain peaks: Krikelas (822 m), at the north-east end of the island; Profitis Ilias (699 m), in the centre; and Korax (607 m), at the south-west end. These peaks are connected by high and sharply crested ridges, so that viewed from an approaching ship the island resembles an enormous prehistoric amphibian, its flanks sloping steeply down from its humped spine, with stupendous limestone cliffs plunging dramatically into the sea at its south-western end.

Amorgos was once heavily wooded, but in 1835 a fire that began on Mount Krikelas destroyed most of the island's forests, so that its treeless hills are now covered only with sage, thyme, marjoram, dwarf oak, and patches of heather.

The present population of Amorgos is 1,873, less than half of what it was in Bent's time, for here as elsewhere in the Cyclades the remoteness and poverty of the island forced its people to leave in search of a better life. But the population has been rising in recent years because of the increased prosperity of Greece, particularly from tourism. As a result there are now daily ferries from Piraeus to Katapola, on the south-western coast, some also calling at the smaller port of Aigiale, farther to the north on the western shore.

There were three cities on Amorgos in classical times. One of these was Minoa, which was on the present site of Katapola; the others were Aigiale, which gave its name to the second port of Amorgos, and Arkesini, which was near the present village of that name near the south-western end of the island. All three of these cities were founded in the Archaic period, probably in the seventh century BC. Aigiale was settled by colonists from Miletos, Arkesini by Naxians, and Minoa by Samians, although its name suggests an earlier foundation by Minoans from Crete. But archaeological studies have indicated that all three of these sites were first inhabited early on in the Cycladic era.

The leader of the Samian expedition that founded Minoa was the poet Semonides (not to be confused with Simonides of Kea). Semonides, along with Archilochus of Paros, is credited with the invention of iambic poetry and 42 fragments of his own iambics survive, the longest and best-known being *An Essay on Women*. This is a bitter exercise in misogyny, attacking women of various types, whom for the most part Semonides compares to animals. The only exceptions were industrious women, whom 'God made from bees', and moody ones, whom he likens to the tempestuous sea.

During the Latin period Amorgos was usually ruled by the Dukes of Naxos, though on several occasions it came under the control of the Ghisi and the Quirini. In 1268, seven years after the Greeks regained Constantinople from the Latins, the Byzantine admiral Licario recaptured Amorgos, along with several other islands in the archipelago. Three decades later the Venetians defeated the Byzantines and their Genoese allies in a maritime war, after which Amorgos was restored to Latin rule, remaining part of the Duchy of the Archipelago until the islands were conquered by the Turks.

Amorgos suffered terribly from piracy during the *Turkokrateia*, and at one point the inhabitants left their island en masse to seek refuge on Naxos, returning only when the corsairs were put down by the French in the late seventeenth century. The last recorded corsair raid was in 1797, when a band of 70 pirates from Mani in the Peloponnesos attacked the island, pillaging the Chora while the local men were off on a fishing expedition.

Most travellers today land at Katapola, which is actually a collection of three small villages at the inner end of a deeply indented bay. These are Xilokeratidi, on the north shore of the bay; Rakidi, on a knoll above the inner end of the harbour, its principal landmark being the large church of Agios Yiorgios; and Katapola proper, to the south, where the landing stage is located, and from where a road leads up to Chora.

The acropolis of the ancient city of Minoa was on a hill above Katapola. The remains of Minoa include a gymnasium, a stadium, a temple of Pythian Apollo, and a necropolis, all excavated by the French School in 1888.

One of the sights of Katapola is its famous spring, whose excellent water is conducted by an ancient aqueduct to a Venetian well-house. High up above Katapola, where the road meets the old cobbled way to Chora, is the chapel of the Taxiarchis, an early Byzantine foundation with many ancient remains built into its structure. Other ancient remnants have been found in the chapel of Agia Eirene on the nearby hill to the north.

The coastal road leads to Xilokaritidi, whose oldest monument is the early Byzantine church of the Evangelistria. The feast day of the church is 25 March, the Annunciation, when everyone from the surrounding region celebrates the *paneyeri* here. The same path that leads to the Evangelistria goes on to Maltezi, where there is a good secluded beach.

Chora is a typical white Cycladic town, set at an altitude of 361 metres above the eastern shore of the island. Its white cubist houses cluster around the ruins of a Venetian fortress known as Apano Kastro, which is perched atop a huge spire of rock in the centre of the town. The fortress was built *c.* 1290 by the Ghisi, who at that time held Amorgos as a sub-fief from the Sanudi of Naxos.

An eighteenth-century mansion in the Chora houses the Archaeological Museum, which has a small collection of antiquities from sites all over the island. The oldest church in town, dedicated to the Panagia Elousa, treasures a miraculous Byzantine icon of the Virgin, which is almost covered with the metal ex-votos known as *tamata*, placed there in gratitude by those whose prayers were answered by the Virgin. There are said to be 40 churches in Chora, of which the smallest is the chapel of Agios Fanourios, which they say can only hold two people, one of whom would presumably be the priest.

The most famous monument on Amorgos is the monastery of the Panagia Khozoviotissa, about a kilometre north-east of the Chora on the coast. The setting of the monastery is spectacular, a white *pyrgos* perched on a ledge halfway up the side of a rocky cliff that drops sheer for 300 metres into the sea.

The monastery was founded in 1090 by the emperor Alexios I Comnenos to house a miraculous icon of the Virgin, which had washed up on the shore of Amorgos two years before, after having supposedly floated all the way from Cyprus. Two other treasures in the monastery are an old iron cross set in silver, said to have been discovered on Mount Krikelas, and an icon of Agios Yiorgios Balsamites, so called because it was found, like the True Cross, in a bed of balsam. The icon of St George was enshrined within its own chapel farther south along the coast in 1619, but because of the danger of corsair raids it was brought for safe keeping to the Khozoviotissa, where it remains to this day. On Easter Sunday the iron cross and the icons of the Virgin and St George are carried in procession from the monastery to a church in the Chora, the first stage in a week-long series of processions around the island; the second descending to Katapola for the annual blessing of the fishing fleet; the third ascending to a chapel on the summit of Mount Profitis Ilias; the fourth going to the shrine of Agios Yiorgios Balsamites; the fifth and last bringing the treasures home to the Khozoviotissa.

The chapel of Agios Yiorgios Balsamites is about two kilometres south of the Chora above the eastern coast. The view from its terrace is extraordinary, including Santorini and Anaphi, the south-easternmost of the Cyclades, as well as Astypalaia, the westernmost of the Dodecanese. The principal point of interest in the chapel is its holy well, which was believed to possess prophetic powers, perhaps one of the last functioning oracles in the Greek world, still consulted by pilgrims. Bent remarks on the popularity of the oracle in the early nineteenth century, when it was occasionally misused for evil purposes.

> At the beginning of this century and during the war of independence this oracle of Amorgos was consulted by thousands: sailors from all over the islands round would consult it prior to taking the important step of matrimony: but during the piratical days that followed, the discovery was made that evil-intentioned men would work the oracle for their own ends. The spot is unprotected and easy of approach from the sea, so the pirates would bribe the officiating mariner to his doom. Despite all of this the oracle is much consulted by the credulous, and reminds one forcibly of the shrine of Delphi of old...

Another road leads from Chora to the port of Ormos Aigiale near the northern end of the island. This part of Amorgos is so narrow that both coasts of the island are in view, with the satellite isle of Nikouria just a few hundred metres offshore to the west. In times past Nikouria housed a leper colony, but this was closed in the 1930s, and since then the island has been uninhabited.

Approaching Ormos Aigiale, one sees just outside the village an old chapel known as Exochoriani, which is built on the site of a classical temple of Athena. Ormos Aigiale is the port for the three pretty villages of Potamos, Aigiale and Tholaria, which are set around the end of a deeply indented gulf in one of the most beautiful regions of Amorgos. There are excellent beaches around the gulf at Levrossos, Psili Ammos and Hoklakas, and at Fokiotria there is a sandy cove with a marine cave where seals sometimes make their home.

Near Tholaria there is an ancient fortress known as Vigla, which has been identified as the site of ancient Aigiale, the third of the three classical cities of Amorgos. Around this fortress there are a number of vaulted Roman tombs, called *tholaria*, from the Greek *tholos*, or dome, from which the modern village takes its name.

There is another old fortress on a rocky crag above Aigiale. The fortress is surmounted by a tiny chapel dedicated to the Holy Trinity, which is still the site of a *paneyeri* celebrated on the seventh Monday after Easter.

A trail leads from Aigiale out to the north-eastern end of the island. En route the trail passes the ruined monastery of Agios Ioannis Theologos, which retains some Byzantine wall paintings. Farther along the trail comes to the chapel of Agios Stavros, from where a path leads to the summit of Mount Krikelas. The trail ends at the north-easternmost cape of Amorgos, where Mount Krikelas terminates in sheer cliffs that plunge directly into the sea, one of the most spectacular sights in the Cyclades.

The southernmost village on the island is Arkesini. The village rests on the north slope of Mount Korax and bears the name of one of the three cities of ancient Amorgos. The site of the ancient city is on the coast north of Vroutsis, on a rocky promontory known as Kastri which is surmounted by the remains of an ancient fortress, which seems to have been occupied from the Classical period on down to the Venetian era. Within it are the ruins of medieval houses and chapels interspersed with fragments of ancient architectural members, as well as inscriptions identifying it as the site of classical Arkesini. Archaeologists have also found pottery sherds dating back to the Early Cycladic period. The only identifiable building is an abandoned chapel dedicated to the Panagia Kastriani, Our

Lady of the Castle, which in times past was the site of a popular *paneyeri*.

A short way west of the village of Arkesini, at Agia Triada, there is a superb Hellenistic tower known as Pyrgos tou Choriou. Sherds found at Agia Triada indicate that the tower stands on the site of a Mycenaean fortress dating from the period 1500–1200 BC.

The village of Arkesini celebrates a *paneyeri* on the feast day of Agia Pareskevi, 26 July. A favourite song that you will always hear at this festival is *Amogiotissa* (The Girl from Amorgos).

> A girl from Amorgos wanted to travel,
> For passage on the ship she paid a hundred crowns,
> Three hundred more to keep her virtue.
> But when the ship was two miles out at sea
> The captain had his way with her and lay with her.
> The girl, from shame, fell in a faint,
> The captain, thinking she was dead,
> Seized her by the hair and threw her overboard.
> The sea cast her ashore on the coast of Italy,
> and the Italian girls going out for a walk
> Found her, washed up on the shore of Italy.
> Then the Italian girls began a funeral dirge:
> 'Ah, see her body, dressed in silk,
> The girdle round her waist,
> Her neck all polished smooth for pearls.'

Versions of this song also have been recorded elsewhere in Greece as well as in southern Italy, and are thought to date back to the fifteenth or sixteenth century. The Italian versions make the girl a prisoner on the ship, but in the Greek songs she is always free and independent, and she is always from Amorgos.

The women of Amorgos no longer wear the beautiful folk costumes that Bent saw when he attended a *paneyeri* here, the most distinctive element being the tower-like headgear known as a *tourlos*.

> One lady especially was resplendent: her *tourlos* was of green and red, her scarf an Eastern handkerchief, such as we now use for antimacassars; coins and gold ornaments hung in profusion over her breast, her stomacher was of

green and gold brocade, a gold sash around her waist, and a white crimped petticoat with flying streamers of pink and blue silk, pretty little brown skin shoes with red and green embroidery on them. She was an excellent dancer too, a real joy to look upon. The men wore their baggy trousers, bright-coloured stockings, and embroidered coats; but the men of Amorgos are not equal to the women. The beauty of an Amorgiote female is proverbial.

So much for Semonides and his diatribe against Amorgiote women.

***

Between Amorgos and Naxos there is a group of islands known as the Lesser Cyclades. These include Iraklia, Schinoussa, Pano Koufonissi, Kato Koufonissi, Keros, the Antikeri, the Makares and Donoussa. The only islands of this little archipelago that have a year-round population are Iraklia, Schinoussa, Pano Koufonissi and Donoussa, the others being inhabited only occasionally by fishermen and goatherds.

When we first went to Naxos in 1962 the Lesser Cyclades were almost completely cut off from the outside world. There were no regularly scheduled ferries other than one that would call at the inhabited isles once a week on its way between Naxos and Amorgos. There were no doctors, nurses, post offices or telephones, nor tourist facilities of any kind. If medical help was needed on one of the Lesser Cyclades the islanders would light a bonfire in the hope that it would be seen by a shepherd on Mount Zas, who would then ride into Filoti on his mule and get word to the Chora, whereupon the town doctor would summon a *caique* to take him out to the island. Early in the 1960s I accompanied Dr Ioannis Iordanis to one of these islands, Iraklia, where he arrived in time to save the life of a young man by extracting his appendix. The entire population of the island was there to wave goodbye to us when we left, the father of the young man having presented Dr Iordanis with a fat sheep as a gift of thanksgiving.

The situation has changed completely in recent years due to the development of tourism on the Lesser Cyclades. This has greatly increased their prosperity as well as the number of those living on the four inhabited islands, which now have regular ferry services. Regular ferries and hovercraft sail from both the Piraeus and Rafina to Donoussa, Pano Koufonissi, Schinoussa and Iraklia; and there are also boats from Katapola in Amorgos. Rooms can be rented on all of the inhabited islands, and there is also a small hotel on Iraklia. There are no cars on the islands, and so you must make your way around on foot (*me ta podia*) or by mule or *caique*, as everyone did on the Cyclades up until relatively recently.

The remoteness of the Lesser Cyclades has preserved evidence of their prehistoric settlements to a greater extent than elsewhere. Colin Renfrew's gazeteer of prehistoric finds in the archipelago lists 19 Cycladic sites on the Lesser Cyclades, including four on Iraklia, two on Schinoussa, four on Pano Koufonissi, two on Kato Koufonissi, two on Donoussa, and five on Keros.

Iraklia, which lies off the southernmost cape of Naxos, is the largest of the inhabited isles in the Lesser Cyclades, with an area of 19 square kilometres. It has a population of 250, divided between two villages: Agios Yiorgios, the port, and the inland hamlet of Panagia, also known as Pano Meria. Paths lead from both villages to the noted cave of Agios Ioannis in the west of the island. The cave is one of the most impressive in the Cyclades, its ten successive chambers containing remarkable stalactites and stalagmites. According to tradition, the cave was discovered by a local shepherd who took cover there during a storm. After he emerged, the other islanders were amazed to see an image of St John on his back, and when they all returned to the cave they found an icon of the saint at its entrance. They then built a shrine within the cave, to which pilgrims come from as far away as Athens on the feast day of St John the Theologian, on 23 June.

South of the village of Agios Yiorgios there is an excellent beach on Ormos Livadi. At the outer end of the bay there is a tiny islet known as Venetiko, so called because it is crowned with the ruins of a Venetian fortress.

Schinoussa has a population of 207, divided into two settlements. One of these is the tiny port of Messaria, on the north-east coast, where there are the ruins of a medieval fortress. The other is Chora, which is in the centre of the island. There are good beaches all around the island, at Mersini, Tsigouri, Livadi, Almyro, Liolio and Psili Ammos.

The church in Chora is dedicated to the Panagia Akathi, taking its name from the Akathistos Hymn. Many girls on the island take the name Akathi in honour of the Virgin, whose *paneyeri* on 15 August is celebrated by everyone in the Lesser Cyclades.

Pano Koufonissi has a population of 250, all of whom live in a single village on the south coast. There is a good beach in the port at Parianos, and even better ones at Pori and Finikas. The village church of Agios Yiorgios celebrates its *paneyeri* on 23 April, when everyone on the Lesser Cyclades gathers here for a procession of the saint's icon along the waterfront, climaxed by a fireworks display, followed by music and dancing into the small hours (*i oras mikres*). Recent excavations have revealed an ancient site elsewhere on the south coast, with ruins dating from the Hellenistic and Roman periods.

Kato Koufonissi is uninhabited except by the occasional fishermen who erect shacks there, not to mention the nudists who come to the island on day trips in the summer to swim. The only permanent building is a chapel of the Panagia, which stands by the pier on the site of ancient ruins.

Donoussa is far removed from the other Lesser Cyclades, lying off to the north-east between the northern ends of Naxos and Amorgos. According to one version of the myth, this is where Dionysos hid Ariadne after he found her on Naxos. The island has a population of 280, divided among four hamlets: Donoussa, Mersini, Messaria and Kaloritissa. The most important of these is Donoussa, the port, which is in a sheltered bay on the south-western side of the island; it is also known as Stavros, from a chapel of Timios Stavros.

Keros, which is about the same size as Iraklia, is uninhabited except for the occasional fisherman or herder in summer. And yet in the Bronze Age it probably had more inhabitants than any other island in the Lesser Cyclades, as evidenced by the five Early Cycladic sites that have been discovered there. These sites have yielded an exceptionally large number of marble figures and vases, products of the so-called Keros-Syros culture that flourished in the period 2800–2200 BC. Two of the most beautiful and unusual works of Cycladic art in the National Archaeological Museum of Athens were found on Keros. These are the extraordinary marble statuettes known as the *Flute-Player* and the *Harpist*, archetypal figures of musicians whom one can easily imagine playing at an island *paneyeri* today, such is the depth and continuity of civilisation in the Cyclades.

Amorgos: population 1,873; area 121 sq km; Mt. Krikelas (822 m); ferries from Piraeus (138 mi); hotels in Katapola, Aegiali and Kamari.

Donoussa: population 280; area 13 sq km; Mt. Bardia (384 m); ferries from Piraeus (114 mi) and Rafina (92 mi); rooms in villages.

Iraklia: population 250; area 19 sq km; Mt. Papas (419 m); ferries from Piraeus (125 mi) and Rafina (103 mi); hotel near Agios Yiorgios, rooms in villages.

Koufonissi (Pano Koufonissi): population 250; area 3.8 sq km; peak (114 m); ferries from Piraeus (120 mi) and Rafina (98 mi); rooms in villages.

Schinoussa: population 207; area 8 sq km; peak (134 m); ferries from Piraeus (122 mi) and Rafina (100 mi); rooms in villages.

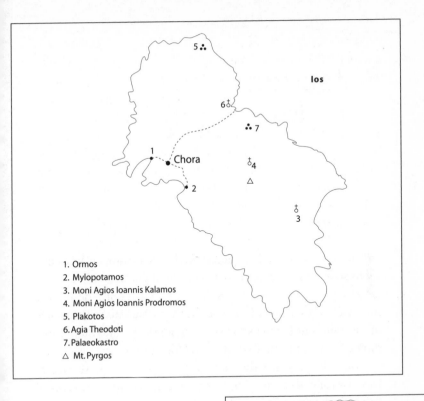

1. Ormos
2. Mylopotamos
3. Moni Agios Ioannis Kalamos
4. Moni Agios Ioannis Prodromos
5. Plakotos
6. Agia Theodoti
7. Palaeokastro
△ Mt. Pyrgos

Sikinos

1. Alopronia
2. Episcopi
3. Palaeokastro
△ Mt. Troullos

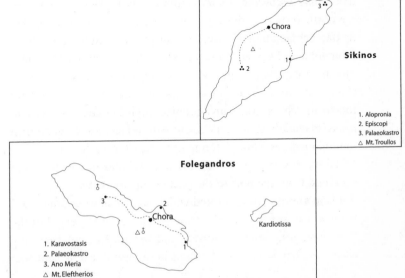

Folegandros

Kardiotissa

1. Karavostasis
2. Palaeokastro
3. Ano Meria
△ Mt. Eleftherios

fourteen
Ios

I os was renowned in antiquity for its association with Homer, for it was supposed to be the birthplace of his mother Klymene, and it was generally believed that both she and her son died and were buried here. According to Pausanias, 'The people of Ios point out Homer's tomb on the island, and Klymene's in a different part of it; they say she was Homer's mother.'

Count Pasch van Krienin, a Dutch officer in the service of Russia, explored Ios in 1770, causing a sensation when he claimed that he had discovered Homer's tomb at a site known as Plakotos, in the northern part of the island. He even went so far as to say that he had actually looked upon the poet's uncorrupted body for a moment after he opened the tomb, but that it then crumbled into dust before his eyes. The count's amazing claim was never substantiated and is not accepted by modern scholars, who maintain that he merely excavated an ancient sarcophagus and gave free rein to his imagination. Nevertheless, the site at Plakotos is still pointed out to tourists as Homer's tomb, and on 15 May each year a festival called the Homeria is held on Ios, at the climax of which a torch is carried from the port to the poet's supposed grave.

Ios in antiquity was covered with a dense oak forest, the wood from which was the island's principal source of income. But the trees have long since vanished, and up until recent years the islanders eked out a living farming, herding and fishing, which in

1950 supported a population of 500, only a sixth of what it had been in Bent's time. Then, beginning in the early 1970s, young backpackers began flocking to Ios in increasing numbers, attracted by its beautiful beaches, transforming it into what came to be called 'the party island'. This revived the economy of the island and reversed the decline of its population, which now numbers 1,834, most of whom live in the Chora. The prosperity has come at a price, for the bars and discotheques and nudist beaches have destroyed the old Cycladic way of life of the island, though in the unspoiled interior one still comes upon landscapes that are just as they were when I first saw them more than half a lifetime ago.

Otherwise Ios is hardly mentioned in the history of ancient Greece. During the Classical period it was subject to Athens, and as a member of the Delian League it paid a tribute of one silver drachma, far lower than the most prosperous states in the Cyclades.

Ios became part of the Latin Duchy of the Archipelago in 1210, ruled by the Dukes of Naxos. In 1269 it was one of several isles that fell to the Byzantine admiral Licario. It remained part of the Byzantine Empire until 1292, when the Venetian captain Domenico Sciavo recaptured it for Marco II Sanudo. The duke then gave Ios as a sub-fief to Sciavo, who constructed the fortress above Chora now known as Kastro. After the death of Duke Francesco Crispo of Naxos in 1397 Ios was bequeathed to his son Marco, along with Therasia, one of the isles of Santorini. Early in the following century Ios was one of several isles that were devastated by Turkish corsairs, who carried away many of the inhabitants into slavery, most of the rest fleeing to other islands. Marco Crispo repopulated Ios with Albanians from the Peloponnesos, and at the same time he rebuilt Kastro, where his subjects could take refuge when pirates attacked the island.

After the death of Marco I Crispo in 1450 Ios passed to the Pisani, a Venetian dynasty who built a second fortress in the north-east of the island, which they ruled until it fell to Barbarossa in 1537.

During the *Turkokrateia* Ios was a notorious lair of pirates, as Tournefort remarked after visiting the island in 1700. 'The

Inhabitants have no notion of anything but the Pence; they are all thieves by profession, and therefore the Turks call it Little Malta; 'tis a harbouring place for most of the Corsairs of the Mediterranean.'

Ferries to Ios call at the little port of Ormos, also known as Yialos, which is at the inner end of a fjord-like bay on the north-western side of the island. A boat leaves the port at Ormos daily in the summer for the beach at Manganari, at the south end of the island, which can also be reached by an excursion bus. There is also a regular bus to Chora which goes on to the beach resort at Mylopotamos, on the next bay south of the port. There are other beaches around the island that can be reached either by road or boat, including Koubara and Kolitsani, on the headlands west of the port; Klima, Pikrinero and Tripiti on the south-west coast; Trias Ekklesias, Kalamos and Plakes on the south-east; Psathi and Agia Theodoti on the east.

Some still prefer to make their way up from the port to Chora by the old stepped path that I first used in 1962. The ascent opens up expanding views of the bay and Chora, which has one of the most picturesque settings of any capital in the Cyclades. A dozen wind-mills on a ridge behind the town make its setting even more striking, particularly since one of them has been restored so that its sails are spinning once again in the *meltemi* as they did in times past.

The rocky crag above Chora is crowned with two white chapels and the ruins of Kastro, the Latin fortress erected by Domenico Sciavo and rebuilt by Marco I Crispo. The acropolis stands on the acropolis of the ancient capital of Ios, which occupied the present site of Chora. This is evidenced by the many ancient architectural fragments that have been incorporated into the oldest church in Chora, Agia Ekaterini – a Byzantine structure which is believed to have been built on and from the ruins of a classical temple of Apollo. An inscribed marble fragment that once stood in front of the church, but which has now vanished, was associated by local tradition with Homer's tomb, and it was this evidence that set Pasch von Kreinen in search of the poet's burial place.

Other notable old churches are those of Agios Ioannis Prodromos, Agioi Anargyroi, Agios Nikolaos, and the Panagia Gremiotissa, as well as the seventeenth-century chapel of Agia Eirene on the headland to the west of the harbour. Chora also has a small Archaeological Museum, its exhibits being principally Early Cycladic and Roman sculpture and pottery found on the island.

Otherwise there is little to see in Chora other than the very pretty town itself, which has two charming little Venetian *plateias* with old street fountains of the Latin period.

At the top of the town there is a panoramic view of the magnificent bay and the lovely countryside around it. Here, more than almost anywhere else in the Cyclades, one is struck by the large number of churches in view, many of them just tiny white-washed chapels. When Bent remarked on this the locals gave him a curious answer. They said that the great number of churches on Ios was not evidence of their piety but rather of their past sins, for many of these chapels had been founded by those who wished to atone for their misdeeds, committed in the days when Ios was known as 'Little Malta'.

The main road continues south-east to the beach resort at Mylopotamos, and from there a network of secondary roads threads its way around the southern end of the island, giving access to the beaches at Klima, Pikrinero, Tripiti, Trias Ekklisias, Kalamos, Plakes and Psathi.

The landscape in the southern half of the island is dominated by Mount Pyrgos, the highest peak on Ios, which has monasteries on both its southern and northern slopes. The one to the south is Agios Ioannis Kalamos, which dates to the late eighteenth century. The other one is Agios Ioannis Prodromos, which is just to the north of the main peak of Mount Pyrgos, built in the sixteenth century on the ruins of a temple of Apollo.

Another network of roads makes its way around the northern end of the island, with branches going to the beaches at Agia Theodoti and Plakotos, the latter being the site of Homer's supposed tomb.

The grave that Count Pasch von Kreinen identified as Homer's tomb was one of the burial places that he excavated around Psaropyrgos, a ruined Hellenistic tower near Plakotos. The count was led to this place by the tradition that Homer had been on his way from Samos to Athens when a storm forced his ship to land on the north coast of Ios in the little harbour below Plakotos, where he died. At a much later time the people of Ios are supposed to have inscribed the following epitaph on his tomb: 'Here the earth covers the sacred head/of the poet who gave heroes glory, divine Homer.'

The beach of Agia Theodoti is on a large bay on the north-east coast. The beach and bay are named for Agia Theodoti, the patron saint of Ios, whose *paneyeri* is celebrated here on 8 September in a large Byzantine church dedicated to her. The church is an object of particular veneration on Ios, because tradition holds that during the *Turkokrateia* the locals once took refuge here when corsairs attacked the island. The pirates tried to break down the door of the church, but those within poured a cauldron of boiling oil upon them, killing them to a man, or so the story goes.

The summit of the white marble mountain south of the bay is crowned with the ruins of Palaeokastro, a fortress-town built *c.* 1517 by Aloisio Pisani. The fortress and the town that it protected, all now in utter ruins, were built entirely of marble quarried from the mountain itself. Bent, who was guided to the site by his host's daughter, Marousa Lorenziadis, writes that 'many roofless houses were still standing, and the brilliant whiteness of the place was quite dazzling in the bright sunshine'. In the midst of the ruins there is a chapel dedicated to the Panagia Palaeokastritissa, Our Lady of the Old Castle, whose *paneyeri* is celebrated on the feast day of the Virgin's birth, 8 September, the same day as the festival at Agia Theodoti. Marousa told the Bents that this chapel belonged to her family, and she persuaded them to 'scribble our names on the wall and on the *tempelon* in Greek and English, which appeared to us both irreverent and vulgar; but we thought what a pleasure it would be to the family next feast day to see these scribblings of ours, so we did as we were bid'.

I looked for the Bents' scribblings when I visited the church, but they seem to have disappeared. The *paneyeri* of the Panagia Palaeokastritissa continues to be celebrated in and around the church, a scene much the same as that which Bent describes.

> Every pilgrim to the festival produces something towards this meal: the well-to-do will bring a lamb or a goat; the poor, rice, olives, and wine. Everything is then common property, and in picturesque groups outside the church they cook their food; into one cauldron is cast the lamb, into another the goat, into another the rice, and the fragrance of the meal ascends in wreaths of smoke towards the blue heavens. There is something patriarchal in a scene like this.

Ios: population 1,834; area 109 sq km; Mt. Pyrgos (713 m); ferries from Piraeus (111 mi); hotels in Ormos, Chora and Mylopotas.

fifteen
Sikinos and Folegandros

S ikinos and Folegandros are among the smallest and most sparsely inhabited of the major Cyclades, mere stepping stones between Ios and Melos, their remoteness keeping them out of the path of mass tourism and preserving their natural beauty and way of life.

Ferries to Sikinos call at the small port of Alopronia on the west coast of the island. The population of the island is only 242, less than a fourth of what it was in Bent's time. Almost everyone lives in either Alopronia or Chora, which is connected to the port by a road that leads across the waist of the island.

Sikinos was originally known as Oenoe, Wine Island, a name that first appears in the *Argonautica* of Apollonius Rhodius. Apollonius, in his account of the voyage of Jason and the Argonauts, tells of how the women of Lemnos, enraged that their husbands preferred the Thracian girls they had enslaved, slaughtered all but one of the Lemnian men. The only survivor was King Thoas of Lemnos, a son of Dionysos and Ariadne, who was put into a chest by his daughter Hypsipyle and floated to Oenoe. There he was taken in by the nymph Oenoe, for whom the island was named, and he became her lover. Oenoe eventually bore Thoas a son called Sikinos, and thenceforth the island was known by his name, according to the legend.

The earliest reference to the island is in a speech by the lawgiver Solon in the sixth century BC, when he contrasted the greatness of Athens to the insignificance of tiny Sikinos. During Roman times it is mentioned only as a place of exile, and in the Byzantine era it literally disappeared from history. The Venetians held the island until 1617, when it finally fell to the Turks.

In Bent's time Sikinos was almost completely cut off from the outside world, with only the occasional *caique* crossing over from Ios. Bent writes that when he and his wife crossed in such a *caique* in mid-winter they were left alone on the deserted eastern shore of Sikinos for four and a half hours, until finally, 'to our inexpressible delight, muleteers arrived, and soon we were on our way to the Chora, across fearful, rocky, pathless hills…'.

Sikinos is still off the beaten track of tourism, but there is now a hotel in Alopronia, and rooms can be rented in Chora. There is a wide sandy beach in Alopronia, and *caiques* leave the port for other beaches farther north along the shore at Agios Nikolaos, Dialiskari and Agios Yiorgios.

Chora is particularly attractive, with its tiers of whitewashed cubist houses shining on the barren hillside north of Mount Troullos, the highest peak on the island, at 552 metres. Chora is actually a twin village, together with its older part, known as Kastro, from which it is separated by a few hundred metres.

Kastro was the capital of Sikinos during the Latin period, when the island was ruled in turn by the da Corogna and Gozzadini dynasties, but there is virtually no trace of their fortress. When Buondelmonti visited the island in 1420, four years after it was ravaged by Turkish corsairs, he found it virtually abandoned. Cretan refugees seem to have arrived in the late sixteenth century and resettled in Kastro, where, as Bent remarks, 'they could be safe from pirates and Turkish supervision; and here they have lived ever since, mingling hardly at all with the outer world, and never likely to be disturbed by the advent of steamer or telegraph'.

Kastro is a veritable fortified village of medieval aspect, the backs of its joined houses forming the outer defence wall, and with only two entryways, one a mere *sottoportico*, which could be blocked in time of siege. Most of the houses have a crypt in the cellar, designed to be used as a hiding place when corsairs appeared.

The oldest church in Kastro is known as tou Stavrou, 'of the Cross', which dates from the late Byzantine period. The village is centred on the church of the Panagia Pandanassa, the Queen of All Things, whose sacred icon is supposed to sweat with agony in times of war. In front of the church there is a pretty *plateia* where the towns-people once congregated in the evening, and where in mid-August they celebrated the Virgin's principal *paneyeri*. But now Kastro has been largely abandoned in favour of Chora, known also as 'To Chorio'.

Chora, which is set higher than Kastro, relied on a single tower to give protection to its townspeople when corsairs appeared. The village church is dedicated to Agios Vassilios, whose *paneyeri* is cele-brated on New Year's Day. There is also a local Folklore Museum with an olive press and other exhibits illustrating life on Sikinos in the past.

The abandoned convent of the Chrysopigi, the Golden Well, is on a hill overlooking the town, looking like a fortress with its high and massive walls overhanging the precipice below. Like other convents and monasteries elsewhere in the Cyclades, the Chrysopigi is supposed to have served as a refuge from corsair raids.

The ruins of the ancient capital of Sikinos can be seen at Episkopi, about five kilometres south-west of the Chora. The site is spectacular, the extensive ruins covering the summit of a steep crag nearly 600 metres above the sea. The setting is still just as Bent describes it in a vivid passage.

> A bleaker and more exposed place can never have existed than the old town of Sikinos. It covered a precipitous height, fully one thousand eight hundred feet above the sea, and from the summit the rock goes down on the north side fully five hundred feet without a break. The rock is of blue marble, covered with a yellow lichen, which gives an exceedingly rich appearance. Here and there out of the crevices grow thick bunches of wild mastic; ravens rush out of their eyries and croak; quantities of partridges too, disturbed by the unwonted noise of human voices, take flight. The foundations of houses, cisterns and public

buildings are extensive, all of the same blue marble stone of the island; one of these was the temple of Hermes and Dionysos, as an inscription tells us.

The temple that Bent refers to is a white marble structure that the German archaeologist Ludwig Ross identified in 1837 as a Doric temple of Apollo Pythios. More recent studies seem to indicate that it is a late Roman mausoleum, which in the seventh century was converted into a church. Then in 1688 a large monastic complex called Moni Episcopi was built around the church. All that remains of the monastery is its ruined *katholikon*, dedicated to the Dormition of the Virgin Mary.

There is another ancient site at Palaeokastro, on the north-easternmost promontory of the island, but this has never been excavated, and even the indefatigable Bent did not seem to have been aware of its existence. The view from the promontory at Palaeokastro is magnificent, looking out across the strait towards Ios, seven nautical miles to the north-east.

The Bents' departure from Sikinos was delayed by a severe storm, and while they waited for the weather to clear they passed the time at a series of parties, one of which was the 'tail end' of a wedding, a celebration that had gone on for five days.

> On the first day, Thursday, when the festivities usually begin, the crier is sent round to summon the guests to the bride's house… On Thursday afternoon they have the ceremony of the mixing of the yeast for the cakes, etc. A reception is announced for the occasion, and guns are let off to announce to all the world the coming event… On Friday they make the sweets, to assist at which all the female friends of the bride are bidden; and they bring with them presents of food and wood, which last commodity is exceedingly rare on Sikinos, where few trees bigger than a fig tree grow. Guns are let off and healths are drunk. On Saturday they make the honey cakes, covered with sesame seeds, and the evening is passed in dancing and other amusements. On Sunday is the usual ceremony of crowning and the church services are followed by dancing in the

evening. On Monday they again have dancing, drinking and feasting to any extent. Today was Monday, and when we went to the house the second wedding feast, the social dinner (*i trapeza*), was just concluded, and they were preparing to dance the whole afternoon.

We ourselves have been guests at one of these five-day weddings, and under similar circumstances, celebrating while a winter storm howled outside. One of the songs we heard was an old Cretan *tragoudi* entitled *Kaloperasi*, 'The Good Life', addressed to the groom.

> Little by little the Lord sends the rain,
> Then comes the quiet snow,
> Cold in the mountains,
> Snow on the hills.
> And the man who has a well-roofed house,
> Fruit in his storerooms,
> Oil in his jars,
> Wine in his barrels,
> Wood in his yard,
> A girl to kiss as he sits by the fire,
> He doesn't care what the north wind brings,
> Rain or snow.

***

Folegandros is the smallest of the inhabited isles of the archipelago, other than the Lesser Cyclades, with an area of only 32 square kilometres, its population numbering 656. The remoteness of Folegandros has made it a place of exile in both ancient and modern times, most recently during the years of the junta (1967–1974), when it served as an open prison for opponents of the dictatorship.

The strait between Sikinos and Folegandros is studded with a number of sea-girt rocks and islets, the largest of which is Kardiotissa, Our Lady of the Heart, named for a chapel of the Virgin. Tournefort identified this as Lagusa, mentioned by Strabo as being between Sikinos and Folegandros, and also by Stephanos of Byzantium, who says that it was named for a son of Minos.

Bent writes of these rocky islets in describing his voyage by *caique* from Sikinos to Folegandros, where he mentions the unusual pall caused by the volcanic eruption of Krakatoa, between Java and Sumatra, which exploded in 1883 and left a cloud of dust in the world's atmosphere for months afterwards.

> A string of islands joins Sikinos to Pholygandros – fantastic barren rocks, which sparkle in the sunshine, and of which we got to know every form and shape during that long day of patient tacking, accomplishing our sail of twelve miles in the same number of hours. Of all the isles in the Aegean Sea Pholygandros can boast of the most majestic coastline; in fact I doubt if it can be equalled anywhere. A precipitous line of rocks, in places rising 1,160 feet above the sea, forms the north-eastern bulwark; as we approached it the sun had set, and the sky was lurid with that strange red light which astonished the world, and particularly the superstitious world of Greece, in the winter of 1883–1884. The water was almost transparent, and its depths looked wonderfully mysterious as we glided in amongst the rocks, some of which were white and looked like Nereids come to drive us from an enchanted shore. Such scenes as this make one realise how easy it is to imagine the phantasies of the Odyssey and of modern folklore.

Ferries land at Karavostasis on the east, from where a paved road leads up to Chora, a drive of some three kilometres. On the way there are continually expanding views of the town, one of the prettiest island capitals in the Cyclades, set on a precipice some 250 metres above the bay.

The Chora is divided into two parts, one of them the old Venetian citadel within Kastro, the other the more recent Cycladic village that began to develop around this during the *Turkokrateia*, a quarter known as Exochorio, or the Outer Village. Locals refer to these as 'Mesa' (Inside) and 'Exo' (Outside), as Bent remarks in writing of his arrival in Chora.

> On reaching habitations we enquired where the demarch lived. 'Outside,' was the stoical reply. 'Outside what?' we

asked. 'Not inside,' was the angry reply; and no further could
we get out of the man. We pursued our way in search of a
more intelligent informant, until at length we discovered
that Pholygandros boasts of only one town, which is walled,
and called 'Inside' (*mesa*), and of a colony outside this wall,
of better-class houses, which is called 'Outside' (*exo*); and
a Pholygandriot knows of no other names but these.

Few of the families on Folegandros date their origins back to the
Venetian period, for in 1715 the Turks sacked Kastro and carried
away virtually all of its surviving inhabitants into captivity. Kastro
was not fully repopulated until after 1780, when Captain Lambros
Katsonis finally cleared the Aegean of pirates. Thereupon a number
of aristocratic families from elsewhere in the archipelago moved
into Kastro, with Greeks of lower station building houses in what
came to be called Exochorio.

The main gate of Kastro was near the *plateia* of the Three Wells,
but the portal was demolished some years ago to create a larger
square from its inner and outer courtyards. There are two main
streets in Kastro: Piso Roua, or Back Street, and Kato Roua, or Front
Street, where the first half of each name is Greek and the second
Venetian. Piso Roua follows the curving line of houses around the
edge of the precipice, while Kato Roua goes along the two inland
sides of the citadel, with *sottoporticos* (another Venetian term)
and passageways connecting the two streets in between.

Piso Roua and Kato Roua intersect at the north-west corner of
Kastro, beside the church of the Panagia Pandanassa, which dates
from *c*. 1700. The most precious treasure of this church is an icon
of the Virgin, whose silver crown and silver-clad right hand were
stripped off by the Turks when they sacked Kastro in 1715. The
church has several other interesting old icons, all done by painters
of the Cretan School in the early eighteenth century.

Other old churches in Kastro are Agia Elousa and Agioi
Anargyroi, which may date back to the Byzantine period, and
Agia Sophia, built at the beginning of the eighteenth century. The
icons in Agioi Anargyroi include works by the Cretan School, and

there is also one that is said to date back to the seventh century, to the pre-Iconoclastic period.

The cathedral of Folegandros, dedicated to Agios Nikolaos, stands just outside Kastro in the *plateia* of the Three Wells, along with churches dedicated to the Taxiarchis and to Stavros, the Cross. Behind the cathedral is the *plateia* of Agios Theoskepasti, named after the church at the back of the square. In the centre of the same *plateia* there are two chapels, one dedicated to Agios Antonios and the other to Agia Ekaterini and Agios Fanourios.

Chora has two portative icons of the Virgin, each of which travels around the town from house to house, spending a year in each one. One of these icons is named Martiatissa, Our Lady of March, and the other is called Mayitissa, Our Lady of May. Both icons are credited with saving Chora from pirates in the late eighteenth century, and each of them is named after the month in which it is supposed to have performed its miracle.

The summit of the precipitous crag to the north-east of Chora is known as Palaeokastro. This is the site of the medieval Latin fortress built by the Dukes of Naxos, which later was the seat of the da Corugna and Gozzadini barons. The site is approached along a path that leads from Chora up along the edge of the precipice. Halfway along the path there is an abandoned monastery dedicated to the Koimisis tis Theotokou, whose *katholikon* served as the funerary chapel of Chora. Bent noticed some ancient fragments here, as well as in a ruined chapel on the summit and another place farther down the hill, all of which led him to identify Palaeokastro as the site of the ancient capital of Folegandros.

There is a cavern known as Chrysospilia, the Golden Cave, in the cliff face beyond Akri Panagia, the promontory that forms the eastern horn of the bay below Chora. The cave is difficult to reach since one must climb up to it via a perilous rock-hewn stairway from the sea.

A secondary road leads north from Chora to the strung-out village of Ano Meria, five kilometres distant. The village has an Ecology and Folk Museum, with exhibits illustrating the old way of life on Folegandros. Ano Meria celebrates the feast day of Agios

Pandaleimon on 27 July, a *paneyeri* that attracts everyone on the island.

Mounts Agios Eleftherios, the highest peak on the island, and Profitis Ilias dominate the southern end of the island and both are crowned by chapels of the saints for which they are named. The chapels were in the past, and perhaps still today, the object of pilgrimages at times of drought. According to Bent: 'When there is a drought, all the Pholygandriotes with the priests and the pictures of the Madonna walk in procession first to the top of Mount Profitis Ilias, where they kneel round his shrine and pray for rain; after which they go and do likewise at the shrine of St Eleutherios.'

The feast day of Agios Profitis Ilias is celebrated in his mountain-top chapel on 20 July. One of the *tragoudia* that you may hear on this *paneyeri* is 'Asmata Pros Tin Vrohin', which literally means 'Songs for Rain'.

> Perperouna walks about
> and asks for rain:
> 'Lord make it rain
> A wetting rain,
> Pools of water,
> Lakes of wine.
> Let each vine-plant
> Fill a basket,
> Every ear of corn a sack.
> May the miller burst with rage
> Because he can't sell dear.
> May the poor man rejoice his heart
> With all his family!'

Sikinos: population 242; area 41 sq km; Mt. Troullos (552 m); ferries from Piraeus (113 mi); hotel in Alopronia, rooms in Chora.

Folegandros: population 656; area 32 sq km; Mt. Agios Eleftherios (414 m); ferries from Piraeus (103 mi); hotels in Karavostasis and Chora.

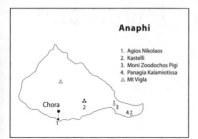

Anaphi

1. Agios Nikolaos
2. Kastelli
3. Moni Zoodochos Pigi
4. Panagia Kalamiotissa
△ Mt Vigla

Chora

Santorini

THERA

THERASIA

NEW KAIMENI

PALAEA KAIMENI

ASPRONISI

Phera

1. Imerovigli
2. Skaros
3. Oia
4. Karterados
5. Messaria
6. Monolithos
7. Vothonos
8. Exo Gonia
9. Pyrgos
10. Episcopi Gonias
11. Moni Agios Profitis Ilias
12. Kamari
13. Ancient Thera
14. Athenios
15. Megalochori
16. Emporio
17. Perissa
18. Akrotiri village
19. Akrotiri archaeological site
△ Mt Profitis Ilias

sixteen
Santorini (Thera) and Anaphi

Santorini, known in Greek as Thera, is to me one of the wonders of the world. I first saw it in 1962, awakening at dawn on the fantail of an old Greek ferry to see that we were steaming into what appeared to be the sea-filled core of a volcano. The first rays of the sun were reflecting with almost blinding intensity off the multicoloured layers of the thousand-foot-high caldera wall, its rim crowned with a succession of white Cycladic towns that looked like troglodyte settlements, burrowed into the uppermost level of the striated mixture of volcanic rock, pumice, ash and solidified lava.

I was looking at part of the rim of a shifting and still active volcano, the fragmentary remnant of a larger island whose core was blown out by a cataclysmic explosion in prehistoric times to create the huge and almost landlocked Bay of Santorini, its subterranean fires, which the locals call Hephaestus, still smouldering through the cusped islet that has formed around its vent at the centre of the harbour.

Santorini is actually a group of islands arrayed in and around the bay. The largest by far is Thera, with an area of 76 square kilometres, followed in order of size by Therasia, Nea Kaimeni, Palaea Kaimeni and Aspronisi. Thera and Therasia are the only inhabited islands of the group, the others being devoid of even goats and rabbits.

Thera is an irregular scimitar, some say a dragon, measuring 20 kilometres along its inner arc and 30 kilometres around its outer periphery. Part of the north-western quadrant of the volcano's rim survives as the isle of Therasia; a speck of the south-western periphery remains as the tiny islet of Aspronisi, White Island; and the core projects out of the centre of the bay as Nea and Palaea Kaimeni, the New and Old Burnt Isles.

The great bay measures ten kilometres from north to south and seven kilometres east–west. Its depth varies from 394 metres, just to the west of Palaea Kaimeni, to 185 metres along the precipitous west coast of Thera, so that ships cannot anchor there but must tie up to buoys connected to weights at the ocean bottom. Large liners and small excursion boats disembark passengers at Skala, the port below Phera, the capital of Santorini, midway along the west coast of Thera. Many other boats also stop at Oia, at the north-western tip of Thera, while most of the inter-island ferries call at Athinos, farther down the west coast from Skala.

The crescent of cliffs stretches for 20 kilometres in length along the arc of Thera alone, varying in height from 62 to 338 metres, with the snow-white towns of Phera and Oia perched on the rim of the caldera more than 300 metres above the sea. The cliff face is a geological cross-section of all the seismic and volcanic upheavals that have been undergone by this tortured island, which some believe to be the only surviving remnant of the lost continent of Atlantis.

The summit of the original isle from which Santorini was formed survives as Mount Profitis Ilias, the highest peak on Thera, rising to an elevation of 566 metres near the south-eastern end of the island. A chain of high hills extends north from there around the western side of the island, their cliffs plunging sheer into the sea on that side, but sloping down to a coastal plain at the middle of the eastern shore, where Santorini airport is laid out.

There are few sources of fresh water on Santorini, the principal spring being at Kamari on the east coast of Thera, from where water is shipped by tanker to Phera and Oia. Since antiquity the islanders have depended on cisterns to collect rain for drinking water, as their wells usually bring up brackish water.

Santorini is covered with material thrown up by the volcano: pumice and a volcanic ash called tephera, or pozzolana, ranging in depth from 20 metres to as much as 67 metres. (Pumice is a porous stone so light that it floats on water, and one occasionally sees large masses of it drifting in the bay; the local tephera is a very white and powdery material, like finely divided ash.) This covering of pumice and ash was laid down by the successive eruptions of the volcano, and one can observe the time-line of these cataclysms on the variegated cliff face around the bay, banded in grey, black, white, ochre and green – a spectacular sight, particularly when viewed across the turquoise waters of the bay at sunrise or sunset, when the precipice of the caldera glows like the damped furnace of Hephaestus, God of the Forge.

Given the aridity of Santorini and the volcanic nature of its soil, one might think that the island is barren, and wonder how it ever supported a population of any size. But it is surprisingly fertile when irrigated, its principal products being grapes, tomatoes, barley and fava beans. Santorini is also renowned for its wine, which has a strong but delicious flavour, with a heady aroma redolent of a whiff of brimstone. The volcanic materials themselves are among the island's main exports. Pumice is used as an abrasive, for electrical insulation and for making lightweight bricks; while tephera is made into a cement that is both water-resistant and impervious to corrosion by sea water, making it very useful for the construction of harbour installations.

Santorini has become an internationally famous tourist centre, with hordes of travellers attracted by the savage beauty of the island and its black sand beaches, the fantastic geological spectacle that it presents, and the fascinating archaeological site to be explored at Akrotiri, where a Minoan colony has been unearthed. These sources of income support a population of 11,984, the vast majority of whom live on Thera, an extraordinary figure for an island that was given up for dead and almost abandoned as recently as 1956, when the volcano last erupted.

Archaeological excavations have unearthed ten Bronze Age sites on Thera and one on Therasia, the earliest of them dating back to the mid-third millennium BC. By the middle of the second millennium BC the island was dominated by Minoan Crete, as evidenced by the excavations on Akrotiri. Around 1500 BC an enormous volcanic explosion occurred, blowing away the entire core of the island, the sea flooding in to fill the void, creating an enormous tsunami across the Mediterranean. The explosion also created a dust cloud that obscured the sun for several years, as evidenced by the layers of fallout it produced and the data of dendrochronology, dating by the analysis of tree rings.

Other eruptions occurred in historic times, the first of definite date being that of 198 BC, which was thought by many to be a sign of divine displeasure. The Rhodians, who were then the dominant power in the Aegean, hastened to build a temple of Apollo upon a new islet that appeared in the bay of Thera, calling it Nisos Hiera, the Sacred Isle, known today as Palaea Kaimeni. Since then a dozen major eruptions have occurred, the most recent in 1956, when there was also a violent earthquake that killed 48 people and injured hundreds of others, destroying some 2,000 houses. The casualties in the 1956 disaster would have been far higher were it not for the fact that the eruption was preceded for several weeks by rumblings and by dense clouds of smoke issuing from the volcano, so that many of the islanders had time to seek refuge in Athens. Many of those who fled never returned for fear of subsequent eruptions, and their ruined and abandoned homes can be seen along the rim of the caldera, particularly in the northern part of Phera, which has the haunted appearance of a ghost town.

The great explosion of *c.* 1500 BC entirely buried the island under a very deep fall of pozzolana, and archaeological excavations indicate that it was uninhabited for about two centuries afterwards. According to Herodotus, the island, then known as Kalliste, or 'Most Beautiful', was resettled by Cadmus, son of King Agenor of

Phoenicia. Herodotus goes on to say that eight generations later a Dorian expedition led by Theras, a descendant of Cadmus, established a colony on the island, which became known as Thera.

Archaeological excavations have revealed that the Dorians on Thera reached a high level of culture and prosperity by the mid-ninth century BC. Around 630 BC the Therans launched an expedition to the Libyan coast, founding the city of Cyrene. Within the next half-century Cyrene itself founded two cities of its own elsewhere in Libya, opening up the north African coast to trade with the Greek world and further enriching Thera, the mother island of these colonies.

Thera was occupied by the Persians during both of their invasions of Greece. After the Persian Wars the Therans declined to join the Delian League, but when the Second Athenian Alliance was formed in 378 BC they felt compelled to take part. At the beginning of the Peloponnesian War the Therans remained neutral, but later they were forced to pay tribute to Athens.

During the Hellenistic and Roman eras Thera had much the same history as the other Cyclades. It virtually disappeared from history during the Byzantine period, one of the few recorded events being a volcanic explosion during the reign of Leo III (r. 717–741), when the cloud of dust obscured the sun for several months, leading many to fear that the world was coming to an end. The explosion was popularly interpreted as a sign of the anger of the gods at the iconoclastic policy of the emperor, and this led to a revolt of the Byzantine fleet in the Cyclades, which was soon put down. The first phase of the Iconoclastic period ended during the reign of the empress Eirene (r. 797–802), who restored icons to the churches of Byzantium, for which she is revered as a saint in the Orthodox Church. The people of Thera expressed their gratitude to the empress by renaming their island Agia Eirene, which in the Latin period was corrupted to Santorini.

After the establishment of the Latin Duchy of the Archipelago in 1210, Marco Sanudo awarded Santorini to Jacopo Barozzi as a sub-fief. In 1269 Santorini was among the Aegean islands recaptured by the Byzantine admiral Licario. Then in 1269 the Venetians recaptured Santorini and awarded it to Jacopo II Barozzi, which was met with opposition from Guglielmo I Sanudo, Duke of Naxos, on the grounds that the Barozzi were vassals of the Sanudi. When Barozzi refused to pay homage to him Sanudo had him arrested and imprisoned on Naxos. Eventually the Venetians intervened and had Barozzi released, after which he returned to his castle at Skaros on Santorini.

While this dispute was going on the Catalans had swept through the Cyclades, ravaging Kea, Siphnos, Melos and Santorini, carrying off many of the islanders to be sold as slaves. The Catalans reached the peak of their power in the years 1311–1389, when they controlled Athens, and during that time a number of Catalonian families settled on Santorini, where some of their descendants can still be found today.

In 1335 Santorini was taken from the Barozzi by Niccolo I Sanudo, son and successor of Guglielmo I. Duke Niccolo then conferred upon the Gozzadini the fortress of La Ponta at Akrotiri, which they held until 1617, long after all of the other isles of the Cyclades except Tinos had fallen to the Turks.

The Latin aristocracy continued to dominate Santorini throughout most if not all of the *Turkokrateia*. Records from the seventeenth century make mention of five *kastellia*, or fortified settlements, which at first were inhabited almost exclusively by the Latin aristocracy, though later they were joined by upper-class Greek families. The Greek peasantry, known as *villani*, lived like troglodytes in the *choria potamias*, or river villages, their houses and churches hollowed out of the volcanic soil, as one can still see today all through the interior of Santorini.

During the Ottoman era Santorini was one of several islands in the Cyclades that had the reputation of being lairs of corsairs, and a significant part of the island's economy was based on the resale of pirate loot.

Towards the end of the *Turkokrateia* Santorini emerged as one of the principal shipping centres in Greece, its merchant fleet used almost entirely for the export of the island's wine. At the outbreak of the Greek War of Independence Santorini's merchant fleet was the third largest in Greece after Hydra and Spetses, growing to 229 vessels by 1856. As the local historian Philippos Kapsipi writes of Santorini's thriving merchant marine in the early nineteenth century: 'Gold and silver poured in, coins were carried in basketsful, rich were the houses of the captains and happy the homes of the boatswains and sailors. And revels lasting from one night to the next were commonplace.'

Santorini's seaborne commerce was ruined by the invention of the steamboat, and by the late nineteenth century the island entered a long period of economic depression that ended only with the beginning of the tourist boom. Nevertheless, as late as 1940 three-quarters of the families on Santorini were involved in shipping, and today many of the islanders still earn their living from the sea, even if only as boatmen for the tourist trade.

Travellers who land at Skala can either take the funicular railway up to Phera, or hire a mule to ride up the winding stepped path that ascends the cliff face. Phera has an extraordinary setting, perched on the edge of a sheer cliff nearly a thousand feet high, its white Cycladic houses contrasting dramatically with the multicoloured caldera and the brilliant blue sea below.

The most interesting part of the town is the area close to the cliff face, a quarter known as Kato Phera. The principal landmark in this quarter is the Greek Orthodox cathedral of the Panagia Ipapantis, Our Lady of Candelmas, which is near the southern end of the town. This is a modern structure built to replace the older cathedral, which was destroyed in the eruption and earthquake of 1956.

The church has no architectural distinction, but it has an attractive arcade where the townspeople congregate on Sundays and summer evenings. In one of the buildings attached to the cathedral there is a small but interesting collection of Byzantine and post-Byzantine icons, theological books and manuscripts, and liturgical objects. A short way to the south-east of the cathedral is the History and Folklore Museum, with interesting exhibits evoking the life of Santorini in times past.

Below the cathedral and closer to the rim of the caldera three old chapels form familiar landmarks on the skyline of Phera. The one to the south, dedicated to Agios Menas, dates to the Byzantine period and is probably the oldest church in Phera. The church in the middle, Agios Ioannis Theologos, was built *c.* 1650; while the northernmost one, Agia Eirene, is a nineteenth-century structure. All three chapels were badly damaged in the 1956 earthquake, and were rebuilt in the following decade.

The old Archaeological Museum is near the terminus of the funicular railway, at the corner of Odos Erythrou Stavros and Odos Nomikos. The museum, founded in 1902 by the German archaeologist Baron Freidrich Hiller von Gaertringen, has exhibits ranging in date from the Early Cycladic period through the Graeco-Roman era, with a few from the early Byzantine era. The new museum, which opened in March 2000, is the second-largest prehistoric museum in Greece, its most outstanding exhibits being objects from the Minoan-Cycladic site at Akrotiri.

Across the street from the museum on Odos Nomikos is the ruined Corogna mansion, dating from 1590. The original owner of this mansion was a descendant of Januli da Corogna of Coruna in Spain, who led a Catalan force that took Siphnos in 1307. One branch of the family continued to rule in Siphnos until 1617, while another moved to Santorini in 1560, subsequently building this mansion in Phera. The coat of arms of the da Corogna family can still be seen over the entryway, its device a crowned eagle.

The Roman Catholic cathedral is on Odos Agios Ioannis, one block to the north of the funicular terminus. This is the seat of the Roman Catholic bishop of Santorini, who also acts as bishop of Syros. The church, dedicated to the Immaculate Conception, was built in 1823; it was badly damaged in the 1956 earthquake and did not reopen until 15 August 1976.

Within the cathedral there are also a monastery and a convent, whose *katholikon* is dedicated to Our Lady of the Rosary. Both the monastery and convent were originally located in Skaros, the medieval fortified town on the rim of the caldera just north of Phera. The two institutions were founded together in 1596, and in the past both were renowned throughout Greece for their cultural and philanthropic activities. The Dominican nuns in the convent still operate a trade school, where girls from poor families are taught to weave and embroider.

At the corner of Agios Ioannis and Odos Firostefani is the Megaro Ghisi, a neoclassical mansion housing the Historical Museum, which has an important collection of engravings dating back to the fifteenth century.

The northern end of Phera is known as Ta Phrangika, the Quarter of the Franks, for it used to be inhabited mostly by Latins and a few European merchants. This part of the town was completely destroyed in the 1956 earthquake, and few of the residents have returned to their homes, so that Ta Phrangika is now a ghost town.

The northern suburb of Phera is known as Firostefani, whose principal monument is the beautiful church of Agios Yerasimos. North of Firostefani on the edge of the caldera is the convent of Agios Nikolaos, dating to 1674.

The first village to the north of Phera is Imerovigli. The *plateia* of Imerovigli is dominated by the church of the Panagia Maltesa, so called because it houses a miraculous icon originally found floating off the coast of Malta and brought here by a Theran mariner. From the *plateia* it is a short walk out to the rim of the caldera, where there is a view of the rocky promontory known as Skaros, a thousand-foot-high crag that forms the northern arm of the harbour at Skala.

Skaros is the site of an ancient city which the Latins chose to be the capital of Santorini, building on its ruins a fortified town they called La Rocca. This was the seat of the Sanudi and Crispi dynasties in turn, as well as of the highest-ranking Venetian nobility. After the Turks took control of Santorini Skaros declined greatly in importance, though the descendants of the Latin nobility lived on there through the *Turkokrateia*. But after the War of Independence Skaros rapidly lost its population, and Bent reports that its last residents left two decades before his visit. He notes that 'the last inhabitant, an old woman, had to be dragged away by main force, so attached was she to the home of her ancestors'.

The main road north from Phera curves around the rim of the caldera, commanding an eagle's view of the great bay and its isles. The road ends at Oia, known in the past as Epanomeria, an extremely picturesque village in a superb setting, clinging to the rim of the caldera at the north-westernmost promontory of Thera.

Oia was once the most populous village on the island, but it was so badly damaged in the 1956 earthquake that many of its inhabitants decided to leave Santorini for Athens and most of them never returned. Many of the houses in Oia are therefore abandoned ruins and so it too has the eerie atmosphere of a ghost town, though one of haunting beauty.

The convent of Agios Nikolaos in Oia was founded in 1674. The village also has an interesting Maritime Museum, portraying the seafaring life of Santorini in times past.

A stepped path leads down from Oia to the little port of Ammoudia, from where boats cross over to Therasia. The island has a population of 250, distributed among three villages, Therasia, Potamos and Agrilia. At the south end of the island there are pumice quarries, which in the mid-nineteenth century provided pozzolana for building the Suez Canal. An archaeological excavation in 1866 discovered an ancient settlement buried 30 feet deep in the volcanic ash. Subsequent excavations have shown that the settlement was a farming community that flourished in the Late Cycladic period, probably contemporary with the much larger city of Akrotiri on Thera.

The main road leading south from Phera goes all the way to Akrotiri, on the south-western peninsula of Thera, with turn-offs to the villages in the interior and on the east coast.

The first turn-off south of Phera leads to the village of Karterados, which was renowned for the number of excellent mariners it produced, although now most of the men in the village remain home to farm or to make their living from commerce or tourism.

The next village to the south is Messaria, where a turn-off on the left leads to Monolithos, a village on the east coast. The village takes its name from an enormous isolated rock (in Greek, *monolithos*), which rises to a height of more than 30 metres. At the foot of the Monolithos there is an old monastery dedicated to Agios Ioannis Theologos, whose *paneyeri* is held here on 23 June. This is within a day or two of the summer solstice, when the noon shadow cast by the Monolithos is the shortest of the year. Archaeologists have discovered evidence of a Mycenaean settlement here dating to the thirteenth century BC, which suggests that the Monolithos might be the site of an ancient shrine, similar to Stonehenge and other megalithic monuments.

Just to the south of Messaria is Vothonas, which in Bent's time was known as Bothro. This is one of the troglodyte villages on the slopes of Mount Profitis Ilias, along with Exo Gonia, Pyrgos and Episkopi Gonias, their houses and churches carved out of the soft volcanic rock in the gullies of the winter torrents pouring down from Mount Profitis Ilias.

At Bothro, Bent met a shoemaker who was the most celebrated bard on Santorini, and who sang his own compositions about island life at all of the *paneyeria*. While he worked, taking swigs from a bottle of mastic, the shoemaker sang for Bent an epic poem that he had composed after the last eruption of the volcano in 1866. Bent reports that 'if the poetry was indifferent the facts were there, for he began':

> In one thousand eight hundred and sixty-six,
> On the seventeenth of January,
> On Tuesday, at four o'clock,
> Haphaestus began his eruption;

And then, as Bent continues, the shoemaker began to describe each event minutely – how professors and steamers came from afar; how Thera was the wonder of all the earth – and now and again before a pause, and as a hint that he wanted a pull at the mastic bottle, he broke his narrative with a pretty refrain:

> O Thera! Loveliest isle of Greece,
> Our peaceful happy home,
> Will this great dread be overpast,
> Or waste wilt thou become.

The Bents' muleteer invited them to his daughter's wedding in one of the *choria potamias*. They arrived to find the bride being dressed for the ceremony in the muleteer's troglodyte house, which Bent says 'was no more or less a cave'. Then the firing of guns heralded the arrival of the groom, accompanied by musicians, followed by the bride's father, two priests and the best man, 'who brought vine tendrils that the maids of honour wove into crowns for the young couple, singing rhyming couplets as they worked'.

> As they made the wreaths the maidens, two on either side of the table, sang songs; the eldest began and sang one verse, then another answered and so on. And in these songs they wished the young couple every good wish, as follows: 'May Holy Procopius be with you today. May holy Tryphon grant you a life of pleasure and peace together...' Then another of the maidens sang as she worked: – 'Adorn the crowns with pearls and flowers/The bride and bridegroom are the moon and stars.' She is answered by another on the opposite side of the table: – 'The bride is Venice, and her swain/Is like that city on the main.' A third then sang a couplet: – 'The bestman, and the bridesmaid too,/Smell as Chiote gardens do.'

Pyrgos is a typical Cycladic community of medieval appearance, with the village houses joined back to back in tiers to form a fortress. Within the village there are three old churches, all with finely carved wooden *iconostases*: Agia Triada, Isodia tis Theotokou (the Presentation of the Virgin) and the Theototaki (Little Mother of God), which is believed to date from the tenth century.

Moni Agios Profitis Ilias is built high on the mountain. The monastery was founded in 1711 by the brothers Gabriel and

Joachim Beloni, two monks from Pyrgos. During the second half of the eighteenth century the monastery became one of the richest and most famous in the Cyclades, and its archives record that in 1780 it owned its own ship, the *St George*, which carried wine that the monks themselves had produced from their vineyard. During the Russo–Turkish War of 1787 the monks lent their ship to the Russian navy, and under Captain Andoni Danezis it sailed into the Black Sea flying the banner of the monastery.

The *katholikon* has a fine *iconostasis* of carved wood made in 1836 by a local artisan named Denis Langadas. The monastery has a small museum, the most interesting exhibits being those associated with the 'secret school' that the monks conducted during the *Turkokrateia*. The library has some 1,300 volumes, as well as an important collection of historical documents associated with the history of the monastery. One of these is a letter dated 1711 from Archbishop Zaccharias Gyris affirming the request of the founders to establish the monastery, which he hoped would be 'a holy place for all men and a common shelter for all Christians'. Theophilos Kaires of Andros was one of those who found refuge there, living in the monastery from 1840–1842.

Episkopi Gonias takes its name from the fact that it was the seat of the Orthodox bishop (*episkopos*) of Thera. The village church, dedicated to the Assumption of the Blessed Virgin, was founded by the emperor Alexios I Comnenos *c.* 1100, which is also the date of its extant wall paintings. When Marco Sanudo took control of Santorini in 1207 the Orthodox bishop was replaced by a Catholic bishop. Nevertheless, it appears that throughout the Latin period both Roman Catholic and Greek Orthodox congregations held services in the church, sharing it peacefully. The treasury of the church has an interesting collection of Byzantine and post-Byzantine icons, as well as old theological books, liturgical vestments and sacred vessels. The *paneyeri* of the Virgin on 15 August attracts celebrants here from all over the island.

West of Episkopi Gonias is Kamari, a coastal village that has now become a summer resort, centred on one of the famous black-sand beaches of Santorini. The name Kamari means 'arches', stemming from the caves that were once visible on the shore, but which have now been covered by the sea. Bent reports: 'At Kamaris we saw the remains of a Roman temple, some statues of inferior workmanship, and the foundations of houses.' The statues have now disappeared but some of the other antiquities can still be seen.

From Kamari a rough road winds upwards on the northern slope of Mesa Vouno, an eastern spur of Mount Profitis Ilias. On the peak of the mountain are the extensive ruins of the ancient city of Thera, on an impregnable site 369 metres above the eastern shore of the island.

Thera was the principal city founded in the ninth century BC by the Dorian settlers from Lacedaemon, and it continued to be the capital of the island up until the early Byzantine era. The ruins were first excavated in the years 1896–1903 by Baron von Gaertringen, who found that the site had been occupied since the Archaic period, though most of the structures visible today date from the Hellenistic and Roman eras. Subsequent archaeological studies of the site have revealed evidence of human occupation dating back to the Early Cycladic period.

At the top of the trail leading up to the north-western end of the site there is a small chapel dedicated to Agios Stephanos. The chapel is built on and from the ruins of a basilica of the fourth or fifth century, originally dedicated to the Archangel Michael. An inscription found here records that Christianity was introduced to Thera in the fourth century, and so it is possible that the basilica that stood here was the first Christian sanctuary on Santorini.

Following the main street leading south-east from the chapel, you come to a levelled-off outcropping of rock, one side of which is carved with figures in low relief. This is the rock-hewn Sanctuary of Artemidoros of Perge, who was admiral of the Ptolemaic fleet when it was based on Santorini in the third century BC.

A short way farther along the main street, a stepped pathway on the right leads uphill to two ruined structures, both of them dating from the third century BC, when the city was garrisoned by Egyptian troops of the Ptolemaic army. The northernmost of the two structures was the Ptolemaic Governor's Palace, and the other is the gymnasium used by the Egyptian garrison.

About 150 metres from here you come to the north end of the *agora*, the market quarter. This vast area, which in its two sections extends for 110 metres and varies in width from 16 to 30 metres, dates mostly from the Hellenistic period. After entering the southern part of the *agora* you see on the right the Stoa Basilike, or Royal Porch, a colonnaded edifice 40 metres in length and ten metres wide, erected in the third century BC by one of the Ptolemaic kings of Egypt.

Above the Royal Portico are the ruins of the residential quarter of ancient Thera, and to its north there is a temple of Apollo. The corner of one of the mansions in this quarter, just between the Royal Portico and the temple of Apollo, has a carving representing a large phallus, with a dedication 'To my Friends'.

Beyond the southern end of the *agora* on the left is the theatre, erected during the Hellenistic era and rebuilt in Roman times. Opposite the theatre a stepped path leads to the ruins of a mansion known as the Basilistai, or Royal House. This was apparently once used as a residence by Ptolemy III Euergetes of Egypt (r. 246–242 BC). Beyond this are the ruins of a Byzantine church built on and from the ruins of a small temple of Pythian Apollo. A short way beyond this are the remains of a sanctuary of the Egyptian gods, dating from the Ptolemaic era, with rock-hewn niches dedicated to the deities Isis, Anubis and Serapis.

An ancient street known as Iera Odos, the Sacred Way, leads to a promontory at the south-east end of the site. Below and to the left are some Roman baths, a Byzantine chapel dedicated to the Annunciation, and the remains of a *heroon*, whose foundations date from the Archaic period.

Continuing along, you now pass on the right a small sanctuary dedicated to Ptolemy III. On the left are the ruins of a temple of Apollo Karneios, the Ram, an attribute that stems from his role as

Protector of Flocks. This was a large Doric temple, 32 metres long and ten metres wide, dating from the period 630–570 BC. It was the focal point of the Karneia, the great festival of the Therans during the Archaic period. The climax of this festival was the Gymnopedia, in which naked *ephebes*, youths in military training, danced on the Terrace of the Festivals, just beyond the temple of Apollo to its south.

Immediately below the terrace there is a grotto that was sacred to Hermes and Heracles, the patron deities of the *ephebes*. At the southern end of the site is the gymnasium of the Ephebes, where the youths trained before their performance and bathed afterwards.

The first village south of Athenios is Megalochori. South of Megalochori a turn-off on the left leads to Emporio and Perissa, the latter a seaside resort on the coast just south of Mesa Vouno with a beach of black sand.

At the outskirts of Emporio there is a Venetian *pyrgos*, still splendid although partially in ruins. The *pyrgos* is of the type known as *goulas*, or tower, an independent fortified building either within or without the walled settlements known as *kastellia*.

On the roadside outside Emporio is the chapel of Agios Nikolaos Marmarites, so called because it is constructed entirely of marble, all reused from ancient structures. An inscription on one of the marbles records that it was part of a Doric temple of the third century BC dedicated to Thea Basilae, Mother of the Gods. Bent examined the church and noted that 'the pillars of the nave have belonged to a Corinthian temple which probably came from Eleusis, the ancient city which once stood here, but almost all traces of which have been washed away by encroachments of the sea'.

The ancient city of Eleusis mentioned by Bent is believed to have been on Akri Exomytis, the southernmost promontory of Santorini, a place still known as Elefsina.

Bent also examined the area around Perissa, particularly the convent of the Zoodochos Pigi. He discovered numerous ancient remains in and around the *katholikon* of the monastery, which he thought might in antiquity have been an important pan-Cycladic shrine. Some of these antiquities can still be seen, though it would seem that many of them have been carried away.

The village of Akrotiri and its famous archaeological site are out on the southern horn of the island. Bent was one of the first travellers to describe the village of Akrotiri, which a century later would emerge as one of the most famous archaeological sites in Greece. He describes it as 'a huge overgrown Venetian fortress village full of labyrinthian alleys...', as it still appears today.

The fortress, known to the Latins as La Ponta, was probably erected early in the thirteenth century by the Barozzi. It was rebuilt by Niccolo I Sanudo after he captured Santorini from the Barozzi in 1335. The following year Niccolo conferred La Ponta upon the Gozzadini, who retained possession of the fortress until 1617.

Bent saw in the Greek New Year while he was in Akrotiri, and he describes the festivities marking the *paneyeri* of Agios Vassilios, St Basil, which in the old calendar is also the Greek equivalent of Christmas.

> It was the eve of St Basil – New Year's Eve in Greece, according to the old style – so the village was *en fete*. The great amusement on these occasions is the 'calends', or songs called *kalandai*, which though twelve days late, according to our notion, really had come. Companies of children and young men club together and wander from house to house singing their 'calend song', carrying with them an ornament somewhat like a Christmas tree, a round thing covered with green and hung with flowers and lanterns.

> Their songs consist of long, chanted stories, beginning thus, 'Today we celebrate the circumcision of our Lord and the feast of the blessed great Basil;' then follow accounts of Christ and Basil, and they finish by saying, 'Many years to you!' and receive each a glass of mastic or some coppers in exchange for their good wishes.'

During the period 1870–1900 several archaeological excavations in and around Akrotiri unearthed evidence of prehistoric human settlements in the area. No further excavations were made at Akrotiri until 1967, when the Greek Archaeological Society began digging there under the direction of Spyridon Marinatos, who headed the project until his accidental death on the site on 1 October 1974. Marinatos was buried on the site, which by then had become world famous, as the buried Minoan-Cycladic city of the Bronze Age emerged from the volcanic ash that had buried it for more than 35 centuries.

Work was resumed at Akrotiri in 1976 under the direction of Christos Doumas and continues to the present day, with expectations that the project will go on for many years. The studies have shown that the original settlement on this site dates back to the Early Cycladic period. The structures unearthed in the excavations were part of a city that reached its full development in the mid-second millennium BC, and was profoundly influenced by the Minoan civilisation on Crete. The city that flourished here until its destruction in the great volcanic explosion of *c.* 1500 BC had achieved a very high level of culture, manifested not only by the beautiful paintings that adorned the walls of its houses, but also by sophisticated 'modern' conveniences such as plumbing and proper drainage. It is estimated that the ancient city had an area of some 200,000 square metres, only part of which has been excavated, and that the number living there at its peak exceeded the present population of Santorini.

The archaeological site is covered over with a corrugated plastic roof, so as to protect the excavated structures from the elements. Numerous translucent windows in the roof admit the light of day, providing a somewhat sepulchral illumination that seems appropriate for a resurrected ghost town. It is a particularly haunting site, for the ancient city looks very much like the villages one sees today in the Cyclades, houses of two or three storeys lining narrow, winding streets that converge here and there in little *plateias*.

The houses of ancient Akrotiri were built in exactly the same manner and with the same materials as the older dwellings one sees today in the villages of the Cyclades. They are constructed of materials available in abundance on the island: small irregular stones bonded with mud often mixed with straw, with walls reinforced by wooden planks so as to be more resistant to earthquakes. The mansions of the rich were revetted with ashlar blocks, which in more modest homes were used only to articulate the levels of each floor and as the surrounds of doors and windows. The ground floor was used for storage and workspaces, including mills for grinding corn. The toilet and washroom were usually located on the ground floor as well, with the waste carried away in cylindrical clay pipes embedded in the walls and connected with sewers dug beneath the streets. The living quarters on the second and third floors were flooded with light through large windows, and at least one room on these levels, presumably the parlour, was decorated with wall paintings.

The Akrotiri wall paintings were all removed upon discovery and are now on exhibition in the National Archaeological Museum in Athens and in the new museum in Phera. According to Professor Doumas, 'The wall paintings of Thera constitute the earliest examples of large-scale painting in Greece, and enrich inestimably the history of European art.' Among them are miniature frescoes depicting scenes of life in ancient Thera, including one in which two women are carrying home water from a fountain in amphorae balanced on their heads, a scene which we ourselves have observed in mountain villages on the Cyclades not so long ago.

***

Anaphi is the most remote of the Cyclades, 145 nautical miles from the Piraeus, floating in the Aegean far off to the south-east of all the other isles that encircle Delos. In fact, Anaphi and Thera originally were not included in the Cyclades by ancient geographers such as Strabo, who instead grouped them among the Sporades, or 'Scattered Isles'. Anaphi became part of the Cyclades only during the Latin period, along with Santorini, as it was then called, when their conquest by Marco Sanudo brought them within the Duchy of the Archipelago.

Other than the Lesser Cyclades, Anaphi is the second-smallest of the archipelago after Folegandros, with an area of 38 square kilometres. The island is literally a mountain-top projecting out of the sea; its highest peak is Mount Vigla, 582 metres high, sloping down to the shore on all sides without an intervening plain. The population of Anaphi is only 282, fewer than that of any of the other major Cyclades, and less than a third of what it was in Bent's time.

The earliest reference to Anaphi is a fragmentary poem written in the fourth century BC by Callimachos of Cyrene, who refers to 'Aeglitan Anaphi, neighbour to Laconian Thera'. Aeglitan means 'the radiant one', an attribute that stems from Apollo's role as a sun god; 'Phoebus', his Latin name, has the same meaning. According to mythology, the temple of Apollo Aeglites was founded by Jason and the Argonauts, dedicated by them in thanksgiving to 'the shining god', who led them there when they were lost while crossing the Aegean on their homeward voyage.

Anaphi is so tiny and remote that it hardly figures in the history of ancient Greece, but it came into its own in a small way during the Latin era, when it was known as Namfio. After Marco Sanudo established the Duchy of the Archipelago in 1210, he awarded Anaphi as a sub-fief to the Venetian nobleman Leonardo Foscolo, whose family held the island for 72 years. The Foscoli lost Anaphi in 1279, when it was taken by a Byzantine fleet commanded by the Anaphiote pirate Giovanni de la Cava. Then in 1307 Anaphi was recaptured for the Latins by Januli Gozzadini, who was awarded the island as a sub-fief by Niccolo I Sanudo, Duke of Naxos.

Anaphi eventually reverted to the Sanudi, passing then in turn to the Crispi, usually ruled by a son or younger brother of the Duke of Naxos. The most notable of the lords of Anaphi was Guglielmo II Crispo, who succeeded as Duke of Naxos in 1453, the year that Constantinople fell to the Turks. Guglielmo gave

Anaphi to his daughter Florence, and then in 1481 the island passed by dowry to the Pisani family. The Pisani held Anaphi until 1537, when Barbarossa raided the island and carried off all of its inhabitants into slavery.

The island was later resettled, and in 1700 the Anaphiotes paid a sum of 500 crowns to the Porte to regain their rights. They were thenceforth left in peace on payment of an annual tribute to the Captain Pasha of the Ottoman fleet when he appeared each year in the Cyclades. Then in 1770 the island was taken by Alexi Orlof, admiral of the fleet of Catherine the Great, and for the next five years it was held by the Russians. At the end of the War of Independence Anaphi, as part of the Cyclades, was included within the borders of the new Greek Kingdom, but only barely, for Crete and the Dodecanese remained under Turkish rule.

During the summer there are several ferries a week to Anaphi from the Piraeus, as well as daily boats from Santorini, 16 nautical miles to the west. But there is only one ferry a week from the Piraeus in winter, and even that service can be interrupted by storms.

Ferries call at the tiny port of Agios Nikolaos on the southern coast of the island, from where a road winds up to Chora, the only community on the island, which has the feeling of being the last outpost in the Cyclades. So it appeared to Bent when he and his wife set out in a *caique* from Santorini on a January morning in 1884, bound for Anaphi, whose peak they could see rising out of the sea 'in the blue distance'. Bent writes of how he and his party landed on the north shore of the island 'about two o'clock in the night', taking shelter in a seaside chapel till the next morning, when he sent his servant to fetch mules to carry them and their baggage to Chora, where they found 'all the population of the place straining their eyes to get a glimpse of the strange foreigners who had come to visit their shores'. Bent and his wife were put up in an empty house in Chora that belonged to the brother of their servant, an Anaphiote, whose family entertained them during their stay on the island.

There were no doctors on Anaphi at the time of Bent's visit, as indeed was the case on most of the islands when we first came to the Cyclades. The *demarch* told Bent that he kept a few medicines that he dispensed at the *demarcheion*, but otherwise, he said, 'our remedies are chiefly the herbs which grow in our mountains'. Bent was impressed with the good health of the Anaphiotes, which he attributed to the self-sufficiency required by their isolation, which we ourselves found to be true of the islanders there and elsewhere in the Cyclades.

> Certainly the lot of the thousand Anaphiotes is an enviable one. No steamer, rarely any letters, splendid air, no doctors. No wonder they live to ninety! The town, too, is exceptionally clean for an island one… Everything is done at home in Anaphi; their windmills grind their corn, their fields produce a sufficiency of grain, their looms make all the materials for their clothes, their hill slopes produce excellent grapes. 'If the rest of the world were to disappear,' said the demarch, 'and Anaphi alone be left, the only thing we should miss would be tobacco;' and relative to the subject of tobacco I asked him if he approved of the new tax the Greek government had recently put on cigarette papers. 'Bah!' explained he with a wink, 'the tax has not yet reached Anaphi;' and the chief functionary of the law chuckled to himself as he rolled a cigarette in smuggled paper.

Chora is a typical Cycladic village of whitewashed houses, arrayed around the upper slope of a hill, some 300 metres above sea level. On top of the hill above Chora are the ruins of a Latin fortress, built by Guglielmo II Crispo before he became Duke of Naxos in 1453.

Chora has been the capital of Anaphi since the Latin period, but there are no antiquities evident in the village. Thus it would appear that the original city of Anaphi was elsewhere on the island, probably at Kastelli, a hilltop site some three kilometres northeast of Chora, where there are extensive ancient remains. The necropolis was on the eastern side of the hill, where a beautiful sarcophagus decorated with reliefs can be seen beside a chapel of the Panagia Docari.

The port of the ancient city was at the seaward foot of the hill, where Bent saw 'traces of houses, a mole, and steps leading down to the sea'. He did not mention the tall cairns piled up by the seashore, all of them apparently ancient, probably erected by Anaphiote mariners as talismans to protect them from the perils of the deep on their voyages. I asked a local fisherman about this and he said that in his grandfather's time it was still the custom to add a stone to the cairn before and after setting out on a voyage.

The two other sites of interest are at the eastern end of the island, where a Gibraltar-like eminence known as Mount Kalamos rises to a height of 396 metres on a peninsula connected to the mainland by a narrow isthmus. The first of the two sites, Moni Zoodochos Pigi, is on the northern side of the isthmus, while the second, the chapel of the Panagia Kalamiotissa, is on the peak of Mount Kalamos.

The monastery of Zoodochos Pigi, also known as the Kalamiotissa, was built in the late seventeenth century on the site of the temple of Apollo Aeglites, whose foundation was attributed to Jason and the Argonauts. The monastery is now abandoned, but in Bent's time there were still three monks living there. Near the monastery there is a cavern known as Drakondospilo, the Dragon's Cave, noted for the beauty and variety of its stalagmites and stalactites.

The chapel of the Panagia Kalamiotissa on the peak of Mount Kalamos belongs to the monastery. It is the goal of pilgrimages on the feast day of the Virgin's Birth, 8 September, when a *paneyeri* is celebrated in the courtyard of the monastery, a festival that has become famous for the distinctive Anaphiote folk dances that are performed there. Bent describes some of these dances, which their host's wife and her beautiful daughter Eutimia performed at a ball they held for their English guests one evening in Chora.

> Dancing is a passion amongst them, and one can easily imagine their love for it when one thinks how shut off they are from the pleasures of the outer world. As for the *syrtos*, they dance it admirably and in a most pathetic manner: the leader bends on his knee in prayer to the adored one, he stretches out his hand to heaven to supplicate the intervention of the divine power in his behalf…

They have several local dances in Anaphi; the *sousta*, danced only by men, is curious: they stand, as in the *syrtos*, in a semicircle, with their hands on each other's shoulders, and then they begin to move slowly backwards and forwards, quickening their steps as they go, until they end in an exceedingly fast motion… Another pretty dance is the *moloritis*; Eutimia and another girl danced it with two men: first they danced hand in hand, like the lady's chain in a quadrille, then they danced separately, the women, of course, demurely, whilst the men performed acrobatic feats, as in the *syrtos*; and they sang little ballads (*mantinades*) as they danced.

Later in the evening they were joined by a 'rough, coarse-looking shepherd' named Andronico, whom the other guests plied with drink until he sang for them, accompanied by a boy playing a goatskin *sabouna*, 'that wretched Grecian substitute for the bagpipe'. Bent writes that '[t]he words of this song Eutimia kindly copied for me next morning, and as they struck me as a production of a curious nature I will append a liberal translation':

> Your figure is a lemon tree,
> Its branches are your hair;
> Joy to the youth who climbs
> To pluck the fruit so fair.
> Black garments, such as now you wear,
> Myself I will cast off
> That I may now clothe you all in gold,
> And take you as my love.

V. C. Scott O'Connor writes of Anaphi in his *Isles of the Aegean*, published in 1929. There he tells of an evening he spent at a house in the Chora as a guest of the *Proidros*, or governor, who introduced him to an old man who said that he had been Bent's travelling companion during his exploration of the Cyclades. Bent remarks on this man in the preface to his book on the Cyclades: 'I took a servant, a native of one of the islands, who became invaluable in assisting me to discover points of folk-lore which without him it would have been impossible to arrive at.' O'Connor writes that the man 'brought with him two faded English photographs of Bent and his wife, and as we sat in the Proidros' room, with a stick in his hand and the lantern he had brought with him beside his chair, recounted some of these ancient adventures in his native Greek…'.

And so life passes in the Cyclades, as stories and descriptions of its ancient way of life are passed on from one traveller to another, from Homer through Bent to O'Connor and then ourselves. Bent caught the essence of the Aegean world on the wind, preserving its traditions so that now we can rediscover them, recalling the words he wrote in his preface: '[P]ersonal intercourse with the islanders in all grades of society; at their work and at their board, proved to us the most infallible method of understanding their life and their super-stitions as they exist today; and the kindly hospitality with which they received us…will remain forever fixed in our memories.'

These are the Cyclades, the islands at the centre of the Aegean world, the lost empire of the sea that awaits discovery at the end of the mule track.

Santorini (Thera): population 11,984; area 76 sq km; Mt. Profitis Ilias (566 m); ferries from Piraeus (128 mi); airport; hotels in Phera, Imerovigli, Oia, Kamari, Perissa, Perivolos, Akrotiri, Vlichada, Messaria, Pyrgos, Megalochori and Monolithos.

Anaphi: population 282; area 38 sq km; Mount Vigla (582 m); ferries from Piraeus (145 mi); hotel in Chora.

Appendix 1: Chronology

(all early dates are approximate)

Late Neolithic Period (5000–3200 BC): settlements on Kea, Melos and Saliagos.
Bronze Age (3200–1150 BC)
Early Cycladic (3200–2000 BC): settlements on all the Cyclades.
Middle Cycladic (2000–1500 BC): Minoan Crete establishes a maritime
      empire with colonies in the Cyclades (*c.* 1750–1600 BC).
Late Cycladic (1500–1150 BC): volcanic explosion on Thera (*c.* 1500 BC);
      Mycenaean colonies in the Cyclades (*c.* 1300–1150 BC). Sea Peoples
      destroy Bronze Age civilisation (*c.* 1150 BC).
Dark Ages (1200–750 BC): great Hellenic migration from Greece across
      Aegean to Asia Minor; Ionians settle on the northern and eastern
      Cyclades, Dorians on Melos and Thera. Geometric Period
      (1000–800 BC). Ionians establish sanctuary of Apollo on Delos (*c.*
      eighth century BC).
Archaic Period (750–490 BC): Naxos (734 BC), Paros (710 BC) and Thera
      (634 BC) found colonies. Lygdamis of Naxos (*c.* 550 BC) establishes
      maritime empire. Unsuccessful Persian siege of Naxos (499 BC).
      Persians occupy Naxos and other Cyclades during invasion of
      Greece (490 BC).
Classical Period (490–336 BC): Cyclades participate in Greek victories over
      Persians at Battles of Salamis (480 BC) and Plataea (479 BC).
      Cyclades join First Delian League of Athens (477 BC). Unsuccessful
      Naxian revolt against Athens (470 BC). Athenians capture Melos and
      slaughter male population (415 BC). Establishment of Second
      Athenian Alliance at Delos (377 BC). Alexander the Great becomes
      ruler of Greece (336 BC).
Hellenistic Period (336–146 BC): After death of Alexander (323 BC)
      Cyclades under rule of Macedonia (318–285 BC) and then under

Ptolemies of Egypt (285–241 BC). Rhodes gains control of Cyclades (197 BC). After being declared a free port by Romans (167 BC), Delos emerges as principal slave market in Mediterranean.

Roman Period (146 BC–AD 330): Roman conquest of Greece complete in 146 BC. Mithradates VI of Pontus invades Greece and sacks Delos twice in period 88–69 BC. Delos soon afterwards abandoned.

Byzantine Period (AD 330–1207): Constantine the Great transfers capital of empire to Byzantium, renamed Constantinople (330); Cyclades become a province of Byzantine Empire. Christianity established in the Cyclades (early fourth century). Islands left undefended against corsair raids and become depopulated. Constantinople falls to Latins (1204). Marco Sanudo of Venice captures most of Cyclades (1207).

Venetian Period (1207–1537): Marco I Sanudo establishes Duchy of the Archipelago (1210) with capital at Naxos, with other isles of Cyclades awarded as sub-fiefs to Latin nobility. Constantinople recaptured by Greeks (1261). Catalans raid Cyclades (1304, 1389). First Turkish attack on Cyclades (1344). Constantinople falls to Ottoman Turks (1453). Ottoman fleet under Barbarossa sacks Paros and takes control of most of the Cyclades (1537).

Ottoman Period (*Turkokrateia*) (1537–1832): Venetian garrison on Tinos surrenders (1715), completing Ottoman conquest of Cyclades. Russian fleet occupies Cyclades (1770–1774). Greek War of Independence begins (1821).

Modern Period (1832–present): Modern Greek Kingdom established (1832), with Cyclades included within its boundaries. Greek refugees from Turkish rule in Crete resettled in Cyclades throughout remainder of nineteenth century. Greek refugees from Asia Minor resettled in Cyclades and elsewhere in Greece during exchange of populations (1923). Cyclades occupied by Italian and then German troops during Second World War (1941–1945), during which many islanders die of starvation. Tourist boom begins in late 1960s.

Appendix 2: Festivals (*Paneyeria*)

1 January:	Agios Vassilios
6 January:	Epiphany
7 January:	Agios Ioannis Prodromos (St John the Baptist)
18 January:	Agios Athanasios
30 January:	Treis Ierarchai (the Three Fathers, SS Basil, Gregory and John Chrysostomos)
1 February:	Agios Tryphon
2 February:	Ipapantis (Candelmas)
3 February:	Agios Spyridon
10 February:	Agios Haralambos
25 March:	Evangelismos Theotokou (Annunciation of the Virgin Mother of God)
23 April:	Agios Yiorgios
8 May:	Agioi Anargyroi
8 May:	Agios Ioannis Theologos
20 May:	Agios Thaleleos
21 May:	Agioi Konstantinos and Eleni
12 June:	Agios Onouphrios
15 June:	Agia Triada
23 June:	Agios Ioannis Theologos
24 June:	Birthday of St John the Baptist
29 June:	Agioi Petros and Pavlos (SS Peter and Paul)
30 June:	Agioi Apostoloi (the Twelve Apostles
7 July:	Agia Kyriaki
14 July:	Agios Nikodemos of Naxos
17 July:	Agia Marina
20 July:	Agios Profitis Ilias
26 July:	Agia Paraskevi
27 July:	Agios Pandeleimon

6 August:	Metamorphosis tou Sotiros (Metamorphosis of the Saviour)
15 August:	Koimisis tis Theotokou (Dormition of the Virgin Mother of God)
27 August:	Agios Phanourios
29 August:	Beheading of St John the Baptist
1 September:	Agios Simeon
7 September:	Agios Sozon
8 September:	Gennesis tis Theotokou (Birth of the Virgin Mother of God); Agia Theodoti of Ios
14 September:	Exaltation of the Cross
25 September:	Agioi Anargyroi, Agios Ioannis Theologos
26 October:	Agios Artemios; Agios Dimitrios
2 November:	Agios Akindinos
8 November:	Taxiarchis (the Archangels Michael and Gabriel)
9 November:	Agia Theoktisti of Paros
11 November:	Agios Menas
21 November:	Eisodia tis Theotokou (Presentation of the Virgin)
25 November:	Agia Ekaterini
30 November:	Agios Andreas
4 December:	Agia Barbara
6 December:	Agios Nikolaos
12 December:	Agios Spyridon
21 December:	Isodia tis Panagia (Presentation of the Virgin)
25 December:	Christmas
26 December:	Agios Stephanos Protomartyr

Apokreos (Carnival) (the three weeks before Lent)
Cheese Week (the last week of Carnival)
Kathara Deftera (Clean Monday) (the first day of Lent)
Agioi Theodoroi (the first Saturday in Lent)
Friday after Easter: Panagia Zoodochos Pigi (Our Lady of the Life-Giving Spring)
Forty days after Easter: Analypsis (Ascension)
Seventh Monday after Easter: Agia Triada (the Holy Trinity)

Appendix 3: Glossary

acropolis: the fortified upper part of a Greek city
Agios (pl. Agioi): male saint or 'Holy'
Agia: female saint or 'Holy'
agiasma: holy well or spring
agora: marketplace; the civic centre of an ancient Greek city
akri: cape or peninsula
apano: up, upper
ashlar: hewn or squared stone
bema: the part of a Greek church containing the altar
caldera: a volcanic crater
capital: uppermost member of a column
cavea: the auditorium of a Greek theatre
cella: temple building
Chora: the principal town of an island
chorio: village
ciborium: a canopy, usually supported on four columns, covering an altar
clerurchs: colonists
Cyclopean: ancient wall of colossal stones
dado: the decorated lower part of an interior wall
demarch: mayor
demarcheion: town hall
dithyramb: a poem in an inspired, wild, irregular strain
Doric: an order of Greek architecture
entablature: the upper part of an order in architecture, comprising architrave, frieze and cornice, supported by a colonnade
exedra (pl. exedrae): semicircular recess or colonnade
ex-voto: a votive offering
heroon: shrine of a deified hero
hoplite: a heavily armed infantry soldier of ancient Greece

icon: religious picture

iconostasis: screen on which icons are placed in a Greek church

Ionic: order of Greek architecture

kafenion: coffee house

kastro: a castle, fortress or fortified town

katholikon: monastic church

kato: below, lower

kore (pl. korai): archaic statue of a maiden personifying Artemis

kouros (pl. kouroi): archaic statue of a youth personifying Apollo

menhir: an ancient upright monolith

Minoan: civilisation that developed in Crete during the Bronze Age, named for the legendary King Minos

moni: monastery or convent

Mycenaean: civilisation that developed in the Peloponnesos during the Late Bronze Age, named for the city of Mycenae

narthex: the vestibule of a Greek church

necropolis: the cemetery of an ancient Greek city

nisiotika tragoudia: songs of the Greek islands

odeion: small theatre

odos: street

palimpset: a parchment that has been reused after earlier writing has been erased

Panagia: the Virgin Mary

paneyeri (pl. paneyeria): religious festival

paralia: waterfront promenade

peristyle: a colonnade surrounding a building

perivoli: garden or precincts of estate or temple

pigi: spring or well

platanos: plane tree

plateia: civic square

portico: an arcaded walkway

pyrgos (pl. pyrgoi): watchtower, fortified monastery or mansion

reredos: an ornamental wood or stone screen behind an altar

satrap: provincial governor in ancient Persia

sottoportico: covered passageway

stele: an upright stone

stoa: a colonnaded walkway

stylobate: platform of a temple

temenos: the sacred enclosure of a temple

thalassa: sea

thalassocracy: maritime empire

threnody: a song of lamentation for the dead

transept: the part of a cruciform church that crosses at right angles to the
greatest length between the nave and the apse

vouno: mountain

Appendix 4:
Bibliography

Apollonius of Rhodes, *The Voyage of Argo*, translated by E. V. Rieu, Harmondsworth, 1959

Barber, R. L. N., *The Cyclades in the Bronze Age*, London, 1987

Barber, Robin, *Blue Guide Greece*, London, 5th edn, London, 1987

Bent, James Theodore, *Aegean Islands; The Cyclades, or Life Among the Insular Greeks*, London, 1885 (republished by Argonaut Publishers, Chicago, 1965)

Bowman, John S., *Guide to Santorini*, Athens, 1974

Burn, A. R., *The Pelican History of Greece*, Harmondsworth, 1966

Carson, Jeffrey and James Clark, *Paros*, Athens, 1977

Charlemont, Earl of (James Caulfield), *Travels in Greece and Turkey*, edited by W. B. Stanford and E. J. Finopoulos, London, 1981

Chatzidakis, Manolis (ed.), *Byzantine Art in Greece – Naxos*, Athens, 1989

Doumas, Christos, *Santorini: A Guide to the Island and its Archaeological Treasures*, Athens, 1982

Finlay, G., *The History of Greece under Ottoman and Venetian Domination, 1453–1821*, London, 1856

Frazee, Charles, *The Island Princes of Greece: The Dukes of the Archipelago*, Amsterdam, 1988

Freely, John, *Naxos, Ariadne's Isle*, Athens, 1976

_____, *The Cyclades*, London, 1986

Grimal, Pierre, *The Dictionary of Classical Mythology*, Oxford, 1951

Guthrie, W. K. C., *The Greeks and Their Gods*, Boston, 1950

Hammond, N. G. L., *A History of Greece to 322 BC*, Oxford, 1965

Herodotus, *The Histories*, translated by Aubrey de Selincourt, Harmondsworth, 1972

Hesiod (with *The Homeric Hymns and Homerica*), translated by Hugh G. Evelyn-White, Cambridge, Mass., 1954

Homer, *The Odyssey*, translated by Richmond Lattimore, New York, 1965

Koukas, George, *Paros–Antiparos: History, Arts, Folklore, Modern Life*, Athens, no date

Koutelakis, M. Haralambos, *Tinos: History, Art and Archaeology*, Athens, 1981

Laiou, Angeliki E. *Constantinople and the Latins*, Cambridge, 1972

Lane, Frederic C., *Venice: A Maritime Republic*, Baltimore, 1973

Lattimore, Richmond (translator), *Greek Lyrics*, 2nd edn, London, 1960

Lawson, John Cuthbert, *Modern Greek Folklore and Ancient Greek Religion*, Cambridge, 1910

Liddell, Robert, *Aegean Greece*, London, 1954

Lock, Peter, *The Franks in the Aegean*, London and New York, 1995

Megas, George A., *Greek Calendar Customs*, Athens, 1963

Meinardus, Otto F. A., *The Saints of Greece*, Athens, 1970

Miller, William, *The Latins in the Levant: A History of Frankish Greece (1204–1261)*, London, 1908

_____, *Essays on the Latin Orient*, Cambridge, 1921

Nilsson, Martin P., *Greek Folk Religion*, New York, 1940

O'Connor, V. C. Scott, *Isles of the Aegean*, London, 1929

Ostrogorsky, George, *A History of the Byzantine State*, Oxford, 1956

Pausanias, *Guide to Greece*, 2 volumes, translated by Peter Levi, Harmondsworth, 1971

Peters, F. E., *The Harvest of Hellenism: A History of the Near East from Alexander the Great to the Triumph of Christianity*, New York, 1970

Petrides, Theodore and Elfleida Petrides, *Folk Dances of the Greeks*, New York, 1961

Petrocheilou, Anna, *The Greek Caves*, Athens, 1984

Philippides, Dimitri (ed.), *Greek Traditional Architecture*, vol. II, Athens, 1983

Phitos, D., *Wild Flowers of Greece*, Athens, 1965

Pym, Hilary, *Songs of Greece*, London, 1968

Randolph, Bernard, *Present State of the Islands in the Archipelago*, London, 1687

Renfrew, Colin, *The Emergence of Civilization: The Cyclades and the Aegean in The Third Millennium BC*, London, 1972

Rodd, Rennell, *The Customs and Lore of Modern Greece*, London, 1892

Sfikas, George, *Wild Flowers of Greece*, Athens, 1976

Stoneman, Richard, *Land of Lost Gods: The Search for Classical Greece*, London, 1987

Strabo, *The Geography*, vol. v, translated by Horace Leonard Jones, Cambridge, Mass., 1969

Stuart, James and Nicholas Revett, *The Antiquities of Athens*, London, 1762–1816

Themelis, Petros, *Mykonos–Delos: Archeological Guide*, Athens, 1971

Thucydides, *History of the Peloponnesian War*, translated by Rex Warner, Harmondsworth, 1954

Tournefort, Joseph Pitton de, *A Voyage into the Levant*, London, 1718 (translation by John Ozell of the original 1717 French edition)

Tozer, M., *The Islands of the Aegean*, Oxford, 1890

Wheler, George, *Journey into Greece*, London, 1682

Woodhouse, C. M., *Modern Greece: A Short History*, 4th edn, London, 1986

Zaroukas, K., G. Sakkas and M. Sarlas, *Mykonos–Delos: A Guide*, Athens, 1981

Index